The John Diaries

THE JOHN DIARIES

By

MARK LE CLAIRE

Cefas Productions Limited

Edited by Cefas Productions Ltd. Formatted on WPS Office, Celtx, LibreOffice and Scribus.

Printed and bound by Deanprint Limited, Stockport, Cheshire

ISBN 978-0-9555019-3-7

To Melissa

Introduction

The John Diaries. And yet I referred to him as John Heal, certainly for the first ten years of this diary. Among all the various acquaintances one makes in life there are always a few peculiar characters that one somehow comes to know, people not to be taken seriously, but whom one tolerates and indulges in a condescending sort of way, despite their evident deficiencies. This was certainly the case with John. Most people found him peculiar and a bit of a joke - someone to snigger at behind his back - and I did too. Coming from the land-locked Midlands and having already lived in Folkestone for about ten years, it struck me that sea-side towns seemed to attract more than their fair share of society's odd balls and misfits, something which I suppose is hardly surprising, given the role sea-side towns have in catering for visitors from elsewhere, some of whom are bound to end up staying. John was another of those slightly odd looking characters one would notice now and then, in John's case his shambling mid afternoon gait clearly suggesting he was feeling somewhat *the worse for wear*, doubtless after an extended *liquid lunch* somewhere, I would knowingly surmise. Fond of a drink myself, this rather predisposed me in his favour. Not that I was in the same category myself, of course. True, I, too, had come to Folkestone and stayed, but I, on the contrary, was not an oddball or eccentric but a talented, artistic person destined for great things; someone who could well afford to accommodate one or two *bit part players* in his life, like John. Little did I ever dream that one day - stricken with ill health though he was - I would end up needing him more than he needed me.

Tall and gangly, John was fairly normal looking, although there was always something slightly disjointed in his movements, whether tipsy or sober, and a dated look to his habitual black trousers and black shoes, his shirt, tie and pullover, worn with blazer or checked cloth sporting jacket, and with a full length coat in winter. His black hair thinning and teeth in a sorry state, John's face bore a perennial pasty indoor pallor, and with his dark, grave, unblinking eyes there was a rather spectral air about him, especially at night. Overall, John could hardly have been described as wondrously handsome, although his polite manner and soft spoken, minor public school voice - as well as a droll, ironic sense of humour which he would unexpectedly prove to have - did temper the initial off putting impression he made. He was in his late twenties and I in my early thirties when we finally met, one afternoon on Folkestone's Leas clifftop promenade. I think I invited him for a drink at the *Over-Seas Club*, the bar in the nearby flat of my friend, Roy Johnson, with whom I lived. John was an extremely private and reserved person, whose personal life and affairs continued to be something of a mystery even after one knew him. In due course I was to learn that he had come to Folkestone to live with his grandmother, who had died some years earlier. He now lived alone in their flat, which no one ever visited, seemingly, and which was now dustily and airlessly sealed off from the world, as I would be witnessing for myself. Though he obviously had little social contact, I knew John wasn't a recluse. One saw him out with his shopping bag, or ambling about the town and on the Leas, and neither was he completely friendless, referring, as he sometimes did, to one or two individuals he knew locally. I assumed that he must also have been used to the social proximity of the people in the wine bars he frequented, though whether he interacted with them was another matter. Somehow one pictured him sitting there, his fourth glass of wine at his elbow on the counter, with both he and those in close social proximity around him refraining from striking up any lively conversation. John's background was *genteel*, and one got the impression of a person of modest financial independence. He had in fact worked for the Saga holiday company in Folkestone for a while, I learned, but by the time I met him his days of having any such conventional employment or career were over. Although he had his grandmother's flat to live in, he was in fact living in constrained financial circumstances, and his income - unbeknown to me at the time - consisted of anything he could derive from his own schemes, usually involving pyramid selling, door-to-door canvassing, or the buying and selling of *collectables* like stamps and postcards, supplemented by support from his long suffering family, in Wiltshire, who several times had to bail him out financially.

Was John autistic? Something was slightly amiss, but one couldn't quite put one's finger on it, though like many autistic people he had surprising talents, like remembering people's telephone numbers, and he had an uncanny memory for past events and conversations. Once, after not seeing him for a long time, I arrived late at his flat to stay the night. We had a two hour conversation over a drink or two and then I went to bed, to wake in the night to hear him pacing about his flat, repeating the whole two hour conversation to himself, word for word, which rather spooked me out at the time. Some years later, by which time I was living in Spain and John was trying to get by on the income from two or three newspaper delivery rounds, and was living a scrimped existence in his flat on a diet of boiled potatoes and biscuits, he had a breakdown and was diagnosed with schizophrenia, after which - with help forthcoming from the state - the questions of his employment and income were finally settled.

When I met John I, too, had no conventional employment and income. Having dropped out of art college, I'd been on my way to Paris to become a renowned artist. I was having an interlude in Folkestone on the way, which, like John's liquid lunches, had become extended. There I was, thumbing a lift back from earning a few quid strawberry picking over at Challock one day, when I was given a lift by Roy in his Alfa Romeo sports car, with the result that I had pretty soon moved into his flat. I worked as a sign writer in a supermarket, and as a steward on the cross channel ferries, then still not having gone to Paris I decided I'd better start being a painter, a resolve that Roy was happy to assist me with. In return for that, inclusive of accommodation in his flat, and food, and the use of a car - not to mention a room rented for a studio - I did the occasional day's van driving work for his timber merchant business in Chilham. In short, Roy was supporting me financially, although I tried not to abuse that generosity unnecessarily, and so like John I had very little money. The thing John and I did both have was time - lot's of time. For years our time was our own, with the freedom to choose whether to go and work on the current oil painting, or go and make door to door charity donation collections, or not. Frequently we chose *not* and went on an outing and bit of a booze-up somewhere instead, me with a little cash to donate and John putting the lunchtime bill on his credit card and mounting total debt. Or, with the pubs and bars closed for the afternoon by the licensing laws of the time, and while most people - or those fortunate enough to have jobs as Britain emerged from the economically gloomy 1970's - were gainfully employed at their work, we would while away the time at the Over-Seas Club, me maybe mixing up some cocktails from a bottle of rum that John had brought with him, and with Roy always looking somewhat disgruntled when he came back from his gainful work at Chilham at 6 pm to find us there. The Over-Seas Club was normally open in the evening, when members - i.e. our friends - were free to visit at any time. Behind the bar I enjoyed being the cocktail shaking barman, and the feeling that Roy and I were generous hosts, with any amount of home brewed beer or lager to dispense, along with supermarket spirits, and litre bottles of plonk, lugged back on our regular day trips to France. It was a happy, carefree time for me - I had Roy to rely on, and a circle of friends, and all the time in the world to be an artist. I also had this odd drinking pal called John Heal, who had come out of his shell a bit since I'd first met him and was now being quite sociable. Everyone I knew thought he was very peculiar, but I got on with John alright - why, I could practically consider him a friend of mine, couldn't I?

Yes, it was all good fun we were having - and pretty innocent fun at that - and meanwhile I continued with my diary, which I'd started a few years earlier. I'd been inspired to begin it after reading the journals of Evelyn Waugh. I knew my diary wouldn't be recording any stylish high society events like his, but something in Waugh's writing style - clear and objective and briskly matter-of-fact - and the also conventionally literate style of other English novelists I'd been reading, like George Orwell and Aldous Huxley – Cyril Connolly, too, and his *Palinarus* - influenced my diary writing and also the style and tone of my future novel, *Vapour Trails in the Blue*. Aside from a love of Scott Fitzgerald's doomed romantic writing from the twenties, I'd also read American authors prominent during the 'sixties of my youth, like Mailer, Heller, Roth and Vidal, and in fact my principal cultural influence had always been the nineteen sixties; its album music, fiction and poetry, all culminating in that decade's *counter culture*, as expressed in the magazines, *Oz* and the *International Times*, heavily influenced as that whole movement had been by the 'fifties beat poets and writers - Ginsberg, Boroughs and Kerouac – still revered as the trail blazing, iconic heroes, or anti heroes. If I hadn't become an out and out hippy myself, I retained hippy-ish ideals, and when I began my diary I decided that if it wouldn't be recording any stylish high society events, or in fact be recording any other notable worldly matters and events that might feature the laudable exploits and achievements of myself, it would simply have to record the events from a lowlier strata of society - my localised arty and hippy-influenced world - but still written in a studied, educated *literary* way - more Aldous Huxley than Henry Miller - aspiring, as far as my abilities went, to what Connolly had referred to as a *mandarin* rather than *vernacular* style.

Introduction

While writing my diary I always felt acutely conscious, as most of us surely do, at times, of the fact that my life hadn't been bound to take this particular path I was writing about. I could have become a celebrated artist, or an odd job man, or magazine editor, or probation officer, or have been on probation myself, or have been and done any one of a million other things. This thought only reinforced the detachment with which I wrote, a detachment which might seem a little heartless to the reader, but even if had taken a different path, I would still have viewed it in exactly the same way, and I suppose it is this fatalistic outlook on life that has always prevented me from changing direction. (Then again, perhaps it is the case that I have changed direction, and have done so numerous times - how could a fatalist possibly tell?) What is certain is that you can't change the past, and we're all bound to take a path of some sort, and afterwards all we have is the memory, and perhaps a few photographs, and sometimes a diary too. So is this the sole reason to keep a diary in the first place - to help recall the past? Without a memory like John's, it can be hard to remember what happened last week, let alone the events of a decade ago. In addition to that primary function, though, a diary does help to clarify the diarists thoughts and come to a decision on things. At the time of writing, a diary can almost seem like a best friend, someone - or thing - to confide in and get things of your chest. Then there is the question of posterity and the prospect of it one day being read by someone else, one's descendents, maybe, or a wider readership - the great reading public, no less! a thoughts which does cross diary writer's mind from time to time, and which is likely to prod that person's ego and vanity into watchfulness. We all like to present our best - or preferred - side to the world, and a diary let's you to do that. The diarist enjoys the luxury of recording and judging everything from his or her own personal point of view, with no one around to argue with you, and unless he or she is a saint, it's hard to avoid the diary being seen, in the diarist's sub-conscious mind at least, an exercise in self justification. *This will justify my life,* is the diarist's secret hope. Vanity is usually the ultimate reason for keeping a diary, which is doubtless true in my case. The reader may wonder what I had to be vain about - unrenowned, financially dependent and hangover incapacitated self professed artist that I was - and I, too, knew full well that the often unenthralling doings of my younger or not-so-young years were hardly likely to arouse much envy or admiration, but I fully expected to be compensated for this one day, when my diary did, indeed, become a record of my later fulfilled, successful, glamorously interesting life, at which point the inconsequential earlier years would be looked on not with disdain but with compassion and understanding - approval, even. *See, how he matured and put all that behind him and went on to great things!* people would murmur. *Amazing, isn't it, what those rich, talented, celebrated people can get away with?*

So the years rolled on, with me continuing to record my life, rich and famous artist (or writer) or not. As well as Waugh - and especially since becoming a diarist myself - I have enjoyed reading various other people's dairies, including, in whole or in part, those by WNP Barbellion, George and Weedon Grossmith (authors of the fictional Charles Pooter diary), Chips Channon, Virginia Wolf, Anais Nin, Joe Orton, Alan Clarke and Gladys Langford. I recently read *A Life Unknown,* an investigative account by Alexander Masters of a diary that was found in a skip. It was from a diary that was a world record fourteen million words long. Mine continued to grow, but it was never in that league. It might be over a million words long, I calculated one day, when I was idly pondering on what might, in fact, be destined to become of my own diary. By then I was in my sixties - probably it was sometime after the failure of *Vapour Trails in the Blue* - when the terrible truth dawned on me. . . that my diary, too, was probably destined for the bin.

Introduction

Unless I did something about it, I could clearly see. Among those diaries I'd read and enjoyed, some of their authors were just about as little known as I was, like Gladys Langford, or the Grossmith's kindly, fictional Pooter, of Highgate Hill, whose very obscurity and deluded self importance was the whole point of the diary, something which exposed the fallacy of my reasoning about my own diary's worth. I hadn't put my past life behind me and gone on to greater things, but so what? Couldn't my diary still be published as it stood? In fact, I had already published a selection of my diaries, covering the years when I was writing and publishing *Vapour Trails in the Blue*, but as far as the bulk of it went I knew it couldn't be published in its entirety; a longer edited selection was called for, and having known John for thirty years, from the age when I was thirty-three to sixty-three – the principal chunk of anyone's life – I decided to publish a selection of my diaries from that period, consisting of every diary entry with any reference to John in it. I resolved to be faithful to this idea and include every such entry, whatever the context or subject matter. It has meant I've had to include some entries that I would rather have left out - usually containing some painful, embarrassing personal detail - and leave out others that I would have liked to include, that probably showed me in a better light. To this end, I have used my acquaintanceship - my friendship with you, John - to publish this present volume. I don't know what you would have had to say about it - me going and blowing your privacy, like this - but even when you were here, I would like to think that you wouldn't have minded so much, after all, or would at least have forgiven me. I hope you do, John, and that you accept my apology (which I'd also like to extend to your family). As for anyone else, who considers it plain wrong of me to have gone and done such a thing, I'll just have to plead guilty, as charged, and live with the shame of it and their censure.

Mark le Claire, Belsize Park, 2021

John at home.

The John Diaries - 1984

Folkestone, Sun, 19 Aug - We were hosts to a motley crew here last night, carnival night. It consisted of ourselves[1] and Vincent[2] and his two Mexican friends, and someone called Gary. My contribution to the assembly was John Heal, an eccentric person whom I have known for some time. Homosexual, ex public school, impoverished, lives in his fantasy world of money-making schemes and friendship with rich, influential people. He is younger than me, but his demeanour and appearance, tall and shabby, has an old fashioned air, which has appeal. Quite barmy but interesting. We had a barbecue and then all took our punch out on the corner of the road to watch the procession. I then went with John to the Executive Club and the Burlington hotel. I went to the Sandgate Road Indian restaurant for a take-away and there I encountered Clive.[3] Returned with take-away to the flat and found Roy gone to bed and the Gary bloke wandering around, to whom I was extremely rude. On Friday evening I went to Tiberius casino,[4] to win and lose nothing. Today I sunbathed on the beach and snorkelled in the sea. Last week I painted on five days and did not drink.

Fri, 24 Aug – August bank holiday. It is 1am. I am in bed. It is very close, still, but I don't feel bad. I went to Dover on Friday evening. I walked twice round Hobart Crescent. It's council houses overlook Dover. The sound of the grass hoppers there was quite deafening. The far end of the crescent is next to some unbuilt upon scrub land, and it was quite dark there, except for the distant presence of Dover Castle, floodlit and floating on its own in the blackness. On Saturday I went to the Executive Club (-60p).[5] Had a swim and snorkel each day this weekend. Last night Roy and I left the flat and got distracted by some noise from the Undercliff. It was coming from the Mermaid café, where a party of black people (on a coach from

---

[1] Roy Johnson and Mark le Claire.
[2] Vincent Crofts, college lecturer.
[3] Clive Botting, biology teacher.
[4] Tiberius casino, Ramsgate.
[5] Fruit machine loss.

Brixton?) were having a party. We went and had a drink there, then walked towards the harbour, to the Beach hotel and Brewery Tap pub. Today I copied up some of this diary. This evening I went with Roy to the Deal pubs. On our return I went to the Burlington hotel, where I met John Heal. There is a thick, summer fog tonight. I have been for one or two day-time car rides to Eastry and back, going and returning by different routes. On one ride I went to one or two pubs, on the other I lay down in a corn field to masturbate.

Fri, 31 Aug – I went to London yesterday, for the preview at Over-Seas House.[6] I arrived at Baker Street underground station soon after 11am, to spend two or three hours visiting galleries in the Baker Street and Tottenham Court Road area. My information was out of date, and most of the galleries had closed down. I went to three pubs, then visited the Curwin Gallery in Windmill Street, my one and only prospect,[7] taxied to the Tate Gallery and saw the *Hard Won Image* exhibition. Bus to Parliament Square, travelling there with two Italian girls I had met on the Tate Gallery steps. The preview was a full blown occasion, with many people and a generous quantity of wine. I met two artists, John Hutton and David Stubbs. My brother[8] arrived with a girl friend, Sue. I had been telling people that my work was available to be viewed on request, and Kim took me at my word and got Carol Wyatt to bring them out. This created quite a stir, so I am told. I retired to the bar while this was going on, and was presently joined by Kim and Sue. I was in a loquacious, extrovert mood, I hope not too overdone. We also met Tim and Graham, of the club itself. Caught the last train at 11.30pm. I felt very tired this morning. Douglas Richmond[9] came up for a coffee in my studio and he visited the flat this evening, as did John Heal and Chris[10] and Clive. Chris

---

6 Premises of the Royal Over-Seas League club, London.
7 Diarist was seeking a gallery to show his art work.
8 Kim Wall, actor, diarist's brother.
9 Douglas Richmond, Scottish ex RAF serviceman, retired property developer, part time chirododist.
10 Chris Crofts, college lecturer,

was just returned from Wales and in good form. I myself did not drink today.

Mon, 17 Sept – On Friday evening we were visited by John Heal, who brought a bottle of gin and by Chris. We had a merry drink of the gin at the bar and then went out, which was probably a mistake. We went to one or two bars, then Roy stood us a meal at Cassidy's Diner hamburger restaurant. On Saturday Roy and I went to Weybridge. Peter Makin[11]had moored his narrow boat, which he had just had built, outside the Pelican pub, to throw a boat warming party. There was lots to eat and drink. Roy and I walked into Weybridge at one stage of the evening, and when we returned I drank several hefty gins. I got drunk, but not incoherently so. However, next morning, having stayed on Peter's boat, I had a major hangover, of the vomiting species. I slept all day, on and off, including on the mattress in the back of the car during the journey home. Recovered enough by the evening to have lamb chops (marinated), mashed potatoes and a glass of wine. This morning I went to Douglas Richmond's flat for a coffee. He talked of his experiences in France during the war. An afternoon visit, here, from Vincent and his Mexican friend, Jorge. Have worked on the crate between times.[12]

Mon, 5 Nov – Walked to a fish and chip shop earlier this evening, so I could see and smell some fireworks and bonfires. Was too hungover to do much in the studio today. Yesterday Roy and I went for a car ride to Camber Sands and Dungeness. John Heal phoned and I invited him for a drink, which was a mistake, as he arrived during our meal (chicken Italienne) and stayed all evening. He had some story about being en route to an all night meeting with lawyers and beneficiaries, to secure his share in an inheritance, and he kept making and receiving

---

[11] Peter Makin, chartered accountant, friend of Roy Johnson.
[12] Diarist was going to send some paintings to America.

phone calls from the flat. On Saturday we had Chris, Clive and Vincent here, for a very entertaining and funny hour, the humour mostly at Clive's expense. We all then went to the Executive Club, then Vincent, Roy and I went to the Pullman Wine Bar, where we met two young people, sixties revisionists on drugs. On Friday afternoon I went with Douglas Richmond to Boulogne for a meal. By the time we got back to Douglas's flat I was drunk and silly. I finally went to the Garden House hotel and met Stella Ing[13] and we visited each other's flats. I got almost as drunk again last night, and haven't been with it at all today. Mrs Gandhi has been murdered. There is a terrible famine in Ethiopia. Last night there was a television programme on the present new wave of expressionist art. Peter Fuller[14]is one of the rare critics of authority to condemn it, and I hope he maintains his stance, or I may not get a look in. My ladies' underwear has arrived - suspenders, panties and black stockings. Had three wanks wearing these today, but I suspect that it will be a short lived enthusiasm.

[13] Stella Ing, daughter of Folkestone nursing home owner, Gordon and Biddy Ing.
[14] Peter Fuller, founder of *Modern Painters* magazine.

Tues, 29 Jan – Am now months behind copying up this journal.[1] On Friday evening John Heal arrived, bearing a gift of a bottle of port. It was *Robbie Burns Night*, and Chris arrived saying they were celebrating this at the Burlington hotel. Chris gave John and myself a lift there, to sample some haggis and drink whisky. All the local regulars, or *goblins*, as one prefers to think of them, were there, and at one stage I got persuaded into dancing *The Gay Gordons*, mid bar – not a success. On Saturday I went to Gillingham, where Nicolet Goff[2] helped me pack my exhibition and I drove with it to Studley, to spend the weekend with my father. Yesterday we took the exhibition[3] to Bromsgrove Teacher Training College and we hung it in the foyer, with the help of Paul Smith, the college art tutor. We did a rush job but it looked OK and quite a few passing students took an interest. That part of the college used to be Bromsgrove College of Further Education, where I spent an uncertain year trying to retake 'A' Levels, knowing, while I did this, that *she* was somewhere just next door at the training college, she, whom I had not seen for a year, and who was now definitely beyond my reach. I did see her in Bromsgrove once, after I had spent a morning, feeling very low indeed, wandering around the nearby countryside. I saw her in the high street and followed her into Woolworth's and the library. Her sudden presence when I felt so low completely threw me – I couldn't even say hello. I decided, yesterday, to return immediately, against my father's advice, as the van was not going well. It broke down at Maidstone with what proved to be a fault in the distributor. Roy had to rescue me and we arrived here late, and I went to bed exhausted and slept till 12 o'clock next morning. The tour, with the addition of the Contact Theatre, Manchester, and the Welsh Water Headquarters at Brecon, now consists of five venues, Gillingham and Boston being the *senior partners*.

---

[1] Diarist always copied up his diary from a first rough draft.
[2] Nicolet Goff, Exhibition Organiser, GAEC Gallery.
[3] *Chance and Certainty*, the diarist's touring exhibition of his paintings.

Mon, 25 Feb – Continued this week lazily doing a few routine chores, serenely unconcerned about things in general. On Friday evening Chris arrived, then John Heal, and Roy and I went with John to the Norfolk Wine Bar. I went solo from there, ending with a short visit to *Oliver's* disco and then a Chinese take-away. Saturday evening I went with Roy to the Burlington hotel, then I went to the Norfolk Wine Bar. Sunday, before a large fried breakfast, I mended my bed then ventured out and met Douglas Richmond, with whom I went to the Garden House hotel. I then went to the Burlington hotel and then, on a sunny very mild afternoon, went with Roy to Hythe, to walk along the seafront. On the way, we met Chris and Margaret with Hugo Oxley, to whom we gave a lift. In the evening Chris arrived and I went with him to a Cheese and Wine evening at the Burlington hotel. The goblins were all there, but who cares? Douglas arrived with his nephew, Paul, who is also a goblin, I think. I had a lot to drink during the day, but remained in a better state than I deserved. However, I could not get up this morning. Did some photography in my studio this afternoon. My Triumph Herald is an MOT write-off, which wasn't at all expected, but Roy and I have quickly found something else, a Volkswagen *Passat* estate car. It seems a good buy, at £135, and will be of practical use in carrying my paintings around. Red, the colour is.[4]   .

Fri, 14 June – On Wednesday I went to London, to see the Tate Gallery Bacon retrospective, and also the Shapinsky[5] exhibition at the Mayor gallery. I also visited the new Anthony Reynolds gallery in Cowper Street, before having a few pints of bitter in a rough pub nearby. In the pub talked to a long haired character in a very shabby suit and tie. I though he was a dosser, but he turned out to be a salaried computer operator, with his own flat in Islington and a taste for fine food, cooked by himself. I then went to the Tate and after buying my Bacon exhibition ticket decided to first go and buy a bottle of wine. As I walked from the Tate along Millbank

---

[4]   A fortune teller had predicted the diarist would have a red car.
[5]   Harold Shapinsky, painter rediscovered by Akumal Ramachander.

I again met Akumal Ramachander.[6] After our flamboyant greetings he said that he had received my slides and had liked the look of one or two of the paintings. We made an arrangement for me to meet him tomorrow at the Mayor Gallery and bring him to Folkestone. I bought the wine and drank some of it sitting in the gardens behind the Tate Gallery, then I went to the Bacon exhibition. Afterwards I went to a lecture at the Millbank Tower on business sponsorship of the arts, preceded by an unexpected wine reception, during which I met the artist, Rasheed Areen, and also made a drunken approach to Waldemar Januszczak.[7] I heard his speech and that of Alan Bownes[8] before leaving. I began having a hangover on the train. Last Saturday's barbecue was attended by the expected crowd, including Vincent's friend, Noel, John Heal, Charles Sturgis,[9] Peter Wagstaff[10]and Colin and Harold. Eight of us, including Etelle[11]and Louise[12]went on to the Golden Pin Club,[13] staying there until beyond 2am.   .

Mon, 17 June – On Saturday I picked up Akumal Ramachander at one o'clock, as planned, from the   Mayor Gallery. We had lunch at Cranks, a vegetarian restaurant off the Tottenham Court Road, then drove slowly along the A20 listening to his cassettes of Indian popular music. With his cheerful oriental uninhibitedness he suggested we stop on the way and take a hotel room for an hour or two - or for the night – an offer I declined. His enthusiasm and persistence obviously goes in all directions, not just on behalf of art. By the time we arrived Roy had spread my paintings around the flat and Akumal soon began to express his appreciation of them. We proceeded to have an *Indian evening*, with Animal's music and a vegetable curry, cooked by Roy and eaten by myself and our guests, which included Chris, Vincent, Etelle and John Heal. Akumal departed on Sunday, assuring me that he was going to

6 Akumal Ramachandar, Indian art and artist promotor and publicist.
7 Waldemar Januszczak, art critic.
8 Alan Bowness, Director of the Tate Gallery.
9 Charles Sturgis, book collector and scholar.
10 Peter Wagstaff, teacher.
11 Etelle de Beare, teaching assistant at school for children with special needs.
12 Louise, teacher, brother of Lindsay Page.
13 Golden Pin Club, *members only* after hours drinking club.

do something for me, either another approach to the Piccadilly Gallery or, more preferably, a meeting with Ronald Alley of the Tate Gallery. Sure enough, he rang today to say that he has arranged this meeting, and so I will be taking my paintings to the Tate Gallery on Thursday morning. Roy and I went to the cinema this evening, to see *Dance with a Stranger.*

Fri, 21 June – The Tate Gallery meeting with Ronald Alley took place yesterday, as did another meeting with Christabel Briggs of the Piccadilly Gallery, both appointments fixed by Akumal. At the Tate I parked in the road alongside it and began unloading paintings, while waiting for Akumal to bring Ronald Alley. I thought I would be taking the work into a side door, but I ended up showing them to him by propping them all up in a line on the pavement, against the Tate Gallery railings, Bayswater Road manner. I doubt whether this is conventional procedure at the Tate, and certainly Ronald Alley seemed rather self conscious about it, but to give him credit he did give his attention to the paintings and we did manage to have a conversation about them. As well as tourists and members of the public several people known to him came past, including Anthony Caro and other Trustees of the Tate Gallery. After this he seemed definitely nervous and during the rest of the conversation would regularly suggest I began to collect the paintings up. He suggested the Piccadilly Gallery as a possibility and said he would try and think of somewhere else, if I had no luck there. Akumal and I went to the vegetarian restaurant, then kept the appointment at the Piccadilly Gallery. I greeted Christabel Briggs, telling her I was pursuing the same line of work. Outside I began unloading paintings from the car, while Akumal carried them into the gallery. Presently I looked up from this task to see Akumal and Christabel Briggs coming out of the gallery, both carrying paintings, a definite sign that her verdict on them was still the same. I tried to get her to have a small work for her mixed summer exhibition, to no avail. I travelled home with uncertain feelings about the day. It was welcome simply to have met and shown my work to Ronald Alley, and I could not reasonably have expected anything definite to have come of this. But my net feeling is still one of anti-climax, as any polite, cautious and tactful reaction to one's work will always undermine one's own enthusiasm and confidence. The police have smashed *the convoy*, near Stonehenge, when they tried to gather again this year for the summer solstice. .

Mon, 24 June – A very typical weekend. On Friday evening I did not drink, and I drove Roy, Vincent and Etelle in the car to *Bottoms*, a new bar at the Carlton hotel. On Saturday evening we had the habitual crowd, including John Heal and Peter Wagstaff, here for a half-hearted barbecue. I left and got a takeaway curry. On Sunday I met Douglas Richmond for a lunch time drink at the Portland hotel, then I went to the upstairs bar at the Carlton hotel, my first visit since falling out of the window.[14] In the evening I went to see a local group, The Maroondogs, at the Pullman Wine Bar, where I talked to three girls. The weather, now and for several weeks, has been awful - rainy and permanently overcast. .

Sun, 30 June – Friday evening found me in low spirits still. In the morning I went to Canterbury, to see the student degree show at the College of Art. The work was of a good professional standard, both in itself and in its presentation. I said a greeting to Nicholas Treadwell,[15] who was looking at the work of a sculptor called Mark Fuller. After returning for lunch I took the car for a garage repair to its exhaust pipe. I then went in it to the Ashford Civic Centre, to see the *Ashford Art '85* exhibition.[16] In the evening, after a visit from Chris and Vincent, Roy and I went to Bottoms, so I could see the attractive bar maid there, called Veronica or Tracy. We then went to Cassidy's Diner hamburger restaurant. It was raining all evening. Yesterday evening began with a visit to the home of Charles Sturgis to sample his home made beer. I returned to find Roy at the bar with Chris, Venetia[17] and John Heal. John had brought a lot of his post cards. I danced with Venetia, then

[17] Venetia Atkinson, companion of Chris, friend of the diarist.
[14] Diarist had jumbed out of a window on a previous visit and injured his knee.
[15] Nicholas Treadwell, Director of the Nicholas Treadwell Gallery.
[16] *Ashford Open Art Exhibition.*

9

went for a drink with John at the Garden House hotel, where we talked to a chap called Roy, who worked at the Leas Pavilion Theatre (threatened once again with closure). I returned to the flat to find Vincent making a late visit. Today I got up at midday and did a further car exhaust pipe repair. Roy and I have just been this evening to Hythe, where we investigated the Yacht Club. The weather has been dire for many weeks, the wettest June for at least fifteen years. .

Sun, 14 July – Yesterday was my birthday. I receive cards from Lesley, Roy and John Heal. Also £5 from Lesley,[18] a Seconda watch from Roy, and two Caribbean Sundae deserts from Douglas. It was a wonderful hot summer day. At lunch time I went to Douglas's flat for gin and tonics, then sun-bathed on the beach with Roy. In the evening we went out for a few lagers and a steak at the London and Paris pub. Have visited Bottoms twice, to see Tracy. On Saturday I got up late, with a hangover, to watch the Band Aid live telly concert, in aid of Ethiopia. On Wednesday I went to Boulogne with Douglas Richmond. We walked along a road through an industrial estate (past the abattoir) to Saint Leonards, where we went to a café and saw Napoleon's house. I wanted to visit Pont de Brique, but Douglas, having walked so far, refused to acknowledge that Pont de Brique was anywhere near. But its church was to be seen near at hand, and so without pressing the point about its identity I said I was going to visit the church. Suddenly we each seemed to be committed to doing different things. We parted, me saying I would see him at the bus stop, but we didn't see each other again that day. I visited the village and caught a bus, which I expected to stop at the place where Douglas was waiting, but it went a different way, so in Boulogne I bought some bottles of wine and caught the first boat home. Later I learned that Douglas had let a bus go past him (as I hadn't returned), which might, after all, have been the one I was on. He had to get a taxi back to Boulogne, where he had a meal by himself before catching a later boat. All the time he was feeling furious with me. This episode was caused by the stubbornness of both of us, though, really, I

---

[18] Lesley Bailey, diarist's sister.

should have deferred to his status as a *senior citizen*, but I knew that he would be alright.

Tues, 6 Aug – It is ten to four in the afternoon. Have spent today and yesterday copying up this journal. I returned to Folkestone on Friday, dropping off *Blue Waves*, and also *Scatterboxed* at Over Seas House, for their annual exhibition.[19] There was very heavy holiday traffic in London, and my arrival there coincided with the car engine deciding to go wrong. I had a terrible time getting the car out of London and home. It is now at the garage. On Saturday evening we saw Chris, Venetia, Vincent, Noel[20] and John Heal. Roy and I went with John to Cassidy's hamburger restaurant. On Sunday Kim arrived here, and he will be staying with us for a month. *Quel coincidence!* - he has got a job in Ramsgate, with the Channel Theatre Company, playing Hal in *Loot!* Last night we were visited by Cathy, our neighbour and theatrical land lady. She brought the actress, Jennifer Oscard, with her to meet Kim. Jennifer is staying with Cathy and is currently at the Leas Pavilion Theatre. I dare say I will have a bit of a job maintaining the fiction with Kim about my job with Roy.[21] *Scatterboxed* has been rejected.[22]   .

Thurs, 15 Aug – After a lie-in each morning, I get up to clear a back log of chores, such as varnishing, copying up this journal, and pasting newspaper cuttings about art into a scrap book. I'm going for a walk each lunch time down to the harbour, where there is a bit of a holiday atmosphere. Last night Roy and I went to an Indian restaurant. Last Thursday I had lunch with John Heal. We went in my car to Rubin's restaurant in Cliftonville. It was one of this summer's rare sunny days, and after lunch we had a walk along the Margate sea front. On Sunday afternoon I gate-crashed a party in Godwin Road, given by Chris's colleague, Sue de Haan. Her house is on my bicycle route to my studio. I had previously noticed a girl from the house walking the dog, whom Chris

---

[19] Royal Over-Seas League club Annual Open Art Exhibition.
[20] Noel. a person the diarist cannot now recall
[21] Diarist did occassional van driving work at Roy's Chilham Saw Mills business.
[22] After submission to the *Athena International Art Awards* open art exhibition, Mall Galleries, London.

thought might be a sister. However there was no sign of her at the party. My latest painting has been rejected. Have sent two more to *Eva '85*, in Limerick. having some unpleasant dreams last night, dreaming of an almighty row with Roy about money, or rather the cost to him of my existence.

Sun,18 Aug – Woke with hangover. Last night we were listening to one of the disco radio stations from Boulogne, and Kim and I responded to the female DJ's invitation to her English listeners to phone. John Heal arrived, and I went with him to the Burlington hotel, then I tried and failed to find Roy and Kim, so went pretty late to the Metropole dinner dance, where at the bar I joined Etelle with ex Burlington barman, David, and also Colin[23] and Harold.[24] This morning I went to the Burlington again and heard that Mr Rousher, the Metropole restaurateur and landlord, died suddenly last night in his Metropole flat, which must have been while we were at the bar being served by his wife, Margaret. Though she was obviously in a daze, I'm sure she started when she saw me again, as if seeing an angel of death. In the afternoon Roy, Kim and I went to Denne Hill.[25] I tried to avoid our having to pay the £1 a head entrance fee, but Treadwell, keen to make a financial killing on a bank holiday, found us and made us pay. I attempted to take the opportunity to harangue him about the quality of his artists, but I made a bad job of this. Immediately I allowed him his best defence by saying *one day you will take on an artist worth some critical approval*, to which he answered *I don't give a damn about the critics*, etc. We made a quick visit to Broome Park and the Butterfly Hot House at MacFarlane's nursery, before returning for a refreshing sleep. We are about to have dinner – roast lamb cooked in garlic.

Fri, 23 Aug – To London yesterday, for the preview of the Tolly Cobbold showing at the Royal Academy.[26] Arriving at Charing Cross at 11.30am, I first of all walked along Pall Mall to identify the location of the various clubs, from the

[23] Colin Williams, Second Mate on Folkestone - Boulogne ferry
[24] Harold Moore, Ladies and Gents' hairdresser.
[25] Country mansion premises of the Nicholas Treadwell Gallery.
[26] London venue of touring *Tolly Cobbold/Eastern Arts Fifth National Exhibition*.

Athenaeum to Boodles and Whites. I see they are mostly closed at this time of year, but offer hospitality to each other's members on a rota basis. I then went to three or four pubs in the Berkeley Square area, then visited the Soloman gallery, in Briton Place, where I introduced myself. Then I visited two or three new galleries which have opened recently near Cork Street. The Royal Academy preview, in their upstairs gallery, was lively and enjoyable. I spent much of the time, in garrulous mood, with Cassie, a girl who works at the Mayor Gallery and Robin Dutt, a young critic who works for *Art Line*. Michael Murfin[27] was there with an exhibitor I met in Cambridge.[28] Earlier in the day I also met prize winner, Lance Smith, in the Royal Academy book shop. I neglected to seek out any gallery owners who might have been there and I did not see my drawing.[29] Having more or less finished my chores, I must now begin to think about another painting, though today I did little beyond recover from yesterday. Slept at the studio this afternoon. The car has been to the garage and is back in a sound mechanical condition. This evening I drove Kim and Roy to the pubs at Wooton, Swingfield Street and Paddlesworth. Last Saturday we watched the carnival procession with Douglas, Vincent and John Heal. I went to the carnival dance, getting in free. Vincent made his entry too conspicuous and did not succeed. In mitigation, I add that I had already flung a fair amount of change at the procession.

Sat, 31 Aug – This week Kim has been at the Marlowe Theatre, Canterbury, playing Hal in *Loot*! I saw it on Wednesday and enjoyed it very much. I was hoping that plenty of people that Roy and I knew would go together as a party. In the end the party was a weird foursome, consisting of Roy, his mother, myself and John Heal. Afterwards Kim and John and I went for a drink in Canterbury, during which it dawned on Kim that John was probably not right in the head. On Thursday evening Chris and Vincent arrived, full of the usual excuses about

[27] Michael Murfin, artist and fellow *Tolly Cobbold/Eastern Arts Fifth National Exhibition* exhibitor.
[28] At the Fitzwilliam Museum, opening venue of the *Tolly Cobbold/Eastern Arts Fifth National Exhibition*.
[29] *The Interrogation of Steve Biko*.

having failed to come with us to Canterbury. On this occasion, I did not feel in a jocular mood and lost my temper with them, calling them *bull shitters* and *wankers*. Despite the considerable truth of these accusations, I suppose I shall have to apologize. Yesterday evening I went to the Leas Pavilion Theatre, to see The Unexpected Guest. The performance was the penultimate one before the theatre closes down tonight, to be maybe turned into a Wild West-themed disco bar. I have been going to the studio each morning to do yet further retouching to *Blue Waves*. Every bit I do dries too dark and has to be gone over again and again. Some afternoons I have been going out taking photos. On Thursday I went to Shepherdswell and yesterday I went to Aylesham. In general my spirits have been very low and unstable this week, though I do feel better now.

Tues, 17 Sept – Yesterday I took *Blue Waves*, or *Sea Dance*, to Chatham, to the Lloyd's of London building in Gun Wharf.[30] I then drove out to Grain and stood at the edge of the sea, looking across to Southend. I went to a café on a camp site of holiday chalets. On Wednesday evening Roy and Douglas and l took the 5.30pm boat from Folkestone to Boulogne. We walked ashore, and went to a couple of cafés, then took a taxi to the port to catch the same boat back, having also just had time to investigate the whereabouts of a sea food restaurant called L'Huitriere. Back in Folkestone, I went to Casanovas[31]where there was a license extension and entertainment from The Maroondogs. On Saturday evening we were visited by John Heal and Chris and Vincent. I ended up going with John, whom Roy can't abide, to the Garden House hotel, where we met Douglas, and then, having telephoned ahead, to the Golden Pin Club. On Sunday there was an all-day event at the Leas Cliff Hall, given by a succession of local pop groups in aid of charity for Africa. I made several visits to this during the afternoon and evening, in between doing chores like going to the launderette, and making return visits to the flat, for a glass of home made beer. Continued the work each morning last

[30] For submission to the *Lloyd's of London Open Art Exhibition.*
[31] Folkestone pub.

week on *Sea Dance*. Am also trying to start up another painting.   .

Sat, 19 Oct – I spent four days this week on my small painting, *The Washing, the Houses and the Chapel Spire (Aylesham)*. On Wednesday I began some preparations for my 1986 tour, which should be going to eight or nine venues. I may use *All My Own Work* for the tour title.[32] At lunch time on Wednesday, Vincent and I went to the Lifeboat Inn, then to the Calcutta Indian restaurant in Tontine Street. The argument has blown over, though Vincent was still very frosty when he and Chris visited last Saturday. On that occasion, we all went to the Garden House hotel, where we met Douglas Richmond. Last night Chris and Vincent visited, then after Chris left John Heal made a sudden ghostly appearance through the open door. We all went with him to the Burlington hotel, then Vincent, Roy and I went to the Metropole, then taxied to Cassidy's Diner. Have just been for a car ride to Canterbury, where I bought a shirt and visited a market in Ivy Street, where I met an artist who works there, whose Christian name, I think, was Terrance.

Mon, 28 Oct – Last Saturday evening Chris and Venetia visited us, and John Heal, who brought a gift for the bar of a bottle of cherry brandy. We all, except Roy, went to Chris and Venetia's house to sample Venetia's elderflower wine. John Heal and I then went to his flat to sip a brandy, then to Cassidy's Diner, then back to his flat to finish our drink. I told John about Roy's dislike for him. On Sunday I went to the Garden House hotel with Douglas. On Friday I had lunch with Vincent at the Hi Tin Chinese restaurant in Tontine Street. That evening Roy and I met Chris, Vincent, Etelle and Louise in the Salisbury hotel. We bought some Indian food at the Courtland hotel, eaten here.[33] On Saturday evening Roy and I met Chris, Vincent and Gilbert[34] in the Salisbury hotel. Roy and I went to the Executive Club and Cassidy's Diner. On Sunday lunch time I met Douglas in the Garden House hotel. I had an afternoon walk on the Leas and seafront. We went on a couple of Rotunda fun fair rides.

---

[32] To be renamed *A Sign-Post Ahead.*
[33] Clifton Mansions.
[34] Gilbert Holiday, businessman, husband of Bernadette (né) Crofts.

Had tagliatelle for dinner last night, with a bottle of red table wine.

Wed, 6 Nov – Last Wednesday I went to the G.A.E.C gallery, in Gillingham, and the Mall Galleries, London, to collect paintings. In London I saw paintings by Stephen McKenna at the I.C.A., and I went to the Albion Studios near Kings Cross station to investigate what I hope is one of the venues for the 1986 tour. Yesterday, having made a good effort to finish *The Washing, the Houses and the Chapel Spire (Aylesham)*, I took it and three other paintings to the Metropole, to submit them for *The Winter Show*. I met the exhibition organiser, Sue Snodin, again, and Stephen Turner,[35] who also happened to be submitting work. He has not, contrary to my expectations, made me his recommendation this year for a South East Arts *Purchase Award*. I have also been organising a *Clifton Mansions Bonfire Night*, culminating last night in a bonfire, attended by about thirty people. Chris let off the fireworks. I had also enjoyed doing things like typing a leaflet, collecting money from the residents, and building the bonfire. Did not do much today beyond returning the van to Chilham[36]and having lunch with Roy in Canterbury, at the Cardinal's Cap. Weather good lately, on the whole.

Tues, 19 Nov – on Friday the preview of *The Winter Show* exhibition took place at the Metropole. It was a pleasure to see the usual gang here for a drink - Chris, Venetia and Vincent - and then go with them to the Metropole. My two paintings, hung by Stephen Turner and Su Snodin, were in a very advantageous position on either side of the door. Afterwards we all went to Julian's[37]bar, where I had a conversation with Brian Oxley, also exhibiting in the exhibition. Vincent, Roy and I then went to the Burlington hotel and Cassidy's Diner. On Saturday afternoon I went for a walk just before dark, taking a circular route from Alkham. In the evening, after a visit from Chris, Roy and I went to the Executive Club (+£1.90)[38]and

---

[35] Stephen Turner, artist and exhibition organiser.
[36] Chilham Sawmills.
[37] Julian Perez, Head Barman, Burlington hotel.
[38] Fruit machine win.

Harvey Wine Bar. On Sunday Roy and I went at lunch time to a new wine bar, Racquets, in Hythe. Later that afternoon I went for a walk and visited John Heal at his flat, taking with me a very small bottle of brandy. He had obviously been in all day, judging from a very fetid atmosphere in his lounge. Later on, after dinner, I went the the Garden House hotel, finding Douglas there. Yesterday I collected 500 leaflets from L.S. Arter Ltd., for use on the 1986 tour, now to be called *A Sign Post Ahead*. I began to assemble the canvas for a new painting today. It is very cold and there has been a light fall of snow. Am feeling faintly glum this evening. 2,500 people have been killed by a Colombian volcano erupting.   .

Mon, 16 Dec – I had an excess of booze and food this weekend, beginning on Friday with what I think must be regarded as *the Christmas party*. This occurred thanks to Etelle and Louise, who arrived here with the food for a buffet, which we had been told by Etelle to expect. The party itself consisted of Roy and myself, Etelle and Louise, Chris and Vincent, John Heal, Howard Atkinson[39] and Clive Pratt[40] and somehow managed to be successful. The next evening Chris, Vincent and I, having decided to all dress in our blazers and ties, went with Roy to the Burlington hotel, but this expedition was not a success. The bar, presided over by Etelle, was staked out when we arrived by goblins and our party was confined to a corner table. Afterwards Roy and I went to the Metropole dinner dance, where we drank with Colin and Harold, who were with an elegant pair of middle aged men, who share a flat at the Grand. On Sunday Roy and I drank some cider, and went at lunch time to the wine bar in Sandgate Road, then to the Golden Pin Club, for something to eat. In the afternoon I visited Douglas Richmond. In the evening we had roast beef and Yorkshire pudding, which was preceded for me with brief visits to the Burlington hotel and Garden House hotel.[41]   .

---

[39] Howard Atkinson, graphic designer, former husband of Venetia Atkinson.
[40] Clive Pratt, manager, Nasons furniture store, Canterbury.
[41] Grand hotel, Folkestone.

Mon, 3 March – Yesterday I began with two large vodka and orange juices, had with breakfast, at twelve o'clock - Roy had cooked a gammon steak, with chips and pineapple and mushrooms. I then walked to the Metropole, and drank several Lowenbraus with Colin and Harold and Bibby and Biddy,[1] an hour I really enjoyed. I hope I did not become too animated at any stage, or make any inappropriate comments, especially as they stood me my drinks. In the afternoon I called on *Long John* Heal, but he was out. I went to see *Little John* Whitehead,[2] which was an interesting experience. He showed me his wood working and metal working tools, lathes and drills in his bedroom workshop. He has never completed anything in his life, but I was fascinated by the metal tools he has made over the years, intended for the mass production of parts for a string of unfinished projects, such as his candelabra. In the evening Chris visited the flat and sat at the bar while Roy and I ate our Robert Carrier[3] *Tournados au Château*. Today I was in a bit of a daze, after yesterday's booze, the equivalent of about ten pints. I began the day with a coffee with Douglas in Debenhams, and then proceeded to my studio to make a bad job of the jockey's hat.[4]

Studley, Mon, 14 April – Have been feeling in an immensely buoyant mood. It is an incredible prospect lying ahead. I feel very good about the idea. I feel certain she will keep her own enthusiasm for it. She has sent a card,[5] saying she will keep me posted on her thoughts. The rest of my Studley visit proceeded as normal. I caught a cold, but I didn't take much notice of it. I especially enjoyed the morning walk around the perimeter of the river meadow.[6] On Wednesday evening, at the Nags Head, I saw Dave Vann[7] and John, his music teacher friend, with whom Dave is able to engage in a highly *camp* double act. On Friday

---

[1] Bibby and Biddy (Ing), female partners, care home owners and managers.
[2] John Whitehead. Deminutive in stature, socially isolated, John lived with his mother until his decomposed body was found in their house after her death.
[3] Robert Carrier, chef, author and restaurateur.
[4] In diarist's current oil painting.
[5] From Pam Michell, social worker, former pupil with diarist at Redditch County High School.
[6] By the river Arrow.
[7] Dave Vann, diarist's school friend, actor and Birmingham drama college tutor.

evening I went with my father to Northampton, to have a drink with Kim, who is there acting at the Royal Theatre. On Saturday, with my father reluctant to see me go, I drove to Pontardawe, an interesting journey via Ross and the *head of the valleys* road. I loaded my paintings, had a drink with John McMullian[8] and stayed the night with his neighbours again. I returned to Folkestone on Sunday. Last week I did two days at the studio. On Wednesday, at one o'clock, I met Akumal at the Tate gallery, and we had lunch in a vegetarian restaurant in nearby Pimlico. He has discovered another artist called Carr.[9] Afterwards, I met John Heal in a South Moulton Street wine bar. We had afternoon tea at the Over Seas Club, me pretending to be a member. We went to another wine bar off Regent Street, called *Shampers*, then I caught the 6.55 pm train. On Friday I went to London again, to transfer a rejected Mall Gallery painting[10] to the Royal Academy, for my Summer Exhibition entry. I went to London by car, going first via the old lighthouse at Dungeness, where I delivered two of Roy's Monk benches.[11] Saw Chris and Paul[12] this weekend.

Birmingham, Tues, 17 June – On Friday, at 10 am, she came to the room[13] and collected some more semen. She was wearing a blue summery outfit, new clothes, l think, as she was off on holiday to Scotland with friends, after her visit to the clinic. She looked very contented. I felt a certain contentment too, if also rather wan as I walked to the coach station. It was a lovely June morning, the city centre now wearing a bright commercial aspect, its pavements quickly filling with healthy, eager looking people. Since then I have been in something of a depression, not relieved by a spell of wonderful weather. At the weekend, I did some repair work on the car. On Sunday evening Roy and I went to *happy hour* at the Burlington hotel, where we sat at the bar and drank several bottles of

---

8 John McMillian, Deputy Events Organiser, The Cross Community Centre, Pontadawe.
9 Robert Carr, painter.
10 Submitted to an open art exhibition there.
11 Items of garden furniture manufactured at Chilham Saw Mills.
12 Paul Crofts, accountancy student, youngest son in Crofts family.
13 In Midland hotel.

Lowenbrau, in the company of John Heal. We were also, unfortunately, in the company of an uncouth and garrulous drunk, who looked like he hailed from an east European circus, or was the brother of Colonel Gaddafi.[14] I think it was on Wednesday of last week when, walking after lunch down Marten Road to my studio, I met Colin and *the girls*, Bibby and Biddy, who now live in the road. I was shown their house and drank gin there all afternoon. This continued in the evening, with a visit by Roy and myself to Colin and Harold's flat, for more gin and something to eat. We all then went out for another drink locally. This could have been on Tuesday.

Mon, 30 June – Have had quite a busy time for a week or two, mixing business with pleasure. On Thursday, the 16th I had lunch with John Heal. On a hot day, we met at the Clifton hotel and went by bus to Hythe, first for *aperitifs* at the Upstairs/ Downstairs restaurant, and then for lunch at Nicola's restaurant, my first visit. I had minestrone soup and a sea bass dish cooked in fennel. John had lambs' kidneys, starting with smoked salmon. John bought the wine - a bottle or more each, mainly Frascati. We had a pleasant time, though we made a messy exit from the restaurant, with some confusion over the bill. We walked to the Imperial hotel for afternoon tea, again bought in some confusion. I lay on a sofa in the deserted lounge bar and went to sleep, and John had departed when I woke. Refreshed somewhat, I walked along the sea front, enjoying the balmy mild air. Arrived Folkestone for *happy hour* at the Burlington hotel. This day, incidentally, started with a painful hangover achieved the evening before, when, while Roy hosted a residents' meeting in the flat, I went with Chris to the Carlton hotel and then solo down the town to the cellar bar at Tofts disco. I must have spent a fairly restful Friday and weekend. I had one or two bouts of depression, due possibly to the weather, which has turned oppressively heavy and overcast. On Sunday Roy and I put an aerial on the roof, braving the fury of the swooping gulls, whose chicks are up

---

[14] Colonel Gaddafi, ex Libyan president.

there. I saw Douglas in the evening at the Garden House hotel, where we found ourselves the sole clients. On Monday I took the 3.40 pm train to London, having received a private view invite from the Mayor gallery, for a Lichtenstein[15] exhibition. The invite proved to be thanks to Akumal, who is in England again. As a Cork Street opening, I viewed the event as being pleasant and routine and unnecessary.[16] I spoke to a few people there, including two well known art world *free-loaders* with identical Christian names, which I do not recall. James Mayor probably always lowers his plummy cultured voice at least two octaves for the benefit of new acquaintances, his other defence being to move away from you as quickly as possible. If he has some enthusiasm for being a host, it certainly doesn't show. His partner, Andrew Murray, is a bit of a twerp, frankly. I was grateful to both of them for my presence there, and for the sandwiches and glasses of wine I consumed. On Tuesday I did a logo for the *Clifton Mansions Leaseholders' Association*, and I also did my office work.

Wed, 9 July – Yesterday I caught the 2.40 pm train to London, where I had a 4 pm appointment with Francis Farmer, of the Contemporary Art department of Christie's auctioneers. He has had the idea to hold auctions of contemporary works that have been obtained directly from artists' studios. He looked at my slides and suggested that I enter *A Day by the Sea* and *His Route Through Leicester Square* for their next sale on the 1st of September. The first auction was not all that successful, and all he is hoping for is to avoid losing Christie's any money. I met him again later at the street party given by the Cork Street galleries. I went there with John Heal, whom I met beforehand in Shampers wine bar. Fifteen galleries were open and giving away wine between 6.30 pm and 8.30 pm, to a large assortment of guests circulating from gallery to gallery, or standing out in the street. It was greatly enjoyable. John and I started at the Mayor gallery, where I again found that I had Akumal to thank for my invitation (not that an invitation would have been

---

[15] Roy Lichtenstein, pop artist.
[16] From a self-promotional point of view.

21

necessary). I spoke to quite a few people, aiming to have a conversation with a different person in each gallery. The only name I recall is that of Claire, or *Tate Gallery Girl*, as I dubbed a girl I recognised, who used to work in the Tate gallery bookshop. A group of art students arrived, wearing, instead of clothes, decorative constructions made of paper mache. As John and I left the party we discovered this group walking behind us; I believe one of them was imitating John's peculiar walk. This caused us to get involved with them, and John and I ended up joining their visit to a pizza restaurant. They were very friendly - respectful, almost - though goodness knows what they made of us both. The ones sitting nearest listened politely to John's conversational nonsense and seemed to regard him with perfect seriousness, which must have been an appauling experience for them. I had a job trying to get John to say goodbye to the students, which I finally managed, to his annoyance. We went to a pub, where I had to abandon him, as he decided he wanted to stay in London. I caught the last train, arriving home after 1 am.

Sat, 27 Sept – I am sitting in the Margate train from London. We have just gone through Tonbridge. It is 6.33 pm. I have been to hand in a painting at the Mall Galleries, for the *Society of Equestrian Artists' Open Exhibition*, and also to visit - taking two other paintings - an advertising organisation called Self Direct near Old Street station. They are putting on an art exhibition for their Christmas party. They gave me a ten pound note for my travelling expenses. Felt stressed and dazed at lunchtime, rushing to catch my train to London, the result, doubtless, of the cocktail party which I gave at the flat last night, to celebrate the end of my *A Sign Post Ahead* tour. I mounted a little display in the flat, in connection with the tour, and I stood behind the bar, shaking cocktails for my guests. The guests were Roy, Chris and Vincent, neighbours Bert and Cathy Bagnell, girls Etelle, Louise and Linda, John Heal, and someone called Eugene, a drinking crony of Chris's, from the Salisbury hotel. Also Douglas Richmond, making twelve people, who had a jovial time, I'd say. Afterwards John and I went to the Portland hotel, then Roy, Vincent and I went to Bottoms, where there was a gay disco night. Last weekend I retrieved the exhibition from Blaenau Ffestiniog. I left Folkestone on Thursday, first meeting Pam at 6 pm in the Hare and Hounds in Kings Heath. I gave her my semen, having just produced it standing in a field gateway in Haye Lane, Studley. Just when I had finished wanking, while I was still in entire disarray, a man walked past with his dog. I gave Pam some more sperm next morning, after staying in Studley, and we had breakfast near Pam's house in a cafe called the Bun and Biscuit. I then returned to Studley, to set off with my father for Blaenau Ffestiniog. In wonderful weather we got as far as Badmouth, where we stayed at the Bryn-Teg guest house. We collected the exhibition on Saturday morning and meandered back towards Studley. Near Shrewsbury, beneath Wenlock Edge, we visited some places in dad's old home territory, then went to one or two pubs on the way back to Studley from there. I left Studley on Monday. I did two studio days this week. Roy has announced that we are going on a canal holiday in the Midlands, to begin tomorrow.

Sun, 26 Oct – Pam is pregnant. It is an exciting feeling, and quite a surprise that it has happened so soon. Is it at our third attempt? I had a feeling it would take us quite a few more months, and perhaps I also had thoughts of a physical relationship developing between us – she still gives me a little ghostly tug. But now she is pregnant I feel ever so pleased and good and right about it. Pam's mother, after first being upset by the news, has volunteered the use of Pam's old cot. How amazing it will be to see it lying inside it! I got the news from Pam on Friday morning. On the way back from my studio at lunch time I called on Douglas, having been invited to his flat for a gin and tonic. I returned a picture to him which I'd framed. When I arrived home I found John Heal making a surprise visit, so I took the opportunity to continue drinking gin with him in the flat, at the *Over-Seas Club*.[17] We left at 4.30 pm and we walked all the way to Hythe, judging our arrival to coincide with opening time at Upstairs/Downstairs wine bar. John has a bar account there[18] and I drank several *Simbuca Romanas* at his invitation, while he was absent making a business call. I then walked all the way back to Folkestone, both journeys made in the presence of a exhilarating autumnal sea storm. On the way to Hythe I had walked much of the time on the beach, alongside permanently serried ranks of crashing waves. On the way back it was dark, and I arrived home drunk, and wet, and joyful. After a shower I went along happily with the rest of the evening, which consisted of a visit by Roy and myself to a jazz evening at Cleggies, where we met Etelle and Louise and Linda, followed by a visit by Roy and myself to Bottoms gay disco night. The atmosphere at the latter is not oppressive, as there is an equal balance of men and women.

Fri, 14 Nov – Another excursion to France yesterday, this time with John Heal at my invitation. We had lunch in Calais at Le Cordial, a little cafe-restaurant near the Post Office. I had lobster bisque and steak frites, John had *maqueraux aux vin blanc* and a pork chop. We visited a couple of cafés, and drank glasses of white wine and talked to the locals. In one of the cafés a man of about fifty five, with a grey beard, sat in the corner singing old French ballads. He had a good voice and he was by no means a drunkard. With him in the corner was a small group of people, including a woman nursing a baby. The rest of the clientèle in the café, standing at the bar or sitting elsewhere, were all in conversation with each other, unheeding the balladeer. The atmosphere of the place was astoundingly French. We got back to Dover at 5.30pm local time and opted to spend some time in the town. We walked along the sea front and back and went to the White Cliffs hotel, where I rang Roy. He collected us at the Arlington Inn, by which time, as the landlord quite rightly spotted, John was rather the worse for wear. He was asleep, in fact, when Roy arrived. In Calais I

---

[17] aka. the bar in Roy Johnson's flat.
[18] ...and later worked behind the bar there for a while.

delivered some slides[19]to the Gallerie de l'Ancienne Post, a gallery I had discovered the previous week, when in Calais with Roy and Douglas.

Sun, 16 Nov – I have sold two paintings. John Heal attended the Christie's sale[20]on Friday, as my observer, and reported back on Friday evening. *His Route Through Leicester Square* went for £320, £20 over the reserve price. *A Day by the Sea*, which was illustrated in the catalogue, went for £380, which was £130 over the reserve. I seem to have been fortunate in that the sale generally seems to have been a success, unlike the previous two of its kind, when many of the lots went unsold. I feel very glad about the news, though also a certain wistfulness about the paintings' departure. I wonder who bought them? One of the successful bidders was an elderly, grey haired man with glasses, and the other was anonymous, according to John. On Saturday evening there was impromptu party here at the flat. The visitors were Chris and Clive Pratt, Andrew Edwards[21](who departed for a party in Whitstable), Etelle and Louise and Etelle's Spanish friend, Salvador, and Vincent and Edward Holiday,[22] making a cheerful hour or two of red wine, cider, disco music and chips on the bar.

Tues, 23 Dec – On Monday Roy and I went to the Self Direct[23]party at the Smiths Gallery. We went with Kim and Marie Pierre,[24] whom we met beforehand at the Nags Head in Covent Garden at 5pm. The party was basically for the Self Direct advertising agency clients. There was a very generous quantity of Champagne. Roy drank two bottles or more and was near to collapse afterwards, as was Kim. On Wednesday Douglas and I went on a non-landing trip from Folkestone to

---

[19] of the diarist's art work.
[20] Auction of British and irish traditionalist and modernist Paintings, Waterclours, Drawings and Sculptures.
[21] Andrew Edwards, Venetia Atkinson's brother.
[22] Edward Holiday, son of Christopher Crofts' sister, Bernadette.
[23] Self Direct advertising agency, sponsor of the *Self Exposure* exhibition at the Smiths Gallery.
[24] Marie-Pierre, Kim's girlfriend.

Boulogne. On the way I did some of my Christmas shopping and on the way back we were in the company of Chris, Clive Pratt and John Gordon and co, who had gone in Chris's car for a meal on Boulogne. Chris's brother, Jim, was the Captain, and he invited us all up on the bridge during the trip back. Vincent and his friend, Phillip, were also on board. On Thursday I snatched a day in the studio. On Friday evening we were visited by John Heal and Vincent. Roy, Vincent and I then went to the gay evening Christmas party at Bottoms, where there was a disco and a juggling cabaret act. Vincent and I danced together. On Saturday I arrived at the Smiths Gallery[25] at one o'clock, having been asked to invigilate at the gallery for the afternoon. This I did with fellow exhibitor, Susan Beckett. We sat behind the desk and handed catalogues to a steady trickle of visitors. I was able to bring all my paintings back afterwards, bar one, which Andrew Wheatley[26] had left elsewhere. Yesterday I took the car to Saltwood Garage[27] for an oil change at 9 am. While they did this I had a cold frosty walk down the lane past Saltwood castle and across the motorway and the A20. I then drove to Margate, to do the rest of my Christmas shopping. I had lunch at the Indian Tandoori on the sea front. I was the only client and I sat in the window, looking out at the Margate sands. It was sunny but there were no sun bathers. Have been a couple of times to the Hi Tin restaurant in Tontine street, once with Chris and once with him and Vincent. On Sunday Roy and Douglas and I went to the Burlington hotel at lunch time. Pam has caught the flu, which unfortunately has developed into the bronchitis she suffers from every winter lately. She is worried about the effect her coughing could have on the baby.

[25] Smiths Gallery, London.
[26] Andrew Wheatley, Exhibitions Organiser, Smiths Gallery, London.
[27] Saltwood Garage, run by Mike Horton, married to Roy Johnson's sister, Julia.

Mon, 19 Jan – A week ago, on Friday, I went to London to collect three paintings, from Ashford, the Mall Galleries and the Self Direct offices. I also ascertained the whereabouts of Blandell Ltd,[1]and visited a new gallery in Islington, called at The Art Space Gallery, speaking to one of the co-directors there. On Sunday evening and Monday there was a very heavy snowfall in Folkestone and throughout Kent. Things have been at a standstill and Roy stayed at home until Friday. I managed a couple of studio days, but have not otherwise used the time very profitably. Should have done more paper work and correspondence, but must have preferred to welcome the interruption to my routine. Spent a lot of time tramping around newsagent shops each day, trying to find scarce copies of the *Sun*, which was publishing coupons enabling readers to cross the channel for a pound. Have got enough coupons for six crossings, which, valid until the 4th of April, will provide some cheerful diversions this winter. On Friday evening Vincent arrived, and Roy and I went with him to the Portland hotel. Etelle and Louise and John Heal and co. were at another table and we affected to remain aloof – Vincent, because he had just had a tiff with Etelle, I, because John Heal demanded a tenner from me before Christmas, for going to the Christie's auction for me. Vincent, Roy and I then went to Bottoms gay disco, which was dreary, as the disco had been cancelled. We then returned late to the flat, where Roy cooked chicken and chips. I did not enjoy the evening in the least. Vincent, or *Adder*, as we call him, was at his most venomous and irritating. I tormented him, by showing him all my cross channel vouchers. He retaliated by hiding Roy's glasses somewhere in the flat. We discovered this the next morning, Roy finding them in an obscure place after a long search. On Saturday evening Roy and I went to the Burlington hotel. Yesterday we went for a rally in my car in the snow. We went to Lympe, Stowting, Brabourne, Hamstreet, Billsington, New Romney and Dymchurch. Pork *Clifton Mansions*[2]for dinner this evening.

---

[3] The diarist was due to have an exhibition of his work in the foyaer of the Barbican Centre, London.
[2] A Robert Carrier pork and caper dish, though cooked with beer instead of cider.

Sat, 7 Feb - It is 1.20pm. I am on a Townsend Thorenson ferry, on a solo *Sun* trip. The newer Townsend ships are not much good. They are like a floating shopping mall and they have no side promenade decks. I have just stood in a long queue to get to the bar, where I bought two and a half pints of Lowenbrau, and I am now sitting in a quiet place. In Boulogne I shall buy some wine and return on the same boat, at 4.30 pm French time. The crossing is smooth and sunny. I was all set to spend a few days in Amsterdam and Brussels, but I've changed my plans, having got some information about an art competition in Paris. I will enter *Sir Gerald Glover* for the Academia des Beaux-Arts *Prix de Portrait Paul-Louis Weiller* exhibition - my stars are predicting good news from abroad at the moment. What of last weekend? On Saturday evening Vincent and his friend, Philip, and John Heal, attended my invitational party at the flat. We sat around a darkened bar drinking wine until quite late. That Saturday evening I went to the Burlington hotel and the Metropole. On Sunday Roy and I had the chicken Wok dish for dinner. This week I went to the studio on two days, and I have also been doing some preparatory work for the Barbican exhibition.[3] My painting activities have come to constitute a one-man business, which I run from my bedroom office. As a business, it is hard to justify its existence, as it is continually losing ninety percent or more of its expenditure, nor have I any idea whether any improvement can be expected. I'm now on the return journey. In Boulogne I went to the Prisunic supermarket and got six free tins of Lowenbrau with two *Sun* vouchers. I decided to keep to my plan, so here I am again on the *Free Enterprise XIII*. I discovered her name just before we arrived in Boulogne, and now I have explored her I do, of course, recognise her as the ship on which I worked one summer as a steward. We used to go from Dover to Zeebrugge. And she does, of course, have side decks, where I remember we used to assemble in groups for lifeboat drill. At the stern there is a top deck where, in harbour at Zeebrugge I well remember

---

[3] The diarist was due to have an exhibition of his work in the foyer of the Barbican Centre, London.

stealing a minute or two at night, just to look at the foreign dockside lights of the port. I remember the scrub-outs we used to have to do, with bucket and mop, in different areas of the ship after it docked.

Wed, 25 Feb - The Paris trip went as planned. I left on the 10am ferry from Folkestone. Douglas and Colin were on board on a day trip. I went via Amiens, unnecessarily, and got lost going through the town, but I emerged on a rural *D* road to Beauvais. I arrived at my hotel between 8 and 9 pm. Not much traffic by that time in Paris, the streets fairly dark and wet. I had a delicious shower, and whisky and cokes, and ate some sandwiches in my room while studying the map of Paris. I lived off sandwiches, as I was aiming to do the trip on the cheapo. I finally went out for a walk around the *cinqieme*. I walked to the square St Medard, where the church looked very beautiful, floodlit and under an inch or two of snow. I walked up Rue Mouffetard (past a few clochards, who were lying around drunk in the wet, not bothering to find a dry doorway) through the arondisement to the Pont St Michel. I ended the walk with a Lowenbrau in two cafes, Aux Deus Magots and La Coupole. Returned to the hotel about 1.30 am. Next morning after breakfast (& hangover) in my room, I walked to the Academia des Beaux Arts, via the *Boul Mich* and the Quai de Conti. Having found where to take the painting, I returned to the car via the Luxembourg Gardens. I dropped the painting off and left Paris. Having time to kill, I had walks in Le Crotoy, Le Touquet, and even Le Portel[4]before catching the 9pm ferry. In Le Touquet I bought some home made tagliatelle. On Friday evening I went, briefly, to a Metropole Arts Centre preview of work by two young local artists. On Saturday evening we were visited by Chris, Venetia and John Heal. John had been drinking wine since lunch time, and was coherent, though wilting. Roy and I went to the Portland hotel and Executive Club. On Sunday, after breakfast, Roy and I went to Charing, so

---

[4] Sea bay suburb of Boulogne.

I could note the dates of Charing and Aldington Point to Point meetings. What did we have for dinner that evening?

Tues, 3 March - The portrait has not been accepted. I heard this disappointing news this morning. I suppose they didn't like my technique, although there's a possibility I was disqualified for submitting a double portrait, instead of single portrait. In the rules I wasn't sure whether *un seul portrait* meant a single portrait painting, or a painting with a single portrait on it. However, I had hoped that if I made a mistake I could rely on the French interpreting the rules in their customary vague manner. I am intending, as already planned, to go all the bloody way there and back in one day, to get it back. On Saturday I went to France with John Heal. We caught the 6 am ferry from Dover. There was an unreal atmosphere at that time in the morning, while it was still dark, the boat full of bleary eyed early risers, enlivened by a party of twenty or so young men, all dressed up identically as Max Wall. They drank pints of lager and moved about the boat imitating Max Wall's funny walk. I wonder how their day went?[5] John Heal and I went two hundred miles or more in my car. We went to Arras and visited a café in the main square, then returned to Bournonville for lunch. Two other tables were occupied by English people. No French people were in the restaurant, then, unbelievably, a coach load of English people on a day trip from London arrived. Apparently, the restaurant has an agreement with a travel firm to cater for a coach full of English people every Saturday. As a matter of fact, the atmosphere improved when the coach load arrived. The cheerful noise of the full-up restaurant was better than if there had only been the three tables of English people. After lunch we visited a wine warehouse in Boulogne, where I bought six bottles of Sylvaner, with a view to starting a collection of them for my Barbican exhibition preview. We caught the 6.15 pm ferry from Calais.

---

[5] *It'll all end in tears*, the diarist recalls another passenger saying.

Thurs, 12 March - On Monday I went to the studio, though I had a day-long gin daze. Since then I've been fiddling about trying to decide on a catalogue design for the Barbican Centre exhibition. I am aiming for something simple, cheap but featuring a colour reproduction. To this end my brain has not been functioning at all. Some of the time on Tuesday was spent with John Heal, whom I met in the town in the morning. We went together to Arter's, the printers, then presently for a drive to Hythe and Romney Marsh. We went to the Black Bull at New church, and the Star Inn, at St Mary-in-the-Marsh, both extremely quiet. It was sunny and warm in the car, and we drove back through Ruckinge and Lyminge. Yesterday I felt very anxious and confused, trying to proceed with the catalogue. I had a walk to Arter's, and on to the Waterworks head quarters, to pay the bill.[6] It is 11.15 am and sunny again outside, so I see. I have not gone to the studio, but will instead spend a third day on the catalogue.

Fri, 20 March - Last Saturday I went to Charing Point to Point meeting. I went on the bus and Roy picked me up by car. A sunny afternoon. I lost £16, plus money for hot dogs and beer. In the evening Etelle gave a birthday party for herself at the flat. She provided the food and people brought wine. The party was attended by Roy and myself, Etelle, her girl friends, Jane, Louise and Sally, Louise's boy friend and her brother, Lindsey, John Heal, Peter Wagstaff and Vincent. Eleven people. The party was quite good, after a slow start. I started the day with a hangover, having the previous evening gone to *happy hour* at the Burlington hotel, then back to the flat, and then with Roy to Cassidy's hamburger restaurant. On Tuesday I had a major outing to London with John Heal. The reason was that we had both received invites to the Mayor gallery preview of paintings by Robert Carr, another of Akumal's discoveries. John and I caught the 10.24 am train from Folkestone and in London we

---

[6] Water bill at Roy's flat.

went first to the Royal Over-Seas League Club. We got there at twelve o'clock, and the bar was almost empty. The atmosphere at that time of day was frosty, and the barman, an unfriendly Greek-looking person, was obviously suspicious of our membership credentials. We then went to Maynard's wine bar, in South Moulton Street, where we stayed until three o'clock. We drank a bottle of Mosel each, and a glass of Champagne, and ate some peanuts. On two occasions I left John and walked up and down South Moulton Street, slipping into a pub at the end of the road for a pint of beer. In the afternoon I had intended to see the *British Art Exhibition* at the Royal Academy, but instead John and I saw the *Lost Tribes of the Amazon* at the Museum of Mankind, an exhibition which I had not had time to properly see before.[7] We then went for afternoon tea at Fortnum & Masons. It was the last half hour and quite quiet, though still light outside. We drank a pot of Darjeeling tea and I ate two coffee éclairs. We then walked along Piccadilly, heading for Shampers wine bar, off Bond Street - how pleasant to do so, just before it gets dark; hearing the gathered starlings above the noise of the traffic, walking blissfully through the homeward bound crowds, seeing the window boxes on the buildings full of early daffodils and polyanthus - walking through you crocus-filled month of March! We walked via the Regent Palace hotel to the wine bar, where we drank some New Zealand wine. We then walked towards Cork street again, via the Regent Palace hotel. It was my first visit and I liked the atmosphere of the hotel, with it's good toilet facilities and large, covered lobby leading to bars, kiosks and restaurants, in which lots of people were creating an agreeable, ambiguous air of half public thoroughfare and half old fashioned, comfortable hotel. Walking along Cork Street, we noticed another gallery private view going on, so we slipped in. It was a bit of a crush inside. After a while I spotted Robin Dutt[8] just leaving. I rushed after him and caught him up

---

[7] On a previous visit.
[8] Robin Dutt, art critic for *Art Line* magazine.

before he had reached the Mayor Gallery. John Heal was behind me, and together we entered the gallery. It amounted to a rather messy, hasty entrance and I think it was this that got me off to a bad start.

Sun, 22 March - To continue Tuesday's tale: the Mayor Gallery private view did not go well for me. I made a hash of it. I was too ebullient, noisy and over bearing. Also, I said one or two inappropriate things. It was an opportunity to see people I knew - Robin Dutt, Ronald Alley,[9] Akumal Ramachander, and even James Mayor. But whereas before they might have had a tolerant impression of me, I think that now they might have the impression that I am an oaf. I upset Akumal, by suggesting that he wanted to sleep with me. Maybe the preview wasn't as bad as I imagined, but I certainly did myself no good. Afterwards John and I wandered around near Piccadilly and went to a pub for something to eat. Before catching the train we split up briefly and I wandered down to the river to walk along the embankment and to look at the dossers, young and old, lying in cardboard boxes underneath Charing Cross arches. We eventually caught the 10.25 pm train and with raving thirsts arrived home at midnight. Next day I attempted a couple of damage limitation phone calls to Robin and Akumal. I also did two days work in the studio, by way of recompense. On Friday morning Paul visited and we went in my car to Hythe. I collected some photographs from Benvics, and then we walked along the canal and returned through the town. We stopped for a drink at the Swan Inn, and had a talk there about Paul's illness. On Friday night Roy and I walked to the Pizza Hut for a meal. Yesterday I had a buoyant springtime walk at high tide along the sea front and out along the ferry harbour arm, to the little lighthouse - the first time I have done this. In the evening Roy and I saw Chris at the Salisbury hotel and the Executive Club. Everywhere was very quiet and I wasted three pounds on the Executive Club fruit machine.

---

[9] Ronald Alley, Keeper of Modern Collection at the Tate Gallery.

Thurs, 9 April - A bad episode took place on Sunday - very bad - though time has now blunted the painful memory. I'm afraid I became a vandal, by tearing down a fence panel belonging to the Lower Sandgate Road Toll-house, and then followed this up by smashing a fruit machine in the Rotunda.[10] I've no idea what led me to this inexcusable behaviour. These events did not happen until after six o'clock in the evening, and I had had a good, enjoyable time during the day, though by six o'clock I was drunk - dead drunk. I had got up early, not having had a drink the night before, and on a beautiful spring day Roy and I had our Sunday breakfast and I then went to the launderette. At lunchtime I went with Douglas Richmond to the Carlton hotel, where I drank a couple of Carling Special Brews (preceded by a pint of cider at the flat). Back at the flat I continued drinking cider, while playing loud music. I made a couple of phone calls and, next, Paul and Denis arrived, and they stayed for an hour or more and drank a pint of cider (Paul, incidentally, stinks the place out after an hour, as he has not been washing, while his mother has been on a long trip to Singapore). After they left I continued enjoying myself. Outside it was sunny, and Roy was gardening, and I knew many people would be walking on the Leas. Eventually I embarked on a walk of my own. I arrived at the toilet beside the toll-house, but it was closed. There were signs announcing the toilet and a light on by the door, and I suddenly felt angry, remembering that several other toilets around the town have closed down recently. I attacked the fence panel, which was beside the toilet door. At the time I must have thought the panel belonged to the toilet, whereas in fact it had been put up by the toll-house to stop toilet users entering their garden. I believe the reasoning behind my anger went something along the following lines: is this a fucking toilet or not? I continued walking towards the harbour, and by the Rotunda I sat down on a bench to rest. I considered making a heroic walk along the beach to Dover then phoning Roy to fetch me from the first

---

[10] Domed circular building on Folkestone sea front.

pub I arrived at, but I realised I would not have the strength to do this, so I decided on going the other way, along the promenade to Sandgate, or Seabrook, to arrive as the pubs opened. I got up and immediately made the mistake of beginning this journey by walking through the Rotunda. In my pocket was a two pence coin, and I sought out the two old fashioned one armed bandits in the place which still accepted 2p coins. I have been quite fond of these two machines and they have been the only ones in the Rotunda I have played on. My coin was not accepted in the first machine and it clatters down into the pot. I put it into the second machine and found that the handle was jammed. I raised my leg and kicked the machine, once, very hard, and very deliberately with the flat sole of my heavy walking shoe (which had once belonged to Roy). I kicked the metal edge of the machine, but the glass panel at the front smashed. The panel had an ornately coloured decoration on it, and the machine was probably a relic from the early 'sixties. A young employee happened to be standing nearby, and he asked me what I thought I was doing. I pretended to be angry about losing my 2p. He went away, leaving me standing in a confused way by the machine. He returned with Peter Woodcock, who is the manager at the Rotunda,[11] and I at once changed my tack to one of abject apology. Peter was obviously disgusted to see who the miscreant was, and he simply walked off, saying the words, *I am **very** surprised, Mark.* I left the Rotunda and sat on the beach for a bit, then I staggered home, full of misery. I wondered how I could try to repair things, and I decided I would return with some cash, to pay for the damage. I got my credit cards and withdrew £100 from machines, on Access and Barclaycard. Peter was not there when I returned, so I walked back to see if he happened to be at the Burlington hotel. Outside the hotel I met John Heal. I invited him back to the flat, and Roy and I invited him to dine with us. Before we did so I slipped out and drove down to the Rotunda, where I

---

[11] Peter Woodcock, social acquaintance of the diarist.

apologised again to Peter. He looked very cheesed off with me. I said I would pay for the damage, but I didn't offer him the money, as he said he would see how much it would cost, and also I was thinking that I needed the money I had on me for the exhibition catalogue. I returned to the flat feeling better and had dinner - the Chinese wok dish - with Roy and John, who were both unaware of what had happened.

Wed, 14 April - On Saturday I went to Saffron Walden with John Heal. We were victims of an April Fool Joke. John invited me to go with him on a British Rail, South East Network *Go Anywhere for a Pound* day. We went to Saffron Walden because he said he'd seen a newspaper article saying that Peter Langan[12]had opened a wine bar extension to his London brasserie there. We got to Saffron Walden, having got up at 6 am and having had a very crowded journey, and of course the wine bar didn't exist. We ended up drinking beer and gin in two or three obscure pubs in the town, and after this we began to see the funny side. We also enjoyed the invigorating breath of fresh Essex air during the two mile walk to and from the station at Aldley End. In London we had a pizza at the Strand Palace hotel, and we visited a wine bar in Covent Garden. Back at the Over-Seas Club we joined the party that was going on, consisting of Roy, Vincent, Denis,[13] Paul, and Etelle and her new friend, Denis. John and I explained that we had had a wonderful time. The party was very cheerful and continued until 1.30 am. I am trying to clean and mend the car, retouch my painting,[14] and do other various little jobs, mostly connected with the Barbican exhibition. On Monday I retouched the woman's face, which was a disaster, as it had not dried properly. I seem to be going through a frustrating, ineffectual time at present.

Sat, 9 May - The exhibition has begun at the Barbican. Roy and I hung the paintings on Wednesday. The exhibition looks fine, with me having planned beforehand where to place the

[12] Peter Langan, chef and restaurateur.
[13] Denis Crofts, brother of Chris, Vincent and Paul Crofts.
[14] Diarist was completing his current painting.

paintings. The spotlights make the exhibition very colourful, especially as the space enables the exhibition to be seen nearly as a whole. On Thursday we went back by train for the lunchtime Private View. John Heal was on the train, but we did not sit together. I had given and sent out one hundred and thirty or more invites, but none of these attended, apart from John, Roy and Kim. There were also two gallery private view free loaders, whom I recognised from Cork Street, one of whom has been featured in a phony critics article in Art Line. I didn't get his name, but he wore untidy hair and beard, and mouldy clothes, and he looked a bit like David Bellamy.[15] I think he lives in Hastings. The other was a small, garrulous middle aged woman, English, but with Japanese teeth and eyes, who talked in a refined accent in an interminable stream. In fact I was highly delighted that they had come, and I treated them royally, and I hope that all of us enjoyed the wine and the conversation. The bearded critic, whom I discovered to be quite thoughtful, made an astute comment about my paintings being ultimately about time. Quite a few other people had a glass of wine and looked at my paintings, thanks to John Heal, who stood at the entrance of the roped off area and invited in any visitor to the Barbican who happened to be passing nearby. Afterwards Kim, John, Roy and I had a meal at a wine bar in the Barbican piazza, benefiting from a change in the law which came into force on Monday, allowing restaurants to continue serving alcoholic drinks with meals throughout the afternoon. At 5.30 pm we arrived at the BBC Club bar, near BBC radio at Portland Place. We were the guests of Kim and we had a couple of drinks there before we split up and Roy and I caught the 7.30 pm train. In Folkestone I arrived feeling refreshed again, so I went solo to the Bay Tree bar[16] and the Metropole. Yesterday I made a very sluggish start to the day and did not do much. I do not intend doing anything while my exhibition

---

[15] David Bellamy, TV presenter.
[16] Bar at the Burlington hotel.

is on, other than things to promote it, such as telephone calls and meetings in London. Thus I also have time to enjoy the month of May. Today we had a second day of wonderful weather. Roy and I went for a walk in our bluebell wood at Billsington.

Sat, 16 May - Not much to report with respect to the exhibition. On Tuesday I remembered that John Heal had mentioned that he had received a Mayor Gallery preview invitation, and I phoned him to ask if I could use it. He arrived about 4pm, and we drank some Pimms and lemonade and some gin. I caught the 5.30 pm train to London, and by then John had decided to come with me. We sat in a carriage drinking a concoction of Kirsberry, duty free gin and orange juice. The train stopped at Westernhanger and a group of men who had been to the races[17]entered out carriage and began a card game, using piles of fivers and tenners. In London we walked from Charing Cross to Cork Street for the preview. No one was there whom I recognised, apart from some of the phony critics, though not those who came to my preview. James Mayor was not there, only his gormless bearded partner. The exhibition was of American Pop Art and Chinese antique furniture. I gave away one or two of my catalogues to people. Afterwards John and I went to the Barbican. I found that my catalogues were not being put out every day, and I have had to ring Margo Ladell[18]about this. We caught the 10.30 pm train from Charing Cross and arrived in Folkestone about midnight. The previous Sunday I had delivered the small Aylesham chapel spire painting[19] to the Chapter House of Canterbury Cathedral, having been invited to participate in an *Artists From Kent* exhibition, in aid of the Kent and Canterbury Cancer Care Centre appeal. On Monday evening Roy and I went to the preview of the exhibition. I met Brian Oxley and Phyllis McDowell[20]and also David Verkaik,[21] who all had works in the exhibition. On Wednesday afternoon I returned the the

[17] At Folkestone race course.
[18] Margo Ladell, Barbican Centre exhibition organiser.
[19] The Washing, the Houses and the Chapel Spire.
[20] Phyllis McDowell, Folkestone artist.
[21] David Verkaik, property owner, artist, the diarist's future painting studio landlord.

Chapter House to be the steward, with co-exhibitor, Pat Castle, and I also met Pat Clarke, the exhibition organiser. During the last couple of days I have purchased one or two urns and ornaments for the garden. It is 3.40 pm, and I am lying in bed writing this. Kim and Marie Pierre are supposed to be coming down for the weekend. There is an (unknown) neighbour's cat, called Corrie, who has spent a lot of time in the flat during the last few months, and of whom Roy and I have become very fond.

Wed, 20 May - The weather has not been very good - not since the day of the walk in Billsington wood. It is midday and I did not wake til eleven. I hear that an unknown woman has been considering making a purchase. I went up on Monday to check the exhibition and I was told this news by the Barbican Centre Information Desk. I also made an unannounced visit to the *Art Monthly* office in Great Russell Street, introducing myself as one of their oldest subscribers. The person sitting in the room, surrounded by magazine publishing chaos, was Margaret Garlake, one of the co-editors. She seemed genuinely pleased that one of her subscribers had made a visit. I also visited three new galleries - the Barbara Carlisle Gallery, in Islington, Marston Schubert Ltd., in Charlotte Street, and the Horizon gallery, in Marchmont Street. I made this pleasing impromptu excursion to London after a dreary start to the day and a visit from Paul, at ten thirty in the morning. I caught the 11.42 am slow train to London, and the 5.35 pm slow train back. British Rail have introduced a £10 yearly *Network Card*, and also a day excursion *Capital Card*, which means that a trip to London is now £6.50 (including London tube and bus fares), instead of the previous £9.50. Kim and Marie Pierre arrived on Saturday afternoon, and, after a meal, Etelle and Vincent arrived, and we ate cheese and bread and stayed in the flat most of the time. On Sunday we went to Canterbury, to collect my painting, returning for a roast lamb dinner. I then went for a walk with

Kim and Marie Pierre to Sandgate and back along the beach, before they departed. The previous Sunday there was a funny little episode which I now recall. I drank several pints of cider in the flat during the early afternoon, and then went for a walk along the Leas. I was walking along the sunken Leas path, somewhere level with the Burlington, when I suddenly determined to make a new secret pathway down to the Lower Sandgate Road. I plunged down into the dense undergrowth near a shelter, where the cliff is very steep but also thick with new Alexanders and dead brambles. I spent an hour carefully inching downwards and then horizontally for a few yards. I decided to return and continue my secret path another day, so I carefully retraced my steps to the top. When I arrived there John Heal was waiting, and he was looking down at me with some curiosity. He, of all people, had been walking past and he had stopped to listen to the sound of the crackling brambles. I have decided to abandon my secret path, as it has already been discovered by my friends.

Tues, 26 May - Another sorry episode to report. In general the *vibes* at the moment are bad. My exhibition ends on Sunday, but I am still expecting that there will be a sale or an important review. Without either of these I will have to deem the exhibition a failure, despite the fact that it will nevertheless have been seen by many, including some influential people, who will remember it. I don't quite know what I was expecting to get from the exhibition. Maybe I was even hoping that it would represent a neat full stop. On Wednesday afternoon John Heal arrived and sat drinking at the bar, while I telephoned London banks and corporations known to purchase contemporary works of art. On Thursday I drove to London, calling first at the *Art Line* office in Garrett Lane. No one there. At four o'clock I arrived at Fortnum and Masons, for Darjeeling tea and cucumber sandwiches with Robin Dutt. Robin has stopped writing for *Art Line*. I then went to check on the exhibition. No news there. On Friday I went to London by train, to show the exhibition to my family. I went to a pub near Smithfield's Market and drank some John Smiths bitter, before meeting Dad, Lesley, Nicky,[22] Kim and Marie Pierre at the Barbican Centre. They all seemed impressed with my exhibition. We had something to eat in the staff canteen, then made plans to meet Lesley and Stewart[23]later at their hotel. Dad, Kim, Nicky and I then played snooker in a club near Archway, to which Kim belongs. We then found our way to the hotel off Baker Street, and had another drink in the hotel room and bar, before walking to a nearby Austrian restaurant. We had a good time there. There was an accordionist strolling from table to table and we had a good drunken sing song and dance. We all had different things to eat. I ate soup and then Austrian sausage and sauerkraut. Stewart paid the bill. We went back to the hotel for a noisy night cap, then Marie Pierre drove us away towards Palmers Green.

Thurs, 28 May - Now where was I? Oh, yes - Kim was very drunk, and Nicky, being only fifteen years old, has just started his drinking. Nicky thought that some comment was against his father, and Kim had one of his unreasonable stroppy moods. A short, sharp nasty argument suddenly happened in the car, with everyone joining in, except Marie Pierre, who had had little to drink. The argument ruined everything. I felt bad because when we had left the hotel I told Lesley that I would look after Nicky, and also I had spotted that Kim was drunk, and I very nearly made a mental note to go carefully with him. Unfortunately, I failed to do either. When we got to Palmers Green Nicky was upset and I went for a little walk and talk with him. When we got back to the house we all managed to patch things up. Nicky is basically similar to Kim. He has bags of confidence and a precocious adult manner that rides rough shod over the social manners which Kim and I had to adhere to at the same age. I would think that Nicky is typical of his

---

[22] Nick Simons, diarist's nephew.
[23] Stewart Bailey, diarist sister, Lesley's, second husband.

generation. He thinks the world of his father, and though we have tried not to let it show,he probably sensed that we took his mother's side during his parents break up. The next morning was dreary - a wet Sunday in Palmer's Green. It was Saturday, actually, but it felt like Sunday. At lunchtime Kim, Dad and I went to the pub with Stewart, which was the only bright spot. I eventually left at five o'clock, calling at the Barbican Centre, where a photographer called Bruno took my photograph in front of my exhibition. I had come across him with camera and tripod taking photographs of the exhibition next to mine. I spent the rest of the bank holiday weekend in Folkestone. I can't remember anything about Sunday. I phoned Pam on Monday. Roy and I went to the *Sellinge Steam Special*, for the first visit for several years.[24] There was a lovely row of little steam engines driving dynamos and water pumps. In the evening a party took place at the flat, with the arrival of Chris, Vincent and Etelle and her boyfriend, Dennis. Etelle brought us some champagne glasses. Since then I have continued to feel pretty wretched. I have made a few telephone calls and sent a few letters. Yesterday started well, with a phone call from a Mr Qovi, who wanted to buy my portrait of President Bhutto. I went with Douglas for a walk in Bilsington woods. In the afternoon John Heal sat at the bar drinking Pimms and lemonade, while I periodically left to make phone calls. The Mr Qovi prospect now looks less certain. The other enquiry is probably not likely to end in a sale. It was from a Mrs Maltpress,[25] of Linton, Cambridgeshire, to whom I have sent some more information. I have a slight sore throat, stomach bug and headache. I feel I have been drinking much too much, lately.

Mon, 22 June - I am now at a stage where I wake up and think: what the hell am I going to do today? So far I have always managed to think of something that is related to my

---

[24] Bi-annual event at Sellinge for steam engine enthusiasts.
[25] Daphene Maltpress, teacher, art collector.

artistic life, mostly administrative stuff, like typing letters, making telephone calls or making relevant purchases, like a box of paper clips. I spent one day last week writing a review appertaining to the Barbican Centre exhibition, for *Art Line*. On another afternoon I drove to Hastings, to see if I could find out anything there about Mr Avivson.[26] I spoke to the woman who bought his gallery and also people who knew him in three nearby shops - a framing and print seller's shop, a shop selling native masks and a bookseller. Nobody said anything adverse about him, which I suspect may have been due to professional rivalry.[27] The journey there was made on one of this month's few sunny days. Otherwise it has been raining every day. It is 4.35 pm, and I still have a headache, caused by drinking all yesterday afternoon and evening. I had quite an enjoyable day, beginning after breakfast with a scotch at the flat, and a couple of bottles of Lowenbrau at the Galleria bar around the corner. It used to be the Lismore hotel, and has just been bought by restaurateur, Nicola, with the bar presided over by Julian. The other customers were an Australian, an Irishman and an English woman, who began singing along to the background Mantovani[28]orchestral tape. One of the songs was about a girl called Perfidia, which struck me as being a memorable name. I went to the Burlington hotel, then returned to the flat and continued with a succession of glasses of home brewed lager. After a couple of hours Vincent, John Heal and Etelle arrived, and we had a glass of fizzy wine in which floated halves of strawberries, making use of Etelle's champagne glasses. Presently, I went for a walk with John on the Leas, then continued by myself through Sandgate and back along the beach and high tide. Yesterday was the longest day, the summer solstice, and during the walk I conceived the idea of eating the evening meal in the garden, after 9.30 pm, while it was still light. We were planning a chicken stew and this was

---

[26] Janus Avivson, Director of the Avivson Gallery, London and Hastings.
[27] The diarist now finds his reasoning here unclear.
[28] Montovani, leader of the Montovani Orchestra specializing in light orchestral music.

eaten in the garden by Roy and Vincent and John and myself. Chris also made a visit. We made use of candles on the table as it got dark. We also ate cheese and biscuits and finished with a glass of port. We then repaired to the bar until about eleven o'clock. I finally went to bed, having been drinking for eleven hours, somehow without overdoing the amount at any stage. This morning, though, I could not get out of my bed. I did, eventually, and retyped my CV before lunch. I got a letter from Pam and walked down to the beach to open it. She is still waiting for the birth. I wrote back to her. The previous evening Roy and I ended our evening with a visit to the Sandgate Road gay bar, taking John Heal with us. We drew the attention of a noisy camp person there, who was drunkenly amusing and tiresome. I think Roy and I went there the previous weekend.

Sat, 27 June - Pam will be giving birth any day now. I wonder if it will be a boy or a girl? I have a feeling it will be a girl, and I like thinking of the idea that she will grow up to be just like her mother when I first knew her. Pam also thinks that a girl is easier to bring up, which, in the circumstances, I think is true. I haven't much considered the idea of a son. Of course, it doesn't matter at all which it is. A healthy baby boy or girl will be a wonderful, exciting thing. If it is a boy it might mean that Pam would need more help and that therefore I would have more of a hand in the child's upbringing. I have had an uneventful week. It is Wimbledon week. It has been raining, it seems continuously this month - a persistent light, summery rain, which I do not mind that much. It is the season of wild poppies, and pink scented wild roses. Yesterday evening I drank rather a lot of lager and whisky. Roy and I went first to La Galleria restaurant bar, where Chris joined us, then Roy and I returned to the flat and drank with John Heal, then we three went for our last drinks at *The Place*, as the Sandgate Road gay bar is known. Today, after suffering an early hangover, I feel good but quite ineffective as regards doing anything useful. Roy and I went to a boot fair at Dover College Junior School. It is now five o'clock and I lie in bed writing this. I am about to have a nap, prior to Saturday evening's proceedings, but first I will read a few more pages of Walter Pater's *The Renaissance.*

Sat, 11 July - I have a son, named Jack. He was born on the 2nd of July, twenty days late after a caesarian operation. Both he and Pam are fine, apparently. I was baffled at first by the news, but I am now quite used to the idea of a son. Pam's pregnancy and Jack's arrival have already given me a lot of pleasure, and I am now greatly looking forward to the future proceedings of the three of us. At the moment I am doing strawberry picking at Roundwood Farm, Lyminge. It has coincided with a week of sunshine and I am really enjoying the work. The pay is not very good, but there is a very relaxed atmosphere in the fields. The events from the previous week include a visit on the Monday to the degree show at Canterbury College of Art. Students' work can be heart achingly fresh and inventive. It was very hot and the students were lounging about in an end-of-term way on the lawn outside. How will their lives unfold? On Thursday, the day Jack was born, I went on an expedition with John Heal. We took the train to Walmer and walked to Kingsdown, by way of Granville Road and the seafront. We went to the Zetland Arms, Rising Sun, and also the King's Head, and then had lunch at the Captain's Table restaurant. For a main course we both had Mousaka, extra large. The restaurant was comfortable and we sat in armchairs drinking brandy afterwards. The new proprietor is an ex merchant navy seaman. It was a hot day, and we staggered out into the sun at three thirty in the afternoon. John stayed on in Kingsdown to do his charity work[30]and I retraced our steps home alone. I remember sitting on a platform seat at Walmer station and staring through

---

[30] John was making door-to-door charity donation collections.

railings into an overgrown ditch. Three very small boys, three or four years old, were playing in the ditch, and I could hear their conversation. The dazzling sun was behind me, so they couldn't see me. They were in their own world, playing in the ditch, which to them was a wonderful, exciting jungle exploration. The different characters of the boys was very apparent. One was the acknowledged leader of the expedition, and one could observe him having to live up to expectations. Sometimes he faltered, or got bored, or had to lead a change of direction to maintain interest. As a trio they would also have almost simultaneous changes of enthusiasm, if suddenly demonstrated by any one of them, when any one of them had the courage to be a leader, like a small shoal of little fish. One of them started to sing a nursery rhyme, which *Miss Willow* had taught at school. Though suddenly remembered, the rhyme had made quite an impression on his imagination. The rhyme seemed to be about animals, and the final line was to the effect that no animal's nose was as big as an elephant's was. The leader gave his attention and admiration momentarily to this important recitation, though you could see that at the same time he was also wondering whether he should do so. Soon after this a mother's voice was heard calling and they all ran away together like little fishes.

Sun, 12 July - I got the news about Jack by letter from Pam on Tuesday, arriving back at the flat after strawberry picking in the morning. I opened the letter on the train to London in the afternoon. I was on my way to see Chantel Burn at her flat near Battersea park. She holds a monthly *open house evening* for the artists for whom she acts as agent. I wanted to exchange the painting of mine that she has held for some months. I withdrew the Hythe landscape and deposited *Scatter-boxed.* Her financial adviser was there and four artists. I did not stay long, as Chantel mentioned that it was the evening of the Cork Street party, which had been unknown to me. I made my departure and arrived in Cork Street at 8.30pm. There was a large gathering of people standing in the street, but I had effectively missed the party, as all the galleries had stopped giving away wine. I did not recognise anybody. Instead, I went to a pub near Piccadilly, and sat drinking a couple of pints of Hurliman lager, which was, as the young barmaid advised me, very powerful. I sat there a long time, looking frequently at Pam's letter and thinking of her and the baby, experiencing a peculiar and rather wonderful sensation. I eventually caught the 10.30pm train from Charing Cross, first collecting the painting which I had deposited there after leaving Chantal's house. The next day I drove to Linton, near Cambridge, for an appointment with Daphne Maltpress. She is a maths teacher in a private school in Cambridge, and her husband works in industry. We had a conversation in her garden for about an hour, during which I drank several mugs of her tea, as it was a hot day. She still liked my *Springtime (with woman and crocuses)* picture, and said the woman in it reminded her of herself. I must have forgotten her saying this when we went back into her house and she wrote out a cheque for £500 and gave it to me. The meeting had gone very sweetly and cordially, but I must have over-relaxed after she gave me the cheque and I was preparing to leave. At his point I made a gaffe. I thought I could afford to make a slightly controversial comment about the picture, And I told her how I sometimes changed the titles of my pictures completely. I showed her one of my catalogues where, at the time, the picture had the title *Springtime (with woman facing an impending major surgical operation)*. Mrs Maltpress looked greatly alarmed, suddenly, to my dismay. She said, jokingly, I hope, that she wished now she had not bought the picture. I did my best to reassure her, but she still looked a little unconvinced as we parted. I drove away feeling as guilty as sin about selling her the picture, and I imagined her hiding it away in her wardrobe. On the journey back, having earlier passed through Saffron Walden, I visited Coggershall, where I found that Langan's new brasserie and bar does actually exist.

Tues, 14 July - It was my birthday yesterday. Roy took me to the Portofino[31]to celebrate. I had paté maison and Coquilles Saint Jacques with mashed potatoes and broccoli. Roy had Eggs Colette and halibut. A litre of house white wine, plus gateau, coffee and Tia Maria liqueur. We sat in one of the window tables. Chris and Margaret[32]arrived at the Indian restaurant on the opposite side of the road, and we waved to them. On Saturday evening Chris visited, and also John Heal. I later joined Roy, who has not much time for John, at the Galleria bar, where he was sitting with Douglas and a Libyan man with whom we got into conversation. On Sunday I picked strawberries in the morning, like last Sunday. In the evening Roy cooked a steak on the charcoal grill. On Monday, my birthday, I picked strawberries and arrived back at the flat at 3.30 pm. The day was extremely sunny and hot. I got cards from John, Roy and my sister, who enclosed £5 for a drink, as usual. I also got a letter from Pam, saying that she is recovering from the caesarian and that Jack is very fine in every way. In the evening Roy cooked a cannelloni dish, and I drank some home brewed beer. Had a brief drink with Chris across at the Salisbury hotel. The sale to Mrs Maltpress is confirmed, by the signing of a bill of sale, which she has returned to me. I had forgotten to take it with me for her to sign, and by sending it to her afterwards I was allowing her the opportunity to change her mind, which, thank goodness, she has not chosen to do.

Fri, 14 Aug - Last Saturday there was a barbecue here. Chris has been doing some summer teaching across at the language school,[33] and he proposed bringing some of his mature students to the barbecue. Only one turned up - a German businessman, named Frederick. The English presence was familiar, and consisted of Roy and myself, Etelle, Peter Wagstaff and Eugene, who drives a taxi and drinks at the

---

[31] Emilio's *Portofino* Italian restaurant,
[32] Margaret Reed, teacher, has long term relationship with Chris.
[33] The Living Language Centre, Clifton Road.

Salisbury hotel with Chris. The lack of new faces was disappointing, and so I went outside and hailed a group of young students standing outside the language school, and about fifteen of them followed me back to the party. They brightened the party for an hour or two, but they were very young and foreign, and so a generation gap was evident. This week I have been giving my thought to Janus Avivson, and the prospect of selling some paintings in America, through his agency. I am keen to sell some work to the client he has in Chicago. However, I am worried that the result will be that I will not see any money and the paintings will simply disappear. I have typed an agreement for Mr Avivson to sign, but it will not really give me any protection if things go wrong in America. I wish to limit things on this first occasion to two paintings, but one of them will be the large *Members of the German Wine Academy*. It will be a case, finally, of proceeding with the deal and hoping it doesn't go wrong. On Wednesday I took the agreement to London and gave it to Avivson at his London home. He is too verbosely reassuring, and does not think in a clear, sequential manner. I suspect I am more aware of what can go wrong than he is. Afterwards I called at Chelsea Art Stores[34]and bought a yard and a half of primed, 84" linen canvas, costing £64. I had, parked in Eaton Square, so walked the length of the King's Road and back. Arrived Folkestone at 8.30 pm and drank some glasses of home brewed lager. Yesterday morning I had a hangover and difficulty getting out of bed. I rose to answer a phone call from John Heal. While I was having breakfast he arrived with a bottle of Guyanian rum and two bottles of wine, to make a punch for the carnival night barbecue. He opened the rum and sat at the bar all afternoon, talking and drinking the rum, mixed with pineapple juice. John is furious with Vincent, as Vincent sent a letter to the Prime

[34] King's Road art materials shop.

Minister proposing John for a *Queen's Award for Industry*, for his charity work. John has since been contacted by people such as the Board of Trade. John thinks that, in revenge, he can manage for Vincent to be sent an income tax questionnaire. Roy returned from work, and was not pleased to be greeted by a bar room atmosphere. John and I retreated to *happy hour* at the Burlington hotel. I returned to the flat and drank further with Chris. Roy and I ate a steak at the London and Paris pub whence I walked home alone. For a week or more my stomach did not feel settled, but it seems alright now. The weather continues to be stubbornly unsummer-like.

Sun, 16 Aug - Last night there was a barbecue here, held to coincide with the carnival procession going by outside. The evening was not a success. I did not see much of the procession, as I stood most of the time in the patio, drinking punch and poking the sausages around. The noise of the carnival was quite deafening, though, in the patio, as it was reflected there from all directions by surrounding buildings. The only visitors to the barbecue were Chris, Vincent, Paul, John Heal, Eugene, and our neighbour, Cathy Bagnell, with one or two of her friends. The party dissolved quite soon. I was not in a good mood and I felt fed up with everyone. Chris and Vincent were equally childish and irritating, Vincent full of mischief and at daggers with John. No females. I went to the Burlington hotel, where a band, The Tony Martin Trio, was playing outside, and where the Bay Tree bar was quite lively. I met Paul, Douglas's friend, and we went together to the Norfolk hotel. I returned to the flat, finding Roy sitting drunkenly alone on the steps. He told me the party had ended acrimoniously. I lay on the bed for some time, and eventually decided to have a midnight swim. I found my way down to the beach in the dark, with towel and swimming trunks, but the tide was out, so I did not proceed. On Tuesday evening Janus Avivson arrived unexpectedly, hoping to collect my paintings. I didn't feel ready to hand them over, and he left disappointed. I am still nervous and unsure about the venture. It could easily all go wrong. However, I still intend to go ahead with it, and I am trying to get the arrangements as much as possible to my own satisfaction. I wish to sell two paintings to the Chicago collector/dealer, and I have suggested to Avivson that he makes an appointment for us to both meet her in Chicago.

I didn't succeed in persuading Pam to change her mind about the birth certificate.[35] She says that it is only a bit of paper and what really matters is that I am a *known person*. I hope she is right, but at the moment I simply feel that a door has been opened for more bad news. I know I wouldn't have been happy about things, if I'd known about this before. Now I'll just have to adjust to the situation.

Mon, 24 Aug - Last Monday I delivered three paintings to Avivson at his Camden flat. I arrived an hour or more late, and he was just going out with his family. Hurriedly the paintings were handed over and the contract signed. I decided on three instead of two paintings, as Avivson said he telephoned the Chicago dealer, Marilyn Nicolet Karos,[36] and found her interested still. Most of our hopes will be on the large German Wine Academy painting, the two others being *The Punter* and *Still Life with Bacardi Bottle*. I had rushed to London, having spent the morning re-typing the contract, and after the delivery I was exhausted, and I relaxed by walking some battered streets in Kentish Town West, where many Italians seem to live. On Thursday I went to London again, by train, for an appointment with Graham Southern, Francis Farmar's[37] successor at Christie's, to arrange for two more paintings to be put up for auction in the Christie's November sale. I also went to the American Tourist Office, to find that it only does business by letter or phone, not by personal visits. I then visited an organisation called the British American Arts

---

[35] Diarist had not been named as the baby's father.
[36] Marilyn Nicolet Karos, furnishings and antiques businesswoman, dealer in contemporary art.
[37] Francis Farmar, director of Christie's contemporary art auctions.

Association, in Covent Garden. I had a useful conversation there with an American woman called Jennifer Williams. The day was exceptionally hot, so I caught the 4.3pm train from Charing Cross, having arrived there earlier at 12.45pm. When I arrived in London I began the visit by walking along Pall Mall, reading the summer closure notices on club doors. I crossed Piccadilly and went to a cocktail bar and a pub off Berkeley Square, drinking three pints of lager. On Friday evening I did not drink, but I did, certainly, on Saturday. I had a morning swim in the sea with Roy, then I went to the Burlington hotel, having a drink there, at the Bay Tree bar, with Chris, an Irishman and Bay Tree regular. I then walked down the Leas to the Bouverie Square betting shop, having been given a tip (which failed) by Chris. Returning here[38]I drank a glass of home brewed beer, then went to my studio for an hour, to do some accounts. In the evening John Heal visited, then Roy and I had a meal at La Galleria, where we both had asparagus soup, followed by brill. We drank a bottle of house white wine and half a bottle of Frascati. The bill, with some bar drinks, came to £40, and the food, compared with San Marco, Nicola's Hythe restaurant, was disappointing. We returned to the flat and then strolled on the Leas, where J observed a person begin to follow me, looking intent on picking me up. I sat down in the shelter where grow the vines, and said hello as he walked past. We had an awkward conversation and I ended up inviting him to the flat to meet Roy. Obviously predatory, he a was also a pleasant, intelligent chap, who lives in Hythe. He sat at the bar for a while, drinking lemonade, then left. While he was at the flat I drank two more pints of home made bitter, which on top of everything else gave me a day long hangover yesterday. On Wednesday morning Roy discovered that a burglar had crept round the passageway alongside the flat and stolen some food out of the freezer, and a gallon of home made cider.

[38] To Clifton Mansions flat.

A man lost his temper in Hungerford this week and shot thirty people, six,teen of them dead. Nihilism can have such frightening consequences, although people with that outlook generally lose it as they grow older. This is getting more difficult, though, today for many people, due to a lack of social contact with friends, relatives and workmates.

Wed, 9 Sept - I have spent a lot of time this week, and last, copying up entries to this journal - just the entries for August! On Saturday I went to Herne Bay, to buy Z-clips from Invicta Arts.[39] I arrived at 1 pm and I went to three pubs. On the way back I called at Denne Hill, to make my last visit before Treadwell moves his gallery. There were some new works on show and I enjoyed some metal space sculptures by, I think, Ian Tolkien. Treadwell himself saw me to the gallery door, and I do believe he actually recalled my name when we said goodbye. On Monday I went to Eastbourne and then on to London, to transfer *Landscape(f igured)*, rejected for the *Coastlines*[40] exhibition, to Christie's, for their November auction. I have re-framed it, and renamed it *Puddles*. The other painting in the auction will be *A Day at the Races*. I had to drive in haste to Eastbourne, but after that was able to relax for the rest of the 200 mile trip. It is now midday and I am expecting a visit from John Heal. We will sit at the bar until mid afternoon, then take a train to London to attend a gallery preview, for which he has received an invitation.

Thurs, 17 Sept - Hello journal! My friend! I would miss talking to you, wouldn't I? I always feel better after our little talks. John did arrive on Wednesday, a week ago. We drank whisky at the bar, then took the 4.25 pm train to London. We sat in an empty compartment in a corridored carriage and had a picnic of smoked salmon paté on bread, swilled down with some sangria. In London I went before it closed to Dillon's bookshop in Covent Garden, then we had a drink at the gay bar in St

---

[39] Art materials shop.
[40] *Coastlines* open art exhibition, Eastbourne.

Martins Road,[41] on my suggestion. We found our way to Berkeley Square, en route to the Mayor Rowen Gallery preview, and bumped into Norman, my bearded Barbican Centre exhibition *critic*.[42] He was on his way to another preview at the Brazilian gallery,[43] which John and I had just passed. At the Mayor Rowan Gallery we had a glass of wine, and I talked to a few people at random. I met Patrick Caulfield, but I had just given away a copy of the Barbican Centre catalogue which I had on me, so I was not able to have a very useful conversation with him. John and I then tried the Brazilian Gallery private view. We went in and immediately came upon the little knot of critics, consisting of Norman, or Carlton, and 'Olly Grey and Polly. I haven't really got their names sorted out yet The gallery, showing an exhibition of photographs, was packed with lively Brazilians of all ages, many from the embassy or trade centre. Waitresses were walking around with trays not of wine, but of tall glasses containing powerful whisky and sodas. This, and some trays of good quality nibbles, amounted to some serious hospitality, but I think the unexpected whisky caused our undoing, or rather John's. We were in an intoxicated state, extremely, when we left the gallery. It had been very hot and crowded and so I took John to the air conditioned quiet cocktail bar opposite for a sedate half hour. We then walked along Piccadilly and Leicester Square to the St Martins Street gay bar, which was now full of quite a different crowd from the earlier home bound commuters. I felt suddenly that I had had enough, and I left John and caught a train, arriving at the flat at midnight. When I left John, I could see he did not wish to come with me, and he did, in fact, suggest going our separate ways Though I myself was tired, I could see that John was very much the worse for wear, and I doubted whether he would finish the evening without incident. I found out on Saturday that he did not get home until the next morning, and that he could not remember the events after I left him very clearly. What seems

---

[41] The *Brief Encounter* pub.
[42] Elsewhere described as an exhibition preview freeloader.
[43] Near the Brazillian embassy.

to have happened is that he left the bar and stumbled in a street somewhere near Charing Cross. He stumbled, or collapsed, and bashed his forehead, and lay unconscious for perhaps three hours. When he woke it was late and he was approached by a West Indian, who bought him a cup of coffee. John said he wanted to catch the *milk train* from Victoria and the West Indian got a taxi. John then found himself in the taxi with two West Indians and two young white kids, who he thinks were kissing each other. The taxi drove around past Victoria and around Chelsea, and John was next aware that hands were restraining him, and he was being robbed. He could not tell who in the taxi were or were not on his side. The taxi ended up at a police station, with the driver restraining one of the white kids, while the others ran off, but John thinks this could have been a ruse, on behalf of the driver. John spent the rest of the night in Bow Street police station, but he told police he could not remember much about the evening. He lost a credit card, a chequebook and about £20 in change. He thought it best not to remember much of what happened, and hopes that the police will not press charges against anybody, and get him involved in a court case. The robbers did, apparently, give him back some of his possessions. I heard this on Saturday, and I went to John's flat with a bottle to cheer him up. At least if our drinking caused John's misfortune, it also made him largely unaware of what was going on. The next day I myself got up late, not with a headache, but feeling pretty black and weary. I wondered what to do with the day, and I had the idea of marshalling some newspaper cuttings about art and artists - some in a pile and some in some scrap books - into alphabetical order, to make a reference file. I thought that this was a brainwave, as I realised I could put other items, like maps, pamphlets and catalogues into the file, along with anything else that interested me.[44] I began this task at once, cutting up newsprint and splitting up the scrapbooks, and I continued over the weekend, reaching the letter J. This humble, though legitimate little past time could be good for a couple of weeks, if I so wish.[45]

Mon, 19 Oct - It is 11.45 am. I had some difficulty getting out of my bed. Monday mornings seem to be a bit of a write off at the moment. Yesterday I drank some cider after breakfast, then Roy and I walked down to the Warren[46]and along the beach, to regard the *Hengeist,*[47] which had been blown there by the storm.[48] We returned to the flat and I sawed some stretcher timber and drank some more cider. At seven o'clock I went to *happy hour* at the Burlington hotel's Bay Tree bar. The chef appeared with two dishes of moules marinière, which were placed on the bar for happy hour customers. I returned to the flat for dinner, *pollo supresa.*[49] At ten o'clock I went to La Galleria, where Nicola, the proprietor, bought everyone in the bar a drink. The people in the bar were myself, an anglicised friendly man from the Middle East, Colin and Harold, and Bibby and Biddy.

Where was I with that day of the breakfast in the USA?[50] Oh, yes - everyone then met at a roadside restaurant for lunch - we three artists,[51] Janus, Phyllis,[52] one of the female Weight Watcher personnel, and a former minister, of Mormon or some other religious fundamentalist variety, now turned fund raiser for the needy of Milwaukee. The fund raiser had undergone a great change in his life, after he lost a lot of weight. He was now a quiet and well groomed man, dressed in a sober dark suit, which all contrasted noticeably with a pair of unusually bright, sky blue eyes. He said he did a lot of public speaking

---

[44] The start of the diarist's *Registry.*
[45] The diarist was to continue with the Registry, despite the advent of the internet.
[46] Natural coastal area near Folkestone.
[47] Folkestone - Boulogne ferry, with sister ship the *Horsa.*
[48] Great storm of 15-16 October.
[49] Portofino restaurant's name for chicken Kiev.
[50] Diarist had been on a trip to Milwaukee.
[51] Diarist and two American artists were in discussions about exhibitio#ng in the Arts Centre gallery that Phyllis Chicorel was sponsoring.
[52] Phyllis Chicorel, Director of WeightWatchers, Inc., art collector & sponsor of the arts.

and raised several hundred thousand dollars a year. The restaurant served good food and was filled mostly with grey suited American businessmen. I had Blackfish, which had been cooked with peppers and spices. After lunch some of us went to down-town Milwaukee. I accompanied Phyllis in her Mercedes. The ride was probably the focal point of my visit. The car, and Phyllis, and the scenery were together the epitome of America. Phyllis spoke candidly, mostly about marriage, love, sex and romance. In Milwaukee we went to a commercial art gallery where the female artist[53] had some of her paintings. She and Phyllis departed, leaving Janus and Geoffrey Rosenberg[54] and me to visit the building which Phyllis has bought in a run down Milwaukee neighbourhood, which is going to be made into an Arts Centre. An art exhibition was there, although workmen were pulling the building apart. Janus and I then dropped Geoffrey off at his house, and we returned to Phyllis's house. Before it got dark we went for a walk along Lake Shore Drive and back. In the evening I sipped gin and tonic and read my book, while upstairs Janus showed the paintings to some more people. The next morning I had breakfast in the house with Phyllis and a girl who is going to help run Phyllis's Arts Centre. Phyllis said she intended to buy *The Punter*, or *The Candidate*, as I've decided to rename it. I got Phyllis to allow me to take a photograph of her, and then I departed, driving slowly along the coast back to Chicago. I returned to the Chicago Days Inn, ready to catch my flight the next day. Since returning to England I have been recovering from my jet lag, and there has been the very bad storm, and I have been re-framing and making the stretchers for a new painting. On Friday Chris and Venetia visited us, and on Saturday we were visited by Etelle and Vincent and his friend, Philip. I have also seen Paul and Douglas and John Heal.

[53] One of the three artists mentioned in footnote 50.
[54] Geoffrey B Rosenberg, mystic, art therapist, textile weaving artist.

Fri, 13 Nov - The painting is being auctioned at Christie's today. John is attending as my observer, and so I will know what happened when I see him this evening. If the sale was overall a success my painting should have sold, as its reserve price was low, compared with that on other lots. Some Impressionist paintings fetched record prices in a Christie's sale in New York a couple of days ago, notwithstanding the stock market crash.[55] John collected the catalogue from me at lunchtime on Wednesday, and I made some wine punch, and we sat at the bar throughout the afternoon. Paul arrived and stayed with us. At five o'clock I went for a walk in another strong storm, then after a shower I joined John at the Bay Tree bar, at the Burlington hotel, for *happy hour*. Back at the flat Roy cooked a lasagne. The previous week Roy and I went on a canal holiday, between Abergavenny and Brecon. We had a pleasant week, creeping along in an electric canal boat, through a scenic, autumnal landscape. In the canal side woods there was much fungi, and I did find some ceps, but the season for them had just finished, and they were black and rotten. We were in Abergavenny on market day, and in Brecon it was Bonfire Night, and we saw a good firework display beside the river Usk. One day I was ill with a bout of food poisoning. On the way back we spent a night with Colin and Harold, who have moved to a small village called Washford, in Somerset. They have bought two old cottages which they have restored. The premises included a shop which is now Harold's hairdressing salon. We visited several pubs with them on Exmoor, and the next morning we all went into Minehead, where Roy ordered a pair of hand made shoes. We had a coffee in the High Street and talked about the relative merits of Folkestone and Minehead. Colin thinks that due to the Channel tunnel Folkestone will soon be full of *roustabouts*. When Roy and I arrived in Folkestone that evening I had a sad feeling that, with people leaving and the advent of the tunnel, it was the end of an era. Later Chris arrived and I cheered up. Yesterday I told him about Jack, which took him aback. Before our holiday, Halloween evening was an ill attended success. I

---

[55] Stock market decline and recession of 1987.

made some garden lanterns with candles and we had a hot dog barbecue. Chris and Venetia were there and John Heal.

Sun, 22 Nov - The painting sold for £480. John said there was bidding from several directions, and that the auctioneer seemed to be making a special effort for the painting. There wasn't much work that had come straight from younger contemporary artists, like myself, in the sale, and much of what work there was failed to sell. Overall the lots in the sale reached their reserve, but John said the atmosphere was subdued compared to last year.[56] It looks like I was lucky, and I feel gladdened by the outcome, and thankful towards the auctioneer. I have also been in touch this week with Mr Qovi, of Blackheath,[57] who was interested in my portrait of President Bhutto. I called on him with the painting at his shop in Blackheath on Wednesday. Unfortunately, he was out, and I continued, as planned, into London. I parked off Tabernacle Street, near the Self Direct[58] agency, and went to Companies House in City Road, to get information on how to register a business name. I then found a proper parking space near Old Street and took the tube to Green Park, whence I walked to Heddon Street for an appointment with Gary Mills, of Allied Artists. I had a painting and some slides with me, but I found that they were an agency dealing in figurative illustrations, mostly for romantic stories in women's magazines. I returned to the car and drove back to Folkestone, thinking the day had been fruitless. Also, when I arrived at the flat I saw on the news that there had been a tragic fire on the London Underground, at Kings Cross, two hours after I went through it on the Victoria Line. I remembered that I had considered changing trains at Kings Cross, instead of at Euston. Next morning, at 8.45 am, I walked around to La Galleria, for a *Beaujolais Breakfast*. A full English breakfast was available in the restaurant, or a continental buffet in the bar. I chose the continental buffet, and ate it sitting at the bar. I drank several glasses of wine and it was fun, but the event was ill attended,

---

[56] The diarist had had work in the previous auction.
[57] Mr Qovi, pine furniture retailer, art collector.
[58] Self Direct advertising agency.

and I was the only person eating from the buffet, and there were just a couple of parties, probably from local insurance businesses, in the restaurant. Also it was supposed to be a charity event and when I left I felt it incumbent on me to stump up the £8 which had been vaguely quoted as the price per head. I left at one o'clock, and when I returned to the flat I got a phone call from Mr Qovi, who had seen my card which I had left at his shop. He stated that he still wished to buy the painting, so next morning I sent him a quote, and also rang to notify him. Again, he didn't seem so definite about wanting it. He seems to blow hot and cold all the time, so I shall drop the matter if he fails to buy this time. After Mr Qovi rang I went to my studio for the rest of the morning and into the afternoon, but I slept there some of the time and did not do much to the current painting. Last Saturday evening Roy and I were visited by Etelle and a Japanese language student, called Kyoko. We all went to the Victoria pub, then Cassidy's Cavern for a hamburger. This Friday they visited again, with Vincent. Last night Chris visited, then Roy and I went to the Clifton hotel, then Cassidy's Cavern. Yesterday morning I had a coffee and a gin with Douglas at his flat, then went to the Burlington hotel, where I drank gin and water in its Bay Tree bar, with Bibby and two of her friends.

The John Diaries - 1988

At the beginning of 1988 the author began keeping a less detailed diary, just recording daily factual events, without much comment or reflection   .

Wed, 20 Jan - Had lunch with John Heal at the Granville hotel, St Margaret's Bay. I travelled by train and bus and met John at the Moat House Inn, Dover. I had the £8 set menu - paté and pork chop. We had coffee and brandy, sitting in the lounge.

Thurs, 21 Jan - A beautiful sunny day. Met John Heal at lunchtime on the Leas. Worked on my Registery.

Thurs, 28 Jan - John Heal arrived mid morning, while I was copying up this journal. I abandoned this in favour of a lunchtime drink with him. We went to the Brevet Club,[1] Tracy's Wine Bar and then to Cleggy's[2] where we a stayed all afternoon. Both pretty drunk, we got a taxi to the Burlington hotel. I stayed there drinking Lowenbraus, while John slept at the flat, to Roy's irritation.

Sat, 30 Jan - I went to John Heal's flat, to help him clear some stuff out of his attic. He is moving soon. I went on to Douglas's flat, for coffee and one of his G & Ts. Roy and I went to La Galleria n the evening. The Christie's catalogue arrived for their 18 February sale.[3]

Tues, 9 Feb - I went to the launderette in the morning. At lunchtime John Heal arrived to collect the Christie's catalogue. We sat at the bar drinking home made wine. Paul arrived, then John and I caught the 3.25 pm London train and drank more wine on the way. I delivered a painting to the Mall Galleries, for the Laing exhibition.[4] We went to the Merlyn Evans exhibition private view, held jointly at the Mayor and Redfern galleries. I talked to various people. I left John at the Brief Encounter and caught the 10.25 pm train.

---

[1] *Members only* club, but in practice open to all.
[2] Formerly the Golden Pin Club.
[3] Auction of *British and Irish Traditionalist and Modernist Paintings, Watercolours, Drawings and Sculptures*
[4] Laing Open Art Exhibition.

Wed, 24 Feb - I spent the morning photographing some paintings indoors, using the new studio lamps.[5] At lunchtime Paul arrived, then John Heal. They sat down at the bar, but soon Roy arrived and he and I went to Dover and then towed my car back to Saltwood garage. A steak in the evening, before which I went to the Garden House hotel, and afterwards to the Leas Club.[6]

Thurs, 25 Feb - I bought a John Bull Printing Set in Ludlow's toy shop, then went to the studio and fiddled with it, making an office stamp. I returned to the flat and after lunch I made some stamp marks in an invoice duplicate book. John Heal arrived, drunk, from the Imperial hotel, Hythe. He drank some home made red wine and left at five o'clock, to go to London, to a Mayor Gallery private view.

Thurs, 3 March - Did some admin. John Heal made an evening visit. We ate pasta, drank some wine and watched a film on telly, *Dance with a Stranger*. I started the day by going with Roy to Saltwood garage, arriving at 8.30 am to collect my car. Drove back to Folkestone but it is still not starting up properly.

Sat, 12 March - To Charing Point to Point meeting. I went by bus with John Heal. It was quite a successful afternoon. I picked three winners out of five races and must have broken even. John spent the afternoon in a mobile wine bar bus. Roy collected us. Saw John again in the evening, and Chris. I went to the Clifton hotel, which spoiled the day for me.

Wed, 16 March - To France with John Heal, on a *Daily Mirror* £3 day trip. We got a train from Boulogne to Etaples and had lunch in the Terminus restaurant - huge bowls of mussels. We taxied to Le Touquet, where we visited the TTL radio studio[7] at the top of the town hall. We got a taxi and train back to Boulogne and had a meal in Le Sainte Beuve

5   A recent photography shop purchase.
6   Formerly of the Leas Pavillion Theatre.
7   French pop/rock music radio station listened to by the diarist and his friends.

restaurant. I had a steak, both of us by then drunk and confused, John making loud demands to the staff in English. We just caught the 11.30 pm boat to Folkestone, me discovering that I had dropped our ticket getting off the morning boat, which was handed back to me as we got back on. We had also visited eight cafés during the day, and I had begun with a *Champagne breakfast*, on the voyage to France.

Thurs, 17 March - Felt blank and weary. A lunchtime visit from John Heal, who said he felt the same. Probably I looked more tired because I had just had a very good, explosive ejaculation, undertaken while I was wearing a pair of black stockings.

Sat, 19 March - In the morning three kids bombed me with some soil as I was walking up the Zig-Zag path.[8] I pocketed some soil and collared them, in due course, as they walked along the Leas. I got off my bicycle and dumped the soil on top of the leading miscreants head. With Roy at lunchtime to The Black Horse, at Monks Horton. Wrote a letter to the local paper about dogs shitting on the Leas grass. Visits from Chris and John Heal in the evening.

Wed, 30 March - It rained all day. I went to the launderette in the morning. John Heal visited in the evening.

Thurs, 14 April - In the morning I helped John Heal move a couple of car loads of items to his new flat, near Kingsnorth Gardens. I returned to Clifton Mansions and drank some cider and did some admin[9] and slept.

Sat, 14 May - Did a dog patrol in the morning.[10] Chris, Vincent, John Heal and a couple of Swiss language students visited in the evening. We had a barbecue.

---

[8] Pathway descending from the Leas towards the sea, made with artificial rocks and caves.
[9] General paper work.

Mon, 23 May - I began the day with a Leas patrol,[10] returning to the flat for a shower and some admin. I'd meant to sleep and then go to the Folkestone race course evening meeting, but John Heal arrived and I spent the afternoon at the bar with him. I left the flat at 5.20 pm and caught a train to Westenhanger. I had a successful evening, winning something on five out of six meetings - won £16. I teamed up with Chris, the Irishman who goes to the Burlington hotel. It was the meeting of the Metropole Gold Cup.[11] Chris gave me a lift back to the Clifton hotel and later I went to La Galleria, for a drink with John Heal.

Sat, 28 May - Did a Leas patrol, then on a day of spectacularly fine weather I had a stroll down the Leas to the Leas Club. I sat out on the grass[12] with many other people. In the evening we had a successful barbecue. Peter Wagstaff brought a friend called Fraser, and there were two Swiss language students, one called Robert, and another from Japan. Also Chris, Vincent, Etelle, John Heal and John Gordon[13] and his wife.

Sat, 4 June - Did a Leas patrol, then I went to Douglas's flat for coffee and a glass of whisky. Had more whisky back at the flat. Showery weather. In the evening Chris and John Heal visited. Roy and I saw John again later, at La Galleria.

Thurs, 16 June - Did a Leas patrol, quite arduous today, not having done a patrol since Monday. Weather very dull. Roy and I cheered ourselves up with a few Lowenbraus round at La Galleria. John Heal was there.

Tues, 21 June - The summer solstice. I did a dog patrol then John Heal arrived at 12.15 pm. We drank at the bar then went to La Galleria. We had a bottle of Sicilian wine and a pasta bar snack. Afterwards I met John again at the flat. We drank more and I then made a *Solstice Cup* each, out of some wine punch. We took this out onto the Leas. Weather overcast but warm

---

[10] Diarist was voluntarily cleaning up dog excrement on the Leas grass.
[11] Horse race sponsored by Sir Gerald Glover.
[12] Leas grass.
[13] John Gordon, social friend of Chris Crofts and Clive Botting.

and sultry. Was drunk. I met John again at La Galleria and got Roy to take us to a country pub, the Welcome Stranger,[14]where I staggered away across a pea field and down the edge of the downs. Back at Folkestone I felt a bit demented and tried to clear up some felled timber left on the Leas after the hurricane

Mon, 27 June - I did a few minor tasks in the morning. At lunchtime John Heal visited and together we drove to Canterbury, as I wanted to shop for a birthday present for Jack. I bought a *toddle truck with bricks* from Mothercare. I also bought some art materials from Crumps.[15]

Wed, 29 June - An expedition with John Heal. We had intended to go to the Henley Regatta, but settled for something less ambitious. He wished to go out of the county, to post some mail, so we went to East Sussex. On the way we stopped at pubs in Westhorne and Tenterden. In Sussex we went to the White Dog Inn, at Ewhurst Green, and the Rother Valley hotel, near Northiam. We then went to Rye, where John sat in a wine bar, while I popped in and out visiting nearby pubs. We arrived back at Folkestone at 6 pm, and I left John sitting on a Leas seat, looking blearily at some literature which he'd got from some Rye estate agents.

Tues, 26 July - Did some filing most of the day. Felt dreary. In the evening John Heal visited, to report on his attendance at the Christie's South Kensington[16] auction. Roy cooked us some curry. I had phoned John from Cheltenham on Friday, to be told that John Brazier's bid was successful.[17] I also phoned Pam, to learn that she is still having a bout of bronchitis. I will not be seeing them this time.[18]

---

[14] The Welcome Stranger, Newingreen.
[15] Sandgate Road stationers and art materials shop.
[16] Christie's South Kensington Ltd., 85 Old Brompton Road.
[17] John Brazier, of South East Arts, was purchasing the painting for their permanent collection.
[18] While the diarist was visiting his father near Birmingham.

Thurs, 28 July - Roy and I took my car to Saltwood garage at 9am. Returned to the flat for my breakfast - two shredded wheat and a boiled egg. I then went to the studio, to tidy it up and begin framing a little painting done by John Heal's mother. Did some phoning in the afternoon and slept. Felt low, went into the town at 4 pm and bought some shoes, Roy having given me £30 for my birthday. In the evening he cooked a sweet and sour pork dish and we drank some whisky.

Mon, 1 Aug - At lunchtime John Heal visited and stayed drinking most of the afternoon, prior to our taking a train to an evening meeting at Folkestone race course. I broke even on my betting. We returned to Folkestone and went to the Burlington hotel and the Metropole.[19] At the end of the evening we were both the worse for wear through drink.

Sun, 6 Aug - Did a Leas patrol. The state of the Leas is not too bad - dog owners away on holiday? At lunchtime I went to La Galleria and then the Burlington hotel with John Heal. We walked down the Leas to the town, where I bought some rum, which we drank back at the flat, Roy annoyed.[20] Later Etelle and Peter Wagstaff visited and we all went to La Galleria. John was there, Peter Wagstaff very camp. During the day I drank beer, Americano, Campari, and rum and pineapple. During the night I was sick as a dog four times.

Sat, 20 Aug - Did a Leas Patrol. It was Folkestone carnival procession in the evening. I made some punch with tequila. John Heal, Vincent and Liz - a girl from the Testwood hotel opposite - visited. We all, with Roy, watched the fireworks[21] and then went to Tiffanies Wine Bar,[22] to a disco upstairs. Felt cheerful.

Sun, 4 Sept - After breakfast - poached egg on toast, with mushrooms, bacon and tinned tomatoes, and marmalade on toast - I went to the Burlington hotel and drank Lowenbrau

---

[19] Formerly the Metropole hotel, now residential flats with public bar & restaurant.
[20] On his return from Chilham Saw Mills.
[21] Carnival fireworks display.
[22] Tiffany's Wine Bar, Tontine Street

and talked to Guillam and Joan.[23] In the afternoon I met John Heal on the Leas. We returned to the bar in the flat. Roy was cheesed off. Chris visited. Grilled trout for dinner.

Wed, 28 Sept - Did USA trip paper work in the morning.[24] John Heal visited at lunch time and drank some vodka. I took him to Canterbury, then returned to Folkestone to go to the launderette. Bought a shirt from Debenhams. In the evening I went to the Cinema Club,[25] to see *Babette's Feast*. With Chris to the Clifton hotel afterwards. Roy cooked a lasagne for dinner.

Thurs, 29 Sept - This morning I went with Roy and his mother to a beginner's Spanish lesson at Earlscliff Adult Education Centre. John Heal visited the flat at lunchtime. I drank some vodka. We walked down the Leas to the town. Sunny day. I got some dollars from the bank. In the afternoon I did my final Leas Patrol.[26] A steak in the evening, with a bottle of Rioja. Finished USA trip preparations.

Mon, 10 Oct - Did some admin. Saw Paul and John Heal at lunchtime at the flat.

Sat, 15 Oct - In the evening John Heal arrived, and presently we took a taxi to Gees Bar in Sandgate. We walked back to the flat, then went out again for a meal at an Indian restaurant in Tontine Street, the Calcutta.

Sun, 16 Oct - John Heal arrived at noon. We went to his office in Canterbury,[27] so I could see a photocopy machine which is to be sold. We then went to the Yew Tree, at Westbere, then to the Barbican Hamburger Diner at Sandwich. Roy arrived from Spain soon after I arrived at the flat, about 6pm. Smoked haddock for dinner.

---

[23] Guillam and Joan, Anglo-Welsh Folkestone hotel bar habitués, with long standing on/off relationship.
[24] For the diarist's next trip to Milwaukee.
[25] Folkestone Cinema Club, founded and run by Clive Botting.
[26] Leaving the last bag of dog excrement to be collected and disposed of by the Council, as per the diarist's arrangement with them.
[27] John was doing some telephone canvassing for a double glazing firm.

Thurs, 20 Oct - A Spanish lesson from 9.45 am to 11.45 am. Felt half asleep. Called on Douglas on the way back and had coffee and a gin and tonic. John Heal visited the flat at lunchtime. He thinks one of his work colleagues is a witch. After he left I drove to Sandgate, to do a bit of glass fibre repair work on the car.[28] Autumn walk along the Lower Sandgate Road. Roy is at present cooking a *chile con legume*. Weather very mild lately.

Fri, 21 Oct - Got the 12.20 pm train to London, calling at John's flat in Kingsnorth Gardens beforehand. In London I went to Janus Avivson's Camden Lock gallery, to report on my US trip. Afterwards, I visited gallery exhibitions in the Cork St area. Got the 6.25 pm train to Folkestone. Roy and I went to the Pizza Hut.

Sat, 29 Oct - In the evening there was a Halloween party, which failed, it must be said. John Heal, Arthur,[29] Chris and Peter Wagstaff were the only guests. There was a barbecue and disco.

Sat, 5 Nov - In the early evening I walked around to enjoy the atmosphere of bonfire night. Called on Chris at *Brockers*.[30] Roy and I went to the Ship, at Sandgate. Drank beer, watched bonfire and fireworks on the beach by the Rowing Club. Back at the flat we let off a few fireworks and ate hot dogs - Chris, John Heal, Roy and myself. Afterwards I went with Chris and Roy to the Clifton hotel and Salisbury hotel.

Tues, 22 Nov - I did some admin, then rang John Heal, suggesting we drank some Beaujolais Nouveau. We bought two bottles for £4.99, which we drank at the flat. We then continued to drink some home made cider, until Roy returned from Chilham. Later I went for an unsteady, frosty walk on the Leas, some snow underfoot.

---

[28] Diarist did it on an area of rough ground used for unofficial car parking.
[29] Arthur, diarist's elderly Clifton Mansions neighbour.
[30] Venetia Atkinson's Brockman Road home.

Mon, 5 Dec - To the studio in the morning. Have begun doing some corrections to *The Drive To The Ministry*. In the afternoon John Heal made a visit, then Paul and Denis. Roy Orbison has died, aged 52.[31]

Fri, 9 Dec - Studio in the morning. At lunchtime John Heal visited and also Vincent, after waving from a window of the Living Language School opposite the flat. John and I drank gin and cider throughout the afternoon. I invited him to France on Sunday.

Sun, 11 Dec - Roy drove John Heal and me to Dover, to catch a morning boat to Calais, using a cheap day return ticket from a *Times* newspaper offer. On the way we drank Champagne. We had a glass or two of wine in Calais, then returned, drinking gin on the way. Roy collected us from Dover. We all had some egg and bacon at the flat, slept, then had dinner later on.

Sat, 14 Dec - I think In went to the studio in the morning. John Heal visited at lunchtime, to enquire about the ferry ticket I had for tomorrow, for a car and two passengers, leaving Dover at 6.30 am. I didn't feel up to the trip, so John and I went to Dover to have the ticket changed for two foot passengers, leaving at 1pm.

Thurs, 15 Dec - A Spanish lesson at 9.45 am. The second half was an *end of term* party, with wine and eating, and even dancing. Afterwards, Roy took John Heal and myself to Dover, to catch the 1 pm ferry to Calais. There we walked around to the beach and then into the town. We had a meal at Le Channel - very good seafood. I had a fish paté and a turbot, grilled. A bottle of white Rhone Hermitage wine. I paid. Roy collected us from Dover at 10.30 pm.

Tues, 20 Dec - Roy took me with him to Chilham, so that I could drive his mother's car from the garage there back to Folkestone. I went via Canterbury, where I bought my last two

---

[31] Roy Orbisan, American singer.

Christmas presents from Next. I was supposed to meet Chris at twelve o'clock in Folkestone for a curry, but needless to say he didn't show. I went solo to La Galleria, where I had a pasta bar snack and a bottle and a half of white wine. Met John Heal on the Leas on the way back to the flat. Chris phoned after I had slept, with some excuse and I lost my temper with him.

Thurs, 22 Dec - A morning coffee and a gin at Douglas's flat. I took John there, having met him on the way. John and I had another drink back at the flat, then we went with Roy to the Testwood hotel, and then to the Brevet Club, where we had a snack. John and I then went to see Chris and Venetia at *Brockers*. We stood in Venetia's kitchen looking gormless and drunk. Tamsin[32]showed us her art work. A brandy at John's flat. With Roy in the evening to the Chinese restaurant in Bouverie Road West, for our Christmas dinner.

---

[32] Tamsin Atkinson, art student, Venetia Atkinson's daughter.

On Tuesday, the 3rd of January the diarist went with Roy on a five day property inspection flight trip to Spain, which precipitated their subsequent long residence in Nerja, with diarist making periodic return trips to Folkestone.   .

————

Folkestone, Fri, 8 Jan - I took down the Xmas decorations in the morning. Did some admin. Roy telephoned the owner of *Casa Don Miguel*.[1] Chicken for dinner. Met John during an afternoon Leas walk.

Fri, 13 Jan - Douglas visited in the morning, then Roy, John and I went to Canterbury, where we had a drink in the Falstaff Tap, and a drink in the Falstaff hotel bar. We then went to Harbledown, where I wanted to visit the Canterbury Press,[2] but it was closed. In the evening Roy and I had dinner at the Burlington hotel. I had a set menu, featuring turkey. Very pleasant evening.

Tues, 24 Jan - Got up at 10.30am. Porridge for breakfast. Did some admin.[3] John visited at lunchtime and sat at the bar for an hour or two. In the afternoon Roy and I took my car to Saltwood garage. Peter Wagstaff visited this evening. Cooked some pancakes.

Sat, 28 Jan - To John's flat in the morning then with him to Douglas's flat for a gin and tonic. Another back here,[4] then John and I went to the Burlington hotel and the Metropole *Mikado* bar. In the evening Roy and I went to the Burlington hotel, where we were joined by Chris, who gave us a lift to Cassidy's hamburger restaurant.

Tues, 7 Feb - In the morning I drove to Hythe, to Benvics, to order a black and white photo enlargement. I also went to Folkestone harbour, to get an EEC Community Movement Carnet. At lunchtime John visited the flat, and Vincent, after his long absence. He has been steering clear of Roy and me

[1] The house in Nerja that Roy was to buy.
[2] Printing and book binding company.
[3] i.e. administrative paper work.
[4] i.e. Clifton Mansions.

lately. Today he insisted on taking me for a ride in his new car, and he is angling for an invitation to come and visit us in Nerja. Chris visited in the evening, then Roy and I went to Cassidy's hamburger restaurant. Had a haircut and walk in the afternoon.

Wed, 8 Feb - At midday Roy and I walked to The Bayle,[5] to attend a Phillips auction, which included half a dozen pictures from his mother's house. These included a horse painting by William Barraud, which fetched £6,500, and the others brought the total to over £10,000. We then walked down The Old High Street to meet Chris, for lunch at the Hi Tin Chinese restaurant. John attended the auction and the lunch. This evening I took my portrait of Paul to the studio, to fix a temporary thin baton frame to it. The mild weather is very wonderful and strange; today I saw daisies, dandelions, pansies and wallflowers out. On Saturday I saw a daffodil out in a garden in Sandgate.

Thurs, 9 Feb - I went on a *Daily Mirror* one pound day trip to Calais, with John Heal. Etelle sold me the ticket. I wished to go to get some booze for the party tomorrow.[6] The crossing was quiet and very sunny. We drank gin and orange. In Calais we walked from where the bus dropped us across the bridge into the other part of the town.[7] We had a dispute about the cost of our drink with a barmaid in a café opposite the railway station. The patron arrived and decided in our favour. Later, I left John in a café to telephone Roy, and I did not find him again until I arrived at the port. Roy collected us from Dover, together with our two litres of spirits and four litres of wine.[8]

Wed, 15 Feb - In the morning Pickford's came and took 50 cardboard boxes of stuff away in a lorry. While they did this I took some more stuff to my studio, then I left the car at a garage, to have a slow puncture repaired. I met John on the Leas on the walk back, and had a cup of tea in his flat in

---

[5] Old quarter of Folkestone.
[6] Farewell moving-to-Spain party, also Etelle's birthday party, held at Clifton Mansions.
[7] Calais' main centre.
[8] Duty Free alcohol allowance.

Kingsnorth Gardens. Lunch with Roy at the Brevet Club. To the cinema in the evening, to see *A Handful of Dust*. Liz[9] called at the flat earlier to cancel going with me to see this film.

Thurs, 16 Feb - At midday John Heal arrived and we went to the Garden House hotel for lunch. A new management there is providing its main restaurant courses as snacks in the bar at the same price. I had a very large bowl of mussel - something not to be found anywhere in the town in the past. James[10] was there as the newly employed head waiter. John and I returned to the flat, in its state of disarray, to drink at the bar. We then walked up to Blackbull Road, where I collected some typing for my catalogue.[11] Visited Bertie's on the way back. Found Chris at the flat on my return.

Folkestone, Sat, 11 March - A walk down the Leas, to post mail for Roy. Felt buoyant, daffodils and warm sunshine.[12] To Charing Point to Point meeting with John. Had two winners. To a pub in Charing afterwards, where I talked to a girl selling French properties. Bought a big bottle of wine in Folkestone and saw John, Chris and Vincent at the flat. There's an item in the Folkestone Herald about the disappearance of Liz (soon to be found safe and sound) .

Mon, 13 March - Collected the car from Mrs Johnson's[13] house, and the typewriter from the studio. Back at the flat Vincent and John visited. John came with me back to Mrs Johnson's house and to Roy's accountants. In the afternoon I did some A4 catalogue photocopying at a shop near the Central Station. In the evening I heated a tin of vegetable curry. Corrie visited me while I was doing this, looking well and staying for an hour.

---

[9] Liz, young girl living opposite Clifton Mansions at the Testwood hotel.
[10] James, well known gay character, did bar work and also modelled for students in life drawing classes.
[11] Diarist was due to exhibit his paintings at Folkestone Library gallery.
[12] Diarist had just returned from Spain.
[13] Roy Johnson's mother.

Wed, 15 March - A trip to Cambridge with John, so I could collect the painting owned by Mrs Malthouse at Linton. We arrived in Cambridge at 11 am, for a walk around the town and to find a pub, where we drank some Green King and Tolly Cobbold beer. I left John in a pub and drove to Linton, where I met Mrs Maltpress again and borrowed her painting. She has bought a holiday home in Nerja. Back in Cambridge, I had a walk in The Backs and met John in a wine bar. We returned via Coggeshall, to look at the late Peter Langan's restaurant. A sparkling day in Cambridge.

Thurs, 16 March - I went to Ostend, to borrow *February Rain*,[14] assisted by John. We caught the 9.30 am Jetfoil from Dover and in Ostend we had lunch at the Taverne Centrum, in Wapenplein,[15] a very good fish soup, followed by a steak-frites, consumed with several glasses of Stella lager. We collected the painting and caught the 5.45 pm ferry back, after the customs had stamped the Belgian EEC Movement Carnet, which I had obtained on a previous trip to Ostend. In Dover it was pouring with rain, with a cold wind, and I had to walk from the Eastern docks to the Western to collect the car. Arrived Folkestone 10.30 pm.

Sat, 18 March - A phone call to Pam at ten o'clock this morning. She tells me she is pregnant again, which is quite a surprise. I feel solemn thinking about her relationship with the man concerned, whoever he is.[16] Saw Chris and John in the evening. Made some bean curry, using a recipe from Chris.

Mon, 20 March - I met John at 9am outside my studio and we took my paintings to Folkestone library,[17] and spent the day hanging them up. I was relieved to see that there proved to be an adequate number of exhibits. There is new lighting and redecoration at the gallery, and the exhibition looked fine. At

---

[14] Painting by diarist.
[15] Main square in Ostend.
[16] Tom, Pam's social worker colleague.
[17] Folkestone Library Gallery.

lunchtime we ate some bean curry at the flat, and listened to librarian, Mrs Ward, talk about my exhibition on Radio Kent. Saw John again, and Chris, in the evening.

Tues, 21 March - I collected John from the library at lunchtime and we returned to the flat for some cold bean curry. I took him back there for the afternoon and then did some more catalogue photo copying. John is, for a small fee, going to sit at the desk at the exhibition and invite visitors to sign the visitor's book. I called at the *Folkestone Herald* and the *Kent Messenger 'Extra'* newspaper offices in the morning, to give them some exhibition info. Saw John and Chris in the evening at the flat.

Wed, 22 March - Did admin in the morning. At lunchtime I collected John, who reported quite a few visitors to the exhibition. The library was closed in the afternoon and we had lunch with Chris and Vincent at the Hi Tin in Tontine Street, then John accompanied me photocopying and then visiting Roy's sister, Julia, at Saltwood garage. Paul visited back at the flat, and we walked on the Leas. In the evening John returned and Chris and Liz visited. I drank a lot of whisky. John, Liz and I played cards - pontoon and then *Spoof.*

Thurs, 23 March - I called on Douglas at 10 am and took him to the fish market - where he bought some fish - then to see my exhibition. At 12.30 pm I collected John and we went to Douglas's flat for a drink. John and I then returned to Clifton Mansions for a drink, then we went to the Garden House hotel and the Burlington hotel. I cleared out the defrosted freezer and slept in the afternoon. John returned in the evening, reporting that the Neville Gallery,[18] of Canterbury, had come and expressed interest in showing my work.

---

[18] Run by Mr & Mrs Neville, of Folkestone.

Wed, 5 April - A rainy day. Paul visited mid morning. At midday I went to the library and took John to the Hi Tin for lunch. Afterwards we walked to Blackbull Road for a beer kit. The home brew shop was closed, so I bought it in Boots. I returned to the flat and attempted to make it - Tom Caxton lager. Should be ready in a week, if it works.

Thurs, 6 April - A morning coffee with Douglas at his flat. In the afternoon I cleared Roy's remaining stuff from his room into the spare room. I dismantled his double bed and moved my bed into his old room. Raining all day. In the evening John Heal arrived, to report that, contrary to expectations, the exhibition had been busy with visitors during the day. Chris also visited. At 7 pm I took Douglas to a house in Cherry Garden Avenue, where he bought two chairs, which I took back to his flat.

Fri, 7 April - l went to the bank and Roy's accountant,[19] and the estate agent[20] in the morning. I brought John from the library to the flat for some lunch. Cleaned the windows in Roy's room in the afternoon. In the evening I was visited by Chris, Vincent, Paul and Denis. Have not taken alcohol since Sunday evening. Gorbachev is on a two day visit to London.

Sun, 9 April - At lunchtime I went to the Garden House hotel to meet Douglas. John Heal was there, and later in the afternoon he helped me take the wardrobe in Roy's room to Douglas's flat, Douglas having bought it for £5.

Wed, 12 April - In the afternoon John Heal came to the flat and helped me put price labels on the items I had washed - mostly glasses, plates, mugs and ornaments.[21] Vincent visited in the evening, and bought some glasses and forks. Before he arrived some people came and bought the bed,[22] for £65.

---

[19] Beresfords Accountants.
[20] Seekers Estate Agency.
[21] Roy Johnson's possessions.
[22] Roy's king-sized bed.

Thurs, 13 April - Roy's sister, Julia, visited in the morning. She took away a couple of pictures and her old toy box. Before this I paid the bed cheque into the bank, along with another that Roy sent from Spain. After Julia's departure I mended some fused bar lights. In the afternoon an elderly man came and bought the calorr gas heater, for £30. In the evening a woman and her daughter came and bought the settee, for £20. John, Paul and Denis were here, and they helped me carry the settee out to the woman's car. Chris also visited and bought some items.

Fri, 14 April - I sorted out some more household items to take to a boot fair on Sunday. I also tidied up the lounge and kitchen and got the bar fridge working again. Vincent and John visited in the evening. A friend of Mr and Mrs Weston,[23] called Molly, whom I have apparently met, wishes to buy the Aylesham chapel spire painting. I have seen Corrie a couple of times this week, once on the Leas and once in the evening, on the way back to the Burlington hotel.

Sat, 15 April - The last day of the Folkestone exhibition. In the morning I went to the municipal dump with some valueless stuff. I went to the library and then with John to Muswell's Café[24] and Bertie's. We returned to the exhibition in the afternoon, for its end, John drunk. In the evening I saw Chris and John at the flat. Lovely weather today. Began to drink the Tom Caxton lager.

Wed, 19 April - Today I went to Cambridge, to return Mrs Maltpress's painting. John came with me. We got to Cambridge at 12.30 pm and went to the few pubs in the town centre,[25] including the University Arms, for its Green King beer. I went to Linton, to deliver the painting, then met John again in Cambridge, in the Tolly Cobbold pub opposite the University

[23] Mr & Mrs Weston, Clifton Mansions retired neighbours.
[24] Sandgate Road, Folkestone.
[25] Or city centre.
[26] Harry Porter, academic, private tutor & mentor.

Arms. We went to another little pub nearby, then returned to Folkestone, arriving at about 11 pm. Called on Harry Porter,[26] Kim's friend, while in Cambridge.

Thurs, 20 April - I went to Beresfords and the bank, and at 11 am called on Molly Willis at her flat in Grimston Avenue. When I saw her I remembered her from Mr and Mrs Weston's drinks parties. She intends to give the painting to her daughter, who I think lives near Portsmouth, as a present. I hung it for her, meantime, in her flat, where it looked fine in the subdued light there. Slept in the afternoon. John Heal visited in the evening, to collect his commission cheque.[27]

Fri, April 21 - To Ostend today, to return the painting.[28] John Heal helped me carry it. We went on the 9.35 am Jetfoil from Dover. In Ostend the customs discovered that Dover had made a mistake on my carnet. We left the painting at the port and went to the Central Tavern, in Wapenplein, for a bowl of fish soup. We picked up the painting at the port and carried it to the office near the docks, where I first got the carnet. They sorted out the mistake and we then carried the painting back to the museum.[29] We then had a few beers before catching the 8 pm ferry. Dover at 11.30 pm and taxi to Folkestone. Our meal on board the Belgian ferry featured freshly picked *spring salad*.

Sat, 22 April - Went shopping for my breakfast, after which I visited Douglas at his flat. In the evening Chris and John Heal visited.

Sun, 23 April - Went with John Heal to a boot fair in a football field in Sandwich. Made about £27. Was back in Folkestone at 2.30 pm. Chris called in the evening.

Sat, 29 April - Made ready some more items for a boot fair. Saw Chris, John and Vincent in the evening.

[27] Diarist had promised John commission on any work sold while he was present as the exhibition curator.
[28] *February Rain.*
[29] Museum Voor Schone Kunsten, Ostend.
[30] Vincent was teaching Engish at the Living Language School.

Sun, 30 April - John and I went to a boot fair at Sellinge, on the site of the Sellinge Steam Special. Made £40 and had a very enjoyable day. Chris, John, Vincent, and one of Vincent's Swedish language learning students visited in the evening.[30]

Mon, 1 May - May Day. After breakfast I helped Douglas take a table to his flat. I then met him at Ward's hotel bar, then I went to the Mikado bar, to meet John Heal. We went on to the Burlington hotel and Garden House hotel. I returned to the flat to clear my bedroom up. John visited again in the evening and we went back to the Burlington, then I went solo to a couple of bars.

Tues, 2 May - An admin day. Ordered my flight ticket to Spain. Did some clearing up in the flat. Have borrowed the Croft family hoover. Took some stuff left over from the boot fairs to John's flat.

Wed, 3 May - Took my paintings from the studio to the flat and displayed them around the lounge, hall way and main bedroom. At 3 pm Janita Elton and Eddie Chambers, of the Usher Gallery, Lincoln, arrived to view them. They are organising an exhibition called *British Artists Abroad*. I provided afternoon tea on the patio. Misty, sunny May weather. In the evening Chris, Vincent and John visited.

Thurs, 4 May - Finished putting in the lounge window.[31] Walked down to the Hi Tin, for lunch with Chris, who did not show. Splendid sunshine. In the afternoon I did some more telephoning and clearing up in the flat. Chris and John visited in the evening. Have had a sore throat that has become a slight cold.

Fri, 5 May - To the bank and Beresfords accountants, where I found that my air ticket had not arrived.[32] Fortunately, I had to go to London, to collect a document for Roy from his solicitor, Lawrence Graham, in the Strand. I caught the 10.19 am train, and in London went to the solicitors, and then to the travel

[31] Diarist had removed the window pane to enable Roy's pianola to be removed after being sold.
[32] Beresfords accountants were providing a mail holding service.

agent, Azure Holidays, who told me the ticket would be waiting for me at the airport. I returned to Folkestone, arriving at 4.30 pm, and took a car load of rubbish to the dump. John visited, and later I went to Harvey's Wine Bar, the Portland hotel and the Happy Frenchman pub. I also took my paintings back to the studio this afternoon.

Sat, 6 May - I took a couple of car loads of household things to the studio, leaving the flat almost empty. John visited in the evening, and also Chris while I was upstairs seeing Mr & Mrs Weston. Vincent made a late visit. Today I also bought a new suitcase and did some packing.

Folkestone, Tues, 4 July - Went strawberry picking.[33] Yesterday I earned £6, today £7. The season has nearly ended, as it began early this year. John visited in the evening, also yesterday evening. This evening we went to the Burlington hotel, to a temporary upstairs bar. When I returned at lunchtime from Roundwood Farm,[34] John told me that the Cork Street party is tomorrow, not today. We decided to go to Martin Mill[35] on the train, but waiting for it at the station I felt weary and changed my mind, leaving John to go by himself. Saw Chris and John again later.

Wed, 5 July - Went strawberry picking, earned £14. On the way back to the flat I collect a few more household things each day from the studio.[36] John and Chris visited this evening, also Vincent and his language school teaching colleague, Amanda. John and I went to the Harvey Wine Bar and the Clifton hotelThere was a rail strike today, so no trip to the Cork Street party.

Thurs, 6 July - Went strawberry picking. The car would not start, so I got the bus to Etchinghill and walked from there. Started picking at 11.30 am. Wonderful summer day, but poor picking. Earned £6.50. Got the return mini bus travelling this

---

[33] After diarist's return from Spain.
[34] Roundwood Farm, Stone Street.
[35] To the Lantern pub.
[36] Diarist was renting a studio room in Marten Road.
[37] Lindsay Page, teacher, brother of Louise.

year between the field and Folkestone. In the evening I ate some baked bean curry. John visited. Am enjoying better sleep, with the cooler English nights.

Sat, 8 July - A hectic time bringing stuff from the studio and preparing the flat for a barbecue, which took place and which was a disaster. John and Chris arrived, and then Adder came with his mother and his friend, Philip, and Paul. Peter Wagstaff and Lindsay[37] also arrived later. Vincent was in a very childish mood. Chris also behaved badly. I also brewed some more beer today - I had brewed some on Tuesday, but it went sour in the bin.[38]

Wed, 12 July - Earned £10.50 today. In the evening Chris phoned, re our visit to the Southcliff hotel, to see Michell play her accordion. Before I went to meet him, Peter Wagstaff arrived, and John Heal, and we all went there in Peter Wagstaff's car. Afterwards we three went to the Harvey Wine Bar, then John and I went to the Clifton hotel, then returned to the flat for some bean curry. Nasty hangover in store. Another car load transported.[39]

Thurs, 13 July - Earned £6. Before returning to the flat, I collecting another car load from the studio. I phoned Dad, Pam, and the Usher gallery, Lincoln, before driving at 6pm, with John Heal, to Broadstairs, where we walked down to the harbour and went to the wine bar half way down the hill. We then went to Ramsgate, to a pizza restaurant on the sea front then to Tiberius casino, where I lost three £5 chips. We then went to Margate, parked near the Lido, and went to a new gay club, called Rumours. We stayed until it's 2 am closure, then walked on the promenade for an hour. I then got a sleeping bag from the car and went down some steps near the Lido to a sandy beach, where I lay down to sleep.

Fri, 14 July - I slept two or three hours on comfortable sand, waking to a grey dawn and the sound of one or two spots of rain on my sleeping bag. I lay watching seagulls wheeling over

---

[38] To this day, the only time the diarist has experienced this.
[39] Of domestic items from the diarist's studio.

the stone cliff above my head. John, who spent the night pacing the promenade and empty streets, and I left Margate at 7 am and arrived in Folkestone one hour later. At the flat I had breakfast, then went to the studio for another car load. In the afternoon I got yet another car load, and also had a sleep. Roy phoned. No visitors in the evening.

Sat, 15 July - After breakfast I went to the studio to move the last things out and tidy the room up. Left £90 cash for outstanding rent, with a room vacation confirmation note. Glad to begin saving the £15 per week. Did some household chores and checked the car.[40] In the evening Chris and John visited. Wonderful weather.

Wed, 26 July - Went to the launderette n the morning. Slept after lunch, then played golf with Dad[41]at the Sports Centre. In the evening Chris and John visited and we all drank home brewed lager. Dad and I then went to the Executive Club and the top bar at the Norfolk hotel.

Thurs, 27 July - In the evening Dad drove[42] Chris, John and myself to Hythe, to the White Heart pub, I think, to see Michelle and her accordion duo. Not a bad trip, the landlord there is German and quite amusing. We dropped Chris off afterwards in Sandgate, pretty drunk, outside Margaret's house

Fri, 28 July - In the evening Chris brought round a silver foil-covered tray, which he put into the oven. It contained some pieces of chicken and potatoes, and when he returned this was eaten with some spicy gravy which he made. Thus we received the meal which he had promised us, and about which he had been on about for days. John and Adder also got in on the free grub, Adder donating a bottle of wine. Quite fun, but not a very relaxed evening, certainly not for Dad.

Sat, 29 July - Not much space here to describe a bad day. It ended - after an awful expedition involving Chris, John, Adder and a couple of Spanish language students to Hythe - with Dad

---

[40] Oil & tyres, for car journey to Birmingham the next day.
[41] Diarist's father was on holiday in Folkestone.
[42] Diarist's car.

and I back at the flat having a terrible row. He accused me of living off Roy for twenty years. I made some terrible accusations concerning his treatment of Mum.

Fri, 4 Aug - Was woken 10 am by a phone call from Roy, then I walked down the Leas to Beresfords, for mail, then to the post office, bank, estate agents and Sainsbury's. Returned to the flat for breakfast. Went for a lunchtime swim - noisy channel tunnel outlet overflow pipe construction work on beach. Returned to the flat. Wrote to Roy. At 6 pm a Mr and Mrs Tebbit came to view the flat, sent by Seekers. Later I drank home made lager with John and Chris.

Sat, 5 Aug - My weekend breakfast is two Shredded Wheat, a boiled egg, and then half a packet of Lincoln biscuits, with lots of tea. During the day I go for a morning walk, and in the afternoon a swim, and in the evening I drink home-brew with Chris and John. Chris, lately, brings tins of strong lager for himself.

Sun, 6 Aug - One evening this weekend Chris brought the ingredients for a mince meat curry to the flat, which was cooked and eaten by himself and John and me, with some left over for another evening meal or two.

Wed, 9 Aug - In the morning two of the Bouverie Square estate agents came and viewed the flat. A lunchtime walk to the harbour, had no whelks today.[43] Did some admin and slept in the afternoon. Drank home-brew in the evening. I have also been going for a swim this week every afternoon at high tide. I've seen Corrie a couple of times, once when she visited while John and Chris were here and I was on the phone to Dad, and once when I went round Clifton Crescent late at night to post a letter.

Fri, 11 Aug - I went into the town to collect my mail and visit all the estate agents, to confirm the £64,500 asking price for the flat. I returned to the flat, then I think I changed clothes and walked down to the harbour, for a half pint of whelks. Some

---

[43] Unlike on previous harbour visits.

admin and sleep in the afternoon, and perhaps a swim? In the evening I drank a large amount of home brewed lager at the flat, with John and Chris. I have tried brewing some Boots *Continental Lager*, which I have begun drinking before it has properly matured. John and I had a last drink at the Mikado bar at the Metropole.

Sat, 12 Aug - Woke feeling sick with a hangover. John arrived at 11am and we drove to West Hythe, to visit a sweet old lady called Mrs Morgan, whose grand-daughter had seen Mrs Morgan's house in my painting at the library exhibition. We then walked around Brockhill Park, at Saltwood, and then the Donkey Derby,[44] at Radnor Park. Met Vincent there and later he arrived with some sausages, expecting a barbecue, which I had to do. Chris and John also were there for this, Chris arguing, as usual, with Adder. This morning I also called on Philip Rutt,[45] at Seabrook, who saw the exhibition.

Sun, 13 Aug - A wonderful breezy, sunny walk at lunchtime along the Leas and through Sandgate and back along the beach. Did some correspondence at the flat. In the evening

Chris arrived with a large dish of chicken curry and rice. We began to eat this, then John and Vincent arrived and joined in, Adder bringing a bottle of wine.

Mon, 14 Aug - Was woken by the doorbell at 10 am, remembering, too late, that it was an appointment with one of the estate agents. Another one came at 10.30 am, then I went down into the town to get some money, photocopies and shoe heels mended. Called on John, suggesting a trip to Leamington Spa. In the afternoon I got ready and waited for a 4 pm appointment with the forgotten estate agent. After this I collected John and drove to Stratford upon Avon, arriving 9 pm. I parked by the theatre and we sat on a bench eating curry and rice, cold, left from last night. I moved the car along past the theatre, then we had a walk around the town, before returning to the car to sleep in it.

[44] Donkey races with child jockeys, held during Folkestone carnival week.
[45] Philip Rutt, art lover.
[46] Stratford pub favoured by Royal Shakespeare Company actors.

Tues, 15 Aug - I had a fitful, cramped sleep in the back of the car, parked by the Avonside hotel, short of the Dirty Duck.[46] Heavy rain during the night, but warm and sunny at 8 am. John had left the front of the car at 5 am to walk about the town. We drove to Leamington and I scanned the local paper and went to estate agents. We visited a firm that let storage and office space and looked at some garages they had, then we ate some of Chris's curry in the park. In the afternoon I drove around more streets, then decided to rent one of the garages I'd seen, in Gordon Street, at £40 a quarter. We left Leamington at 5 pm. We drove to Henley on Thames, for some more curry by the river, then went on to Folkestone, arriving midnight.

Wed, 16 Aug - Awoke feeling a bit blank. Did a few chores, such as shopping and some admin. In the evening John arrived and we phoned Vincent, who took us to Hythe, to the Venetian Fête.[47] Took plastic bottles of home brew, did not pay to enter. The fête was held on a barren stretch of canal, with too many bank side coloured lights, and a loud loudspeaker system with

a brash yuppie commentator - all too over-organised, with floats looking rather lost and bewildered and no magic in the event nowadays. John and I split up and I enjoyed the walk back in the moonlight, along the canal to Seabrook and then along the promenade, a high tide plashing over occasionally, but I did not have any bad luck getting wet.

Sat, 19 Aug - Folkestone carnival day, wonderful weather. After breakfast I walked to the post office, to post some credit card cheques and a cheque for the Leamington garage rent. A swim in the afternoon, and Peter Wagstaff visited. In the evening I watched the procession with Chris, John and Vincent. We returned to the flat for curry - made by Chris - together with neighbours Maureen Pilkington and her friend, David.[48] To the Burlington afterwards, to see Julian behind the bar, and I was joined there by John and Vincent.

---

[47] Procession of floats on the Royal Military Canal, held every four years.
[48] David Simpson.
[49] Formerly Miles Haven bar.
[50] For Diarist's possible future use.

Sun, 20 Aug - A wonderful hot, mediterranean day. Went out for a *Sunday Times* and returned for a weekend breakfast. Afterwards a walk along the Leas and down through Sandgate. Had a swim in the company of Adder and his mother, who were on the beach by Beachcombers.[49] Walked back to flat then drove all over town, noting *Accommodation To Let* phone numbers in newsagents' windows.[50] Chris and John visited in the evening. Ate some more of Chris's curry.

Thurs, 25 Aug - I went to the bank, Beresfords and the post office. I also went round all the estate agents and gave them a key each to the flat. Nine agents now have keys. I also took the car to the garage in Plain Road, to see if they still wanted to buy it, and they said they would tomorrow morning. In the evening I used the car to take my paintings to John Heal's flat, where he will store them for £7 a month.

Sat, 26 Aug - Tried to start the car at 9 am, ready to take it to the Plain Road garage, to sell it for £50, as arranged. It was raining and the car wouldn't start. I ended up with a flat battery, and I also failed to start it with some home made jump leads from Roy's car.[51] John visited in the evening. My latest home-brew is a failure, but we had to drink it anyway.

Sun, 27 Aug - I was out fiddling with the car at 8 am, failing to start it with jump leads from Roy's car. John, who doesn't drive, then steered the car as I towed it to Sandgate Hill, where I failed to start it as it rolled down a little way. Towing it back, the string tow rope kept breaking and two police cars began buzzing around, so I eventually abandoned the car on the hill, by Coolinge Lane. John visited again in the evening.

Folkestone, Sat 4 Nov - A shivery night, wearing old clothes and only a car blanket.[52] Spent the day chopping some old wood and getting the stove operational. Chris visited. In the evening John visited and presently I left him to go and see one or two bonfires on the beach, and to visit several Sandgate pubs. John had some visitors while I was away.

[51] Roy had yet to sell his ageing BMW.
[52] Diarist had just returned from Spain.

Sun, 5 Nov - Bonfire night proper. I had my Lincoln biscuit breakfast, then walked to Chris's garage, to retrieve the bag of bedding, which had been in Roy's car there, until Chris removed it for some reason. Later, after dark, I walked around the town and decided to buy some booze instead of fireworks. Chris came to the flat with a box of them, and there was a greatly enjoyable little display and barbecue, attended - though not all at once - by Etelle, John, Chris, Vincent, Peter Wagstaff, Venetia with her grandchild, and Tamsin, with her boyfriend, Paul.

Folkestone, Fri, 17 Nov - I went shopping and to the bank and to Beresford's for my mail. Felt contented.[53] Bought a bottle of Beaujolais Nouveau, and drank half of it in front of the wood fire in the evening, before the arrival of John, and then Adder and, I think, Chris. John and I went to the Garden House hotel, then the Burlington, arriving there too late to get a drink, then we went across from the flat to the Living Language Centre, where Adder was attending a fancy dress students' banquet in the basement there.

Sat, 18 Nov - For breakfast I had two Shredded Wheat, a boiled egg, toast and marmalade and half a packet of Lincoln biscuits. Transferred the beer from plastic bucket to a plastic polypin. In the evening I was visited by Chris, Adder, John Heal and Peter Wagstaff, which started with another bottle of Beaujolais.

Sun, 19 Nov - A repeat of yesterday's breakfast, excepting for a fried egg and two fried sausages instead of an egg boiled. Cleaned the cooker inside and out. A walk to Sandgate and back via Folkestone harbour and the Old High Street. In the evening Chris arrived with a rice snack, which was eaten by himself and me, Adder, John Heal and Peter Wagstaff, Adder and Wagstaff rowing at each other.

Thurs, 23 Nov - I drove Roy's car to a scrapyard near Aldington, to seek MOT repairs, and was redirected through lanes to Kingsnorth, to a council house there occupied by a

---

[53] Diarist had just returned from a USA trip.

Mick Crabb, who said he could do the repairs for £300. Drove back to Folkestone via Hamstreet and Lympne - autumn leaves and bright clear sunshine. I re-garaged the car and shopped at Sainsbury's. on the way back to the flat. Met John on the Leas. Had muesli then Sainsbury's lentil and bacon soup lunch . Chopped some wood, or rather sawed it, and slept. John visited in the evening and we drank home-brew.

Fri, 24 Nov - To the bank and Beresfords in the morning. Adder called at lunchtime to cancelled a party he was supposed to be organising here tomorrow evening. He is presently trying to take over the garage that Chris rented, and where Roy's car has been left of late. He is worried I will leave the car there after I return to Spain. I won't be doing this, but I hope his doubt will result in events that will mean I do not have to pay him the garage rent this month. A quiet evening at the flat. Saw John, I think.

Sat, 25 Nov - A frosty afternoon. Walked to a Cheriton toy shop, to buy a Christmas present for Jack. Met Etelle as I returned to the flat again. She took me to the flat she is sharing in Westbourne Gardens, where she gave me a brandy and a meal. In the evening no one came to the (cancelled) party, except John. He and I went to Cleggy's, where we stayed til about 2 am. Was given a lift back to the flat by Graham, a person I played pool with there.

Sun, 26 Nov - John visited at noon, to wake me up, sell me a copy of the *Sunday Times*, and share my breakfast. I felt very blank afterwards, but went for a sunny, frosty walk to Cheriton and back, taking a few photographs. In the evening Chris arrived, unexpectedly with a rice dish, containing pieces of chicken and pheasant. This was eaten by Chris and John and myself, the remains to be eaten by myself tomorrow, on the train to Birmingham.[54]

---

[54] Diarist was going on a family visit.
[55] St Mary's parish church, Studley.

Studley, Tues, 29 Nov - A walk to the church[55]after eating some porridge. Returned to pack my bag and to eat a pasty, chips and curry sauce meal. Lesley arrived during this and I said goodbye to her, and to Dad soon afterwards. Bus to Birmingham, trains to London and Folkestone, where I arrived at 7 pm. I walked from the station to the garage in Broadmead Road and found that Vincent had changed the padlock on the gate. Met John as I approached the flat, and inside I got the fire going and we drank some beer.

Wed, 29 Nov - Did some preparations throughout the day towards tomorrow's departure.[56] Before lunchtime I took my guitar and the beer making equipment to John's flat, then called on Vincent in Julian Road. He tried to pretend he'd changed the lock because the old one was all rusty. I gave him my keys to the garage, but I said I could give him no rent for this month, as he had already taken the garage over. Thus the amusing little garage intrigue ends as hoped. In the evening Chris visited, and John, and I drank gin and beer with them, me happily neglecting my travel preparations.

Nerja, Sat, 23 Dec - Roy dropped me at Malaga airport, before going on to spend Christmas with his mother in Portugal. The Dan Air flight arrived in London at 1 pm and I arrived by train at Folkestone about 4.30 pm. The flat was very empty looking but had been aired by John. I walked down to the town to buy a gift for Rosie,[57] plus mince pies, which I ate walking along. Phoned Dad then called on Venetia - at home with her granddaughter. Chris arrived at the flat later and we drank home brew left over in the cellar. I was glad to see him. I went afterwards to the Burlington hotel, where Julian was behind the bar and where an Xmas function was going on. Return to flat to dig out mattress and blankets. USA has invaded Panama and deposed drug profiteering head of state, Noriega.

---

[56] To Spain.
[57] Rosie Michell, Tom's daughter and Jack's half sister.

Studley, Tues, 2 Jan - Another damp day. Bought Dad some medicine for his cough. Lesley called at the house during her office lunch break. I got some chips and she ate some too, with curry sauce. I poured the rest of the curry sauce over a few left over bits of turkey, of which I began, but the sauce failed to disguise the fact that the meat was inedible. After Lesley left I departed at 2.45 pm, Dad unhappy and sentimental. Bus to Birmingham, trains to Folkestone, arriving about 8 pm. Phoned John from the station and he arrived later at the flat with the telephones.[1] The flat was completely empty when I arrived, until I dug a few bits and pieces out of the cupboard.

Folkestone, Thurs, 4 Jan - A 10.30 am dental check up by Tom Green.[2] To the library, to try without success to find anything about air conditioning in old *Which* magazines. Returned to the flat to sort out a couple of bags of fuel from the wood store - am almost to the last of the wood from Chilham now.[3] Lunch, stuck some *sticker soles* on shoes, slept. Began *Put Out More Flags*, having skimmed the last confusing quarter of *Black Mischief*. Got the fire going. Presently, John arrived, then Chris and we drank some lager. Am masturbating plentifully, usually twice a day, once three. I do it while indulging in my sweet little fantasies, usually about tickling or spanking grown up girls.

Fri, 5 Jan - Got 10.19 am train to London. Arrived Camden Lock at midday, to call on Janus Avivson at his gallery. The gallery was closed, so I called at his house in Ferdinand St. The door was answered by a cagey girl in a dressing gown, who informed me that he was in Amsterdam. Thwarted in this attempt to confront Avivson, I decided to see if my grandmother was in at nearby Hampstead. The door of the Wells House flat was opened by aunty Phyllis, and Nanny,[4] who lives with her there, was sitting inside in an armchair. At ninety she is still very fit and well, with just a little rheumatism

---

[1] John stored the telephones when the diarist was away.
[2] Diarist was socially acquainted with Tom Green and his wife, Helga.
[3] The fuel had come from Chilham Saw Mills.
[4] Diarist's grandmother.

in the legs. We had some tea and Christmas cake and she insisted on giving me a fiver on my departure, half of which I spent on buying this journal[5]in Hampstead. Folkestone about 6.30 pm. Saw John and Chris at the flat.

Sat, 6 Jan - I phoned Janus Avivson, who agreed that he had received a 400 dollar cheque from Phyllis. He said he paid it into a local bank and was waiting to get more money from her. I said 300 dollars of the money was mine. He then said the money was to cover the agreed £250 travelling expenses, though this is only due after several thousand dollars worth of work has been sold. I got him to assure me he would send me the money he owes. I don't expect him to do this and I will be glad to use it as a reason to terminate our relationship. In fact the end was when he lied to me last year about not receiving any more money from Phyllis. I walked into Folkestone and took a look at the sales. Bought a £20 ski jacket in The Old High Street and a £15 pair of walking shoes in Sandgate Road. John visited the flat in the evening.

Sun, 7 Jan - Chris visited just as I was halfway through my Lincoln biscuit breakfast. He was full of enthusiasm for *The Phantom of the Opera*, having been to London yesterday to see it with Margaret. I then went for a pleasurable walk down through Sandgate and on along the promenade to a point below the Clarendon Inn. Bought a Penguin paperback[6]in a Sandgate second hand shop, oft visited in years past. Came back along the beach and up the Zig Zag Path. In the evening Chris arrived with an oven tray containing rice, shrimps and chicken pieces, plus curry sauce. We had a drink across at the Tudor Bar of the Salisbury hotel then returned to eat the dish, aided by John.

Mon, 8 Jan - An 11 am appointment at the doctor's surgery for a polio inoculation booster. From there I walked into the town and made one or two more purchases in the sales - a pair of red

---

[5] Blank paged hardback note book.
[6] Diarist collected early Penguin paperbacks.

shoes (£13.49), a pair of pumps (£2), some white summer trousers (£4.99), a jumper (£6.99) and a pair of socks (99p). In the afternoon I began to pack and to put some of the few household items in the flat away in a bedroom cupboard. In the evening Chris and John visited. Chris, who had a cold, drank from a small bottle of whisky he brought with him. I drank home brew. John just sat at the bar with his head bent round, gazing at the fire.

Nerja, Tues, 27 Feb - To the studio[7] but I was dismayed to find the digger and lorries back in action. I fear they will be there all week. I walked down to the beach and back to the house to write in this journal. Roy and his mother have gone to the Tuesday market.[8] The day continued with me beginning to drink beer at lunch time. Roy and his mother departed to play golf. I tried to phone John in Folkestone but failed, due possibly to yesterday's heavy UK storms. I walked to the Fontainebleau hotel[9] to fail to get through from there. Walked back via Churchill's Bar, to have several beers with the owner, who is one half of the Lawrence Duo[10] and a tenor of unfulfilled talent.

Sun, 18 March - A 9.15 am departure from the house.[11] *Sprout*[12]in playful breakfast mood. At Malaga Roy and I walked to a café off the airport, as the flight was put back an hour. The Caledonian flight finally left at 2 pm and arrived at Gatwick at 2 pm GMT. Very mild sunny weather, similar to Spain. Trains to Folkestone, during which I read various discarded Sunday newspapers and looked out of the window before it was dark, at daffodils, and blossom and weeping willows just in leaf - everything advanced again this year. Sat next to an attractive - though overweight - Australian girl in charge of delightful little boy and girl, all of them eating jam tarts and on a

---

[7] Diarist was renting a caravan studio on some disused ground.
[8] Nerja weekly street market.
[9] Run by Ian Anderson, the hotel was a focal point for Nerja expats.
[10] Nerja vocal cabaret act.
[11] *Casa Don Miguel.*
[12] Adopted street cat.

Christopher Robin-type Sunday expedition. Folkestone 8 pm, saw Adder and John.

Mon, 19 March - Found some porridge and tea in the cupboard for breakfast. Unpacked and wrote a *things to do* list. Adder made a brief visit. I visited Mr and Mrs Weston upstairs then tried and failed to contact Mike Goody,[13] who is buying the flat. He is also converting Mrs George's[14] old flat and a bloke working there came and got the gas heater for the shower working again. John then arrived with my guitar and some home brewing equipment. I walked with him down the Leas then continued down to the harbour and back through the town to Sainsbury's. In the afternoon I brewed some Boots lager. At dusk I walked down near the toll house[15] and returned with two large windfall logs. Julian spotted me carrying them, to my embarrassment. John visited in the evening and we drank some lager left in store from Christmas.

Wed, 21 March - Did more things on my *things to do* list. Got my old bedroom ready for use as a temporary studio. As well as the failed drawing[16] I have also brought with me pastels and photos and I will try to do some more work on the current pastel, with a view to getting it adequate enough to enter for the RA Summer Exhibition. John and Chris visited in the evening. Drank some duty free Larios gin from Malaga airport.

Thurs, 22 March - I began by putting a car in front of the supermarket looking about to disappear around the corner. Drank some gin in the evening with, I think, John and perhaps Chris.

Sat, 24 March - Worked on the drawing in the morning, after porridge and boiled egg breakfast. Bought a piece of hardboard from Allcrafts[17] for the back of the picture. In the evening Chris and John visited. Chris took John and me to Sandgate,

---

[13] Mike Goody, new neighbour and Clifton Mansions lease holder.
[14] Mrs George, deceased elderly neighbour and friend.
[15] Former toll house on Lower Sandgate Road.
[16] An uncompleted graphic work.
[17] Builders' merchant shop.

where we went to the Ship. I drank a pint of Burton Ale - a mistake when mixed with gin and lager. John and I then went the Providence Inn and the Royal Norfolk hotel (revamped and renamed), then we walked in darkness along the Lower Sandgate Road to Cleggy's. Ray let us in and we stayed 'til about 1.30 am. I played pool with some people.

Sun, 25 March - Got up at midday, felt very weary. Walk to the newsagent for a newspaper then returned to the flat to be sick, plans for a fried breakfast abandoned. Ate some porridge and slept again, had a boiled egg at 6 pm. Roy phoned and in the evening John and Chris visited. Chris brought a tray of rice and chicken bits, into which he tipped a jar of mussels. I managed one useful thing today in cutting out the mount and doing a reasonable job with a worn out blade.

Wed, 28 March - I worked on the drawing in the morning and afternoon - about five hours in all. I also finished sawing the frame joints. In the evening John visited and we drank some home brewed lager. I drank five pints. The remains of Chris's Sunday rice dish has kept me going each evening - ate the last of it this evening. Am keeping the fire going each evening by continuing to go and search for timber every other night.[19]

Thurs, 29 March - Worked on the background in the morning and the foreground in the afternoon.[20] John sat sipping lager at the bar throughout the afternoon, and I periodically broke off from my work in my old bedroom to visit him. He departed at 6 pm but returned later and I drank some home brewed lager with him. I've finished assembling the frame and am assured now of having the pastel ready.[21] Framing it, using inadequate tools, has also been a fiddling, lengthy task.

Sat, 31 March - To Boulogne with John on the last day of a £6 day trip offer. We got the 7.45 am *St Anselm* from Folkestone, which was crowded. In Boulogne we bought cheese and pâté

---

[18] Ray, manager/licensee.
[19] Beachcombing or from skips.
[20] Viz. diarist's current pastel.
[21] To submit to the RA Summer Exhibition.

from the market, and bread, and two litres of the cheapest wine. We sat on a seat on the ramparts of the Old Town and had a picnic. It was sunny but our backs were to a breeze and after finishing eating we found a more more sheltered spot and sat finishing the wine, while reading a plastic bag full of newspapers discarded on the boat. John went for a walk and when he returned we were both drunk (we had also been to one or two cafés). We managed to walk back to the harbour for a 5.30 pm return. John was in poor shape during the voyage. In Folkestone we parted outside Cleggy's. I had a drink with Chris at the Salisbury hotel. Saw John again at the flat. Got some chips from Tontine Street.

Sun, 1 April - Rose at 11 am and walked to the paper shop for the *Sunday Times* and a carton of milk - Sunday morning April sunshine. Returned for porridge, fried egg, sausages and bread then toast and marmalade - an enjoyable success. Sawed wood, tidied flat then went for a walk up the Leas and down to Sandgate and along the esplanade, as far as the Sandgate hotel. People were sunbathing. Returned to the flat and presently got the fire going and showered. John visited. We drank some home brewed lager. I ate some cold chips left from last night, then bread and cheese. Watched telly then had a late walk to retrieve a few pieces of wood from a nearby roadside skip.

Tues, 3 April - I went to Folkestone Job Centre and also looked in local newspapers in an attempt to find a temporary job until Easter. The two possibilities seem to be being a fruit packer or else a field worker, planting strawberry plants (but this is at the farm where I got the sack).[22] Made some phone calls at the flat. John visited in the evening. We both drank tap water.

Wed, 4 April - At 11 am I went to the Marton Recruitment employment agency in Sandgate Road, to see about the fruit packing job. I was told there should be something available soon. At lunchtime today (or tomorrow)[23]I saw some builders

---

[22] Diarist had been dismissed for supporting another picker who had been campaigning to be paid more money.

throwing old timber down from a building into a skip in Clifton Crescent. They were old floorboards and joists and they said I was welcome to have the timber for firewood, so I commenced bringing armfuls of it round to the flat. Drank some home brew in the evening with John.

Thurs, 5 April - I got up early and went to the Sandgate Road employment agency at 7.45 am, in the hope that I would get on the fruit packers' bus, but there was no one to be seen. I waited until 8 am then walked back to the flat in an increasingly peculiar way, arriving just in time, thankfully, to have an urgent shit. I went back to bed and slept 'til mid morning. I then went shopping at Sainsbury's and called at the agency, which informed me that I would be starting on Monday at 6.30 am. Saw John in the evening and, I think, Chris.

Fri, 6 April - I spent the morning buying, packaging and sending some Easter Eggs by post to Pam. I also went to the bank - have had to begin drawing credit card money for any further expenditure. In the evening Chris and Venetia visited. John then arrived and we left him tending the fire while Chris drove Venetia and me to *Brockers*, making a quick visits to the Salisbury hotel on the way. At *Brockers* Venetia showed me the work that Tamsin is doing on the Foundation Course at Canterbury College of Art. Venetia gave me a glass of her Elderflower wine. My Tom Caxton *Pils* strong lager needs black current juice tipped in, to disguise the taste.

Sat, 7 April - Woke at 10.30am and walked to the post office, for a *Daily Mail* then returned to cook a comprehensive breakfast. Sawed some wood, tidied the flat, went for a walk into the town. At 6 pm Chris arrived with some ingredients to begin cooking a rice and chicken dish. John arrived, bearing some sticks and odd bits of wood. I got the fire going, then showered and changed. Peter Wagstaff arrived with a bottle of wine. Chris returned and completed cooking the dish Vincent

---

[23] Diarist wrote his diary weekly, on a Sunday.

made a last minute appearance with a bottle of wine. We had a cheerful time for an hour or two.

Sun, 8 April - I did a load of washing by hand in the bath instead of going to the launderette, to save money. An afternoon walk up the Leas and down to Sandgate and back along the shore, past the Rotunda market to Tontine Street - bright sunshine with a fresh easterly breeze. Purchased some apples in the little grocery shop opposite the Salvation Army. Walked back to the flat through the quiet town centre, in contrast to the animated Sunday market and Rotunda amusements and rides. Sawed some wood and got a bit more from a skip. Lit the fire and showered. John visited, then Chris. We ate the remainder of Chris's rice dish. Watched golf on the telly.

Thurs, 12 April - Up at 5 am. Arrived in the van[24] at EKP[25] for another *no work* announcement, except for a job for just one man in the stores. Most of the blokes were not interested in this, and I ended up tossing a coin for it with the only other person who was. I wouldn't have minded going home, but unfortunately I won the toss. I walked to the cold stores for fruit, but there wasn't anything for me to do, as the foreman had already hired a bloke with whom I stood all day, very occasionally lifting a metal support brace onto loads being carried by fork lift trucks. The day eventually ended at 5pm. I was very sleepy all day, especially during lunch and tea breaks. In the evening John arrived, then Vincent. A spaghetti meal cooked by Chris was expected, but it never arrived.

Fri, 13 April - John arrived at 11.30 am, in response to my breakfast invitation last night. I fried some food. Wet day, lit fire and drank lager. An afternoon walk to the bank and to shop for Easter Eggs.[26] In the evening John returned, then Chris bearing the ingredients for the spaghetti dish, which he began to cook. I showered then Chris returned to finish

---

[24] Diarist was driving the Marton agency workers' van.
[25] East Kent Packers Ltd.
[26] For diarist's family.

cooking and the result was shared by the three of us. Drank the last of my Malaga gin. John had the news that Mike Stonestreet[27]has died. I went to the Garden House hotel and read in a local newspaper that he died a week ago, aged fifty two. It should not really come as a shock, but it is hard to believe that it has happened to such a character.

Sat, 14 April - Did packing in the morning. John arrived at midday to collect the bag with my cheque books and the flat telephones. I reheated the remainder of Chris's spaghetti for our lunch. I departed the flat at 2.55 pm and caught the 3.20 pm London train, then the 6.15 pm Paddington to Hereford, arriving at Evesham at 7.50 pm after a pleasant rural journey on a comfortable Inter City train. Kim and Dad met me at the station and we went to the pub in Harvington and the Little Lark in Studley.

Studley, Mon, 23 April - A morning walk across the field to the church foot bridge then along the river Arrow to the brook footbridge and back round in a circle to the church - bursts of bright new sunshine on jewel-like celandines, dandelions and red campions. A pasty, chips and curry sauce lunch. Lesley called in. Said goodbye to Dad at 2.45 pm to catch a bus to Evesham, then trains to Folkestone, arriving about 9.30 pm. Bought bread, milk and a tin of beans and sausages at the shop near the station. I later went with John to the Garden House hotel where there was a nasty drunk.

Wed, 25 April - A 6 am start to the day, after breakfast collecting together things to be transferred to the Leamington garage, the main ones being my studio armchair, calor gas heater (both given to me by Mrs Kerr[28]) and the Zed-Bed frame - things together not of much worth. I walked to U-Drive van hire near Folkestone West station and collected a van, then returned to the flat and met John. We loaded the van and drove

---

[27] Mike Stonestreet, Folkestone builder & developer, charismatic hellraiser.
[28] Mrs Kerr, retired pub landlady, landlady of a studio the diarist had previously rented in Sandgate.

to Leamington where we unloaded, then we drove to Lincoln. Approaching Newark I realised we would be late, so I phoned the Usher gallery and a curator waited with my painting after the gallery closed, for our 6pm arrival. We loaded, parked then had a curry picnic in the Usher Gallery grounds and walked round the cathedral. A drink in Cambridge on the way back. Arrived Folkestone 2 am, after a five hundred and thirty mile round trip.

Thurs, 26 April - I slept until 10.30 am, but woke with a headache after yesterday's marathon effort. Did some preparations for my Saturday departure. A 4 pm unexpected visit from Etelle and Louise, interrupted by the predictable arrival of John. I drank some home brewed lager and watched telly in the evening.

Fri, 27 April - A Shredded Wheat, toast and marmalade and Lincoln biscuit breakfast before walking to the doctor's surgery for my last inoculation, which was a tetanus booster. Walked from there to the bank, Woolworth's and Beresford's accountants to get them to deal with the final flat bills. Returning to the flat I called on Cathy Bagnell next door. In the afternoon I walked down to the harbour with Roy's branch trimming cutter. It was attached to a metal pole and I went to a workshop under the harbour railway arches to get it detached from the pole, which they did for nothing. Back at the flat I showered then called on Mr and Mrs Weston upstairs. I also saw Terry Sexton, the builder who is buying the flat. He said he was going to spend £10,000 on it. I went to the Burlington hotel and drank five or six Pils lager, Julian serving behind the bar. Etelle called in at the bar. Back at the flat Chris did a rice dish, eaten by ourselves and Vincent and John.

Sat, 28 April - I awoke to one of my heavier hangovers, which affected my stomach worse than my head. Chris got me out of bed with another farewell call at 9.10 am. John Heal arrived at

9.30 am and I got him to begin bottling left over home brew, and carrying this round to his flat, while I tried to come to and have some breakfast. After this I managed to pack and clear the flat up. John is going to store my bedding and the few household things. We left the flat at ten to one, after I had made my ceremonial farewell to each room and had kissed the bar. We walked to the station and I caught a train going straight to Victoria, another from there to Gatwick, then a Monarch flight to Malaga, arriving at 10 pm local time. Roy met me and we drove to Nerja, stopping for a soft drink in Torre del Mar.

Nerja, Sat, 26 May - Before breakfast I walked up to Capistrano,[29]shopping for bread and cakes and also cat food. *Gatti*[30]disappeared while I was away last time and *Sprout* now prefers a house around the corner. We now have another tomcat called *Bunter*, and an unnamed female cat has now appeared, with three kittens. Also before breakfast I rang John, who informed me that my R.A. Summer Exhibition entry has been rejected. In the evening I drank a few whisky and cokes with Roy. We went to the nearby Ancladero and Nautilus bars then returned to the house for a meal. I then went to the Nerja Club hotel for a couple of more drinks.

Sun, 27 May - Lazed around the house and pool, very woolly in the head. I walked down into the town to post a cheque to John, who is going to get my Royal Academy reject. In the evening Roy cooked Robert Carrier's Chicken Leoni again, this time with the asparagus. I prepared a prawn avocado. Sipped white wine and watched *Inspector Morse* after the meal on Gibraltar television. Before the meal I went round the the Nerja Club hotel, for a beer and to pay barman, Antonio, 100 pesetas, owed from last night.

---

[29] Pioneering Nerja residential estate, built for foreign property owners.
[30] Adopted street cat.

Studley, Fri, 6 July - Slept til gone 11 am. I drove in Lesley's hired car to Leamington with the second hand frames.[31] Approaching Warwick I stopped for a pee in a field gateway, which afforded a view across a corn field to the town, with its church and castle. Approached Gordon St via The Parade. A car was parked in front of my garage, its owner obviously having noticed that the door wasn't used much. I was able to open it just enough to get the frames inside. I had a walk through Jephson Gardens to the top of The Parade, where I phoned John, but no answer. Returned to car, felt desolate, but probably I will remember this morning with fondness. Back in Studley I bought a tin of spaghetti from Leo's supermarket, ate then slept one and a half hours. Did the week's finances.[32] Bread, chess & onion for tea. Still feeling grim, I washed then drank some Larios gin and bitter lemon. Drove with dad to the Boot Inn then we returned to the Nag's Head. Recent news: 50,000 dead in Iranian earthquake. World Cup football on. Gorbachev being challenged by critics.

Mon, 9 July - A last morning walk up towards Studley castle. Spent an hour trying to finish a watercolour of the scene back towards the church. A pie and some chips with curry sauce for lunch. Lesley visited and I departed afterwards, taking a 2.50 pm bus to Birmingham, a National Express bus to London and a train to Folkestone, arriving at 9.15 pm. As arranged I went to John's flat and he is putting me up in his spare room, where the conditions are cramped, due to my stored paintings and other stuff of his surrounding the bed.

Folkestone, Tues, 10 July - Spent the morning trying to locate Chris to talk about me using his flat. I went to South Kent College and Venetia's home and made some phone calls, and at least I did verify that he is here somewhere. In the afternoon John and I took the 3.30 pm train to London, to go to the annual Cork Street party. We drank some of my Larios gin on

---

[31] Bought in a Studley second hand shop.
[32] Personal financial budget.

the way. We arrived in the street too early, so we went to a pub and when we returned we found the party was invitation only, so we had to gatecrash, pretending we were with a party of guests. I met Robin Dutt and Michael Murfin[33]there. Drank a lot of wine and latched on to a French woman and ended up talking demented rubbish to her. Lost John, got last train home after another pub drink. Slept rough on a Leas pathway.

Wed, 11 July - An uncomfortable night trying to keep warm with the aid of my thin jacket and a copy of yesterday's *Times*. Slipped into shivery unconsciousness once or twice. I *struck camp* at 5.30 am and walked down the Leas to a cash dispenser and to the bus station to examine a time table. I then went to John's flat, but no answer to door, as expected. Still wearing my respectable clothes, I caught a bus to the first stop past Etchinghill then walked to Roundwood Farm strawberry field. I picked six trays of strawberries and what with this and the Leas brambles my clothes were in a mess afterwards. I returned to John's flat to find him in and hear that he had been arrested last night in London for drunkenness. Had a wash and to bed at 9 pm. This evening I phoned Chris and we met on the Leas and talked about the flat. He says it will be available as from the middle of next week. We had a drink at the Clifton hotel.

Thurs, 12 July - 7.17 am bus to New Barn Corner to begin an hour's walk to the Lyminge forest strawberry field. Got a lift up the lane to Stone Street. I turned right opposite Roundwood Farm and found a path between the forest and a cornfield and then through the forest itself, going through an area that had recently been felled, which contained an undergrowth of roots and saplings and tall flowering weeds. I picked strawberries from about 9 am to 2 pm, earning £11.20. I walked slowly back to New Barn Corner, sticking to fields and pathways and noting potential water colour scenes. In Folkestone I went to Sainsbury's supermarket and arrived at John's flat at 6.30 pm.

---

[33] Michael Murfin, painter.

Drank a pint glass of tea, washed, ate curried beans and sausages, went to bed, to read, at 9 pm.

Fri, 13 July - A Central station bus to New Barn Corner. Thumbed a lift up lane to Stone Street to walk on foot path and along road and through Lyminge forest. Brilliant morning sunshine and blue sky. Worked 'til 12.30 pm, picking six trays of strawberries to earn £8.40. Retraced path back to New Barn bus stop, arriving 1.50 pm. Awaiting the bus I sat and ate my lunch - some bread, cheese and onion and a carton of milk. Felt content to be living again in the present. In Folkestone I went to the bank before returning to John's flat to wash and change. Got a 6.30 pm train to Ramsgate, for a visit to Tiberius casino in celebration of my birthday. I felt sure I was going to win, but I lost four five pound chips, betting on red or black even chances. Bought a bag of chips, got 10.30 pm return train.

Sat, 14 July - A day of rest and mental deflation. Phoned Roy from a phone box near the station. Wrote in this journal. In the afternoon I visited 2a, Clifton Mansions, to find the telephones still in place and working. I am not staying in the flat, so as not to give a further excuse for delay to Terry, Roy's potential purchaser, although in reality it looks as if the deal has fallen through.[34] In the evening I drank some home brew (kept by John from last time), listened to the radio and ate some tinned food and went to bed early.

Sun, 15 July - Went strawberry picking in the morning. On the way back I began a watercolour of a scene off to the right between Farthing Common and New Barn Corner, featuring the hillside with the Etchinghill aerial on it. I preceded this by lying down in the cornfield at hand to have a wank, naked on the bed of flattened sheaths under a blinding sun. Back at John's flat I washed and heated the contents of a tin of minced beef and a tin of potatoes for my *Sunday dinner.*

---

[34] The flat was purchased in 1993 by a Mr Gooding.

Tues, 17 July - Strawberry picking and watercolour painting. Earned £9.80 today. I usually Manage to thumb a lift after the bus drops me, along the lane to Farthing Common, then I walk along the North Downs Way footpath with its view, then through Lyminge forest to arrive at the strawberry field about 8.45 am. John is not much of a host, which is exactly as I expected. I am giving him £2 a day for bed and electricity, the electricity being for a tepid, shallow bath and a kettle of water to make tea. He lives an incredibly frugal existence, as only the impoverished, genteel middle class are capable of doing. He has not given me a key. However, I have ensured that the conditions here are of no consequence, by being out all day and then going to bed early.

Wed, 18 July - Strawberry picking and watercolour painting. After arriving back at John's flat for a wash and change, I walked to the Ship Inn, Sandgate, having left a note at Chris's flat to say I would be there. I drank three pints of Burton Ale, while waiting for Chris, who didn't show. Walked back to meet John on Leas. We went to the Metropole Mikado bar and the Garden House hotel, where we conversed with James, a local veteran queen, who is always friendly, though obsessed with talking about thrashing men. On the way home John said again that his mother would be coming to his flat on Friday.

Thurs, 19 July - I walked from John's flat to Margaret's bungalow in Sandgate, arriving 8.30 am to learn that Chris was away for the day. Walked back to the Central station to see if he was on the 9.40 am train. Decided he would be likely to be back early, so I kept leaving John's flat every hour to meet trains from London at the station. No joy by 4.30pm, so I began carrying my possessions to the porch of Chris's flat, between meeting more trains. About 5.30 pm I discovered Chris at his flat, learning that he went to London from Folkestone West station. Was glad to hear his confirmation that I can use his flat. Completed the transfer of my possessions, to bed exhausted with blisters on feet.

Fri, 20 July - Strawberry picking, followed by some watercolour painting on a very warm day. Back at Chris's flat I washed and changed then walked to the Metropole Arts Centre, for a glass of wine at an exhibition preview. Very mild evening. Met Vincent driving his car on the way into the Metropole, and John walking on the Leas on my way back. Back at the flat I managed to heat a tin of spaghetti bolognese, before falling asleep, physically exhausted.

Fri, 3 Aug - To John's flat to arrange for him to take my supermarket pastel[35]to London tomorrow, to submit it to the Mall Galleries *Pastel Society Open Exhibition*. Made some potato salad from a Betty Falk[36]recipe and had some of this in the late afternoon, with sardines, tomato and celery. Did some slide photography of the pastel. In the evening Chris took us[37]to the East Cliff Pavilion bar, then to two harbour pubs. Dad and I then went to the Lifeboat Inn before walking back to the flat. Incredibly hot it has been this week - record temperatures. I think the potato salad and sardines were tomorrow or the next day. Today I did a ham and egg noodle snack.

Thurs, 16 Aug - Did some more tasks like going to all the estate agents to inform them of another flat price reduction. Began making more beer. In the evening I drank some home brewed beer then went to the Happy Frenchman pub to hear a rock group, then I went the the Harvey Wine Bar. John has visited to inform me that the pastel has been accepted for the Mall Galleries exhibition.

Sat, 18 Aug- After breakfast a bus to New Barn Corner, taking with me the framed watercolour. I walked from there to Skeete and called at the two adjoining cottages, as the house featured proved to be. One was named West Cottage. No one was in either, so I went to the large house and farm further along the

---

[35] Nerja urban scene subject matter.
[36] Betty Falk, recipe book author.
[37] The diarist and his Folkestone holidaying father.

track. I spoke to the son of the woman who lives there, a Mrs Barclay. I left the picture with him, to see if his mother would be interested in buying it. In the evening Chris cooked a chicken curry at his flat, which he shared with me and John. John and I then went to the Burlington hotel to watch the carnival procession. Julian was on behind the bar. To the Clifton hotel's Tracy's Bar afterwards.

Sun, 19 Aug - Shredded Wheat, fried egg, bacon and bread and some biscuits for breakfast. Wrote to Pam and to Roy. A walk to the Zig Zag Path on the Leas, where I met John. He was walking along the procession route looking for lost coins. In the evening Chris visited me at his flat. He's going to Scotland tomorrow. I ate the rest of his curry.

Sat, 25 Aug - At lunchtime, after breakfast, I drank a mixture of home brewed beer and tinned lager. There was a downpour of rain, warm and tropical. I read a pile of *Sunday Telegraph* magazines purchased at the Capel cliff-top tea hut on my way home one evening last week. Visited Venetia at *Brockers*. In the evening John visited. I drank some home brew and I do not think I went out.

Sun, 26 Aug - In the evening Peter Wagstaff visited. He and Etelle have just been staying with Roy in Nerja. He told me about it in the Bay Tree bar and at *Bonkers*, the pub which is part of Godden's[38]disco. In the evening he visited again, as did John Heal and the three of us went to the gay evening in the bar of *Bottoms*, in the Carlton hotel. Afterwards we went to the Norfolk Wine Bar.[39]

Mon, 27 Aug - A bank holiday. I went into the town, toying with the idea of buying some trousers. Instead I purchased some boxer shorts and a couple of sale price shirts, £5 each, from Fosters. The boxer shorts are to wear in Spain, to combat the *dhobey itch*. In the evening Wagstaff arrived and dragged me reluctantly to John's flat, to collect him then go to

[38] Jimmy Godden, Folkestone amusement arcade and property entrepreneur.
[39] In the basement of the Norfolk hotel, later the Harvey Wine Bar.

Canterbury, to the gay evening in a bar of the pub opposite the bus station. Wagstaff met someone he liked the look of, to whom we gave a lift home. Quite an enjoyable evening, after all.

Nerja, Thurs, 30 Aug - Up at 6am to gather the household items and begin, at 8am, to carry them to John's flat for storage. Made about five journeys, going back and forth across Kingsnorth Gardens. I then began packing my bag and suitcase and doing some last minute financial admin. Got into a mess and panic with this, during which Wagstaff made an inopportune visit. Went to the bank then post office, buying stamps and a phone card. Spent an hour or two tidying Chris's flat, then got the 5.15 pm train to London, thence to Gatwick, for a 9.55 pm British Caledonian flight to Malaga, arriving 1.30 am local time to be met by Roy. Warm breeze. We stopped for an orange juice at Torre del Mar. I slept in the cooler downstairs room at *Casa Don Miguel.*

Fri, 14 Sept - Did some admin and domestic chores. Phoned John Heal re the arrangements for the collection of my drawing from the Pastel Society exhibition. In the evening we went to the Don Manuel restaurant-bar and the Barbados bar. In both bars people were saying farewells to Nick,[40] Geoff's,[41] partner at Don Manuel, as he was about to go to the airport, to go back to England due to illness.

Studley, Sun, 4 Nov - I left Studley at 9.40 am for an autumnal sunny drive to Leamington Spa, to my Gordon Street garage. Everything there was in good order, with little evidence of damp. I loaded the car boot with the boxes of household cleaning items and inside the car a hoe and broom. Drove to Coventry and after getting lost on the ring road I picked Kim up outside the theatre,[42] then we drove down the M1 to Kim's Palmers Green flat. Had a sandwich with him and Marie-Pierre,

---

[40] Nick Charrington, restaurateur, thought to be from brewing family.
[41] Geoff, restaurateur, ex semi-professional rally driver & tennis player.
[42] Belgrade Theatre.

then went on into London, traffic heaving, got lost before crossing Blackfriars bridge. Did 90 mph along the M20, touched 100 going down Routham Hill. At 4.30 pm I arrived at John's flat and loaded up the flat stuff stored there. John helped unload it at Clifton Mansions then I got the hire car back to the Burstin hotel depot on time, before 5 pm. Walked back to the flat, past the Sunday Market.[43] John was at the flat, then Chris arrived. Drank beer and was happy.

Mon, 5 Nov - Tried to get organised in the flat during the day, had a walk into the town to shop for food. There's some wood still left in the store, to be sawed for the wood stove. Chris arrived soon after it got dark and we arranged to meet at 7.30 to 8 pm at the Ship Inn, Sandgate. I showered then got the barbecue going, before leaving the flat to walk down to Sandgate, enjoying the bonfire night atmosphere. Met Chris coming out of the pub and we drove to Venetia's, Chris relating a story about a row with Margaret over a box of fireworks. Met Venetia's Spanish mature language student staying with her. Walked back to the flat, where I was met by John standing by the dying embers of the barbecue, then Chris soon arrived with two fireworks. We eventually managed to cook a few sausages. A poor evening, apart from the walk to Sandgate.

Wed, 7 Nov - Began cutting the ivy right back (that which grows in the corner of the patio), a harder task than expected. Drank a couple of pints of home brewed beer in the evening, that had been stored by John since the summer.

Thurs, 8 Nov - Continued with the ivy task, sawing through its thick arteries. Have now left just an 18" high clump of it growing. Paul visited and we discussed going to Folkestone races on Monday. Have this week taken to going on an evening walk in the area at about 10 pm to smell wet leaves and read menus outside local restaurants. Am eating things like beans and chopped onion with curry powder. John visits most

---

[43] Held on Folkestone seafront.

evenings, also Chris. One evening this week while John was here I tried phoning a *dial-a-date* number, to no useful result.

Fri, 9 Nov - Was woken by the alarm clock so I could phone Pam at nine o'clock, as arranged last night. Had a hasty conversation with her, the noise of bawling children in the back ground. Arranged to ring again re a meeting next weekend. Lay in bed another hour, ate porridge, walked into town and down to the harbour where I examined the available shell fish, having discussed a sea food meal with Chris last night. Return to the flat for lunch, slept in the afternoon, did some admin and sawed wood. Chris and John visited in the evening.

Sat, 10 Nov – A Porridge-then-fried-sausage-egg-and-bread breakfast. Rain threatening, so I cancelled a plan for a country walk. Did a few little repairs - plug on kettle lead, new battery on door bell, screwed loose bar stool seats back on. In the evening Chris arrived with a pork dish, with vegetables and egg noodles. He went off to see Margaret, or Venetia, then returned to finish heating the food, which we ate with John's help. After Chris and John left I went to the Harvey Wine Bar, but didn't feel very comfortable in the very young crowd there. Went to the less crowded Tiffany's Bar (or Tracy's, as I have sometimes mistakenly called it). Vincent visited in the afternoon.

Sun,11 Nov - Porridge then fried sausage, egg and bread for breakfast. At 11.30 am Chris arrived and he took me to Etchinghill, where he left me to enjoy an autumnal walk back to Folkestone, going via lanes to Acrise. Visited Acrise Place - presently being converted into flats - and the church. Hunted fungi in nearby woods and succeeded in finding some small ceps, although they were rotten and partly eaten by squirrels. Went across army training fields and more woods to Paddlesworth, then via Arpinge to the lane going down past the waterworks to the roundabout at the end of the motorway.[44] A wonderful afternoon. In the evening John visited to watch telly and we drank gin & lemon and beer. I cooked up the remains of Chris's food with some spaghetti.

Thurs, 15 Nov - I placed one or two more figures.[45] In the afternoon I decided to replant the palm tree, which has outgrown a little shelf in a corner by the patio steps. Began preparing to drop it down into a bigger space made by sawing three joists and putting them above each other across the corner. The first thing I did this morning was to go the the Metropole for details of the Arts Centre's *Shepway Artists' Christmas Show*, then I went to John's flat, having had the idea of submitting one of my summer watercolours to it. I arranged for John to do this for me on Saturday. Sir Geoffrey Howe, deputy Tory party leader, resigned and made a speech condemning Thatcher and now Michael Heseltine has challenged her for the leadership. An international agreement has been signed formally putting an end to the Cold War.

Studley, Tues, 20 Nov - I left Studley at 10.45 am, taking a bus to Birmingham, coach to London and train to Folkestone, arriving about 6.30 pm. In London I dragged my suitcase along The Mall to Charing Cross, finding that the new Left Luggage lockers there, which have replace the old Left Luggage department, cost a minimum of £2.50 to use. Instead of doing this I dragged the suitcase to Cork Street and back, to visit the Piccadilly Gallery, where I asked Christabelle Briggs[46]for a catalogue of Michel Muffin's last exhibition. I then told her I was in Spain doing some pastel drawings. She said she didn't much like pastel work, but that I could nevertheless send her some slides. Near Folkestone station I bought a tin of beans, some tinned sausages and bread and milk. Had a wank on arrival at the flat. John visited. Saw on TV that Michael Heseltine won just enough votes to force another ballot in the Tory party leadership battle.

---

[44] i.e. where the motorway ended at the time.
[45] In the diarist's current pastel work.
[46] Christabelle Briggs, Director, Piccadilly Gallery.

Wed, 21 Nov - I placed two or three more figures in the drawing. At lunchtime I walked into the town and visited an estate agent and Sainsbury's. Purchased a sink plug in Bouverie Square covered market. Did some admin in the afternoon, then slept. After dark I retrieved some timber from a skip in Clifton Crescent and sawed half a bagful of it. Showered, after which John visited and we spent the evening drinking home brewed lager, me laying on my mattress and John sitting at the bar. Occasionally I rose to saw another lump of wood for the fire, then I made a brief, solo expedition to the Harvey Wine Bar. After John left I cooked some potatoes, sauerkraut and tinned sausages.

Thurs, 22 Nov - Margaret Thatcher resigned as Prime Minister today. Did some more work to the drawing in the morning. Made some preparations towards Sunday's departure, such as booking a rented car to drive to the airport. In the afternoon I hammered wooden batons across the three joists, to unite them, then attached wires to prevent the joists falling away from the replanted palm tree. I cooked up some spaghetti in the evening, which John helped me eat.

Fri, 23 Nov - Did a little more work on the drawing.[47] At least I have now got it all basically planned out and blocked in with colour. Went to the bank and post office at lunchtime. In the afternoon I achieved the task of dragging the palm tree off its concrete shelf and down into the corner space prepared for it. The space will need a lot more earth than I anticipated, and having got the tree in place I will have to finish putting in more earth tomorrow. The tree looks much more comfortable in its new place and will have a chance of living much longer. I bought the tree[48] as a little plant during a trip to Torquay with Roy. At 7 pm John arrived and at 7.30 pm I went to the Metropole *Shepway Show* opening, where I stayed a short while and had a chat with Brian Oxley.[49] A drink at the Bay

[47] Diarist's current pastel drawing.
[48] A Chusen palm.
[49] Brian Oxley, Hythe art teacher and artist.

Tree bar on the way back to the flat. At the flat I found John, joined by Chris and Vincent. I was nearly drunk. Chris left and John and I teased Adder about his new teaching job at Havering.

Sat, 24 Nov - Was woken 8.30 am by the alarm, then I had a phone call from Douglas. Left the flat after 9 am in a very blank, dazed state of mind, to walk down to the Burstin, to pick up a hire car. A lovely gale was blowing, with wind and rain, and cars driving past with snow on their bonnets. Collected the car and returned to flat for breakfast. At noon I arrived at John's flat with a box of groceries and bottles of beer and home brew making equipment for him to store. We then embarked on a ride in the car. I drove to Lyminge airport, encountering some snow and hail on the way. We visited the departure hall and café, then proceeded to Dungeness. There I walked out on the shingle by the old light house to the water's edge for a hangover curing blast of channel air. We then returned to Folkestone, where in heavy rain I finished replanting the palm tree. In the evening John arrived again, then Chris with a hot curried spaghetti dish. We ate this and drank beer. Packed and stored things in cupboards before bed at midnight.

Nerja, Thurs, 20 Dec - A subdued day. Did some preparations towards my departure. Stayed in the house with Roy in evening, for a meal and quiet drink. Phoned John Heal.

The John Diaries - 1991

Studley, Wed, 2 Jan - Left Studley by bus at 2.45 pm after goodbyes to Dad and to Lesley, who visited the house in her lunch break.[1] 4.30 pm coach to London, during which I listened to music on Kim's Christmas present, a portable tape player and radio. Walked from the coach station to Victoria, where it began to rain heavily. Stood eating a handful of chocolates, while wondering whether to take the tube. On finishing the chocs the rain had abated, so I continued walking along Buckingham Palace Road and down the Mall to Charing Cross. Rang John. Train to Folkestone, arriving 10 pm, bought milk, bread and a tin of beans and sausages at the mini market near the station. Called at John's flat and collected my tea and packet of porridge. Walked to Clifton Mansions and dug out the mattress and bedding from the cupboard (including my old pillow).

Thurs, 3 Jan - Ate porridge then walked to John's flat, returning with a suitcase full of groceries and plastic bottles of home made beer. Spent the rest of the morning doing financial calculations. Sent £300 of Nanny's money[2] to a credit card company, bringing my total debt down to £2,599. Met Chris on arrival at the flat after visiting John, and we decided to have lunch at the Hi Tin.[3] I met him and Vincent at the restaurant at 12.45pm. Afterwards we walked to the harbour and along the lower Sandgate Road. I went solo on to Sandgate, where I bought a book at the bric-a-back shop. Earlier, walking down to the restaurant, a young loud mouth had jeeringly commented on my red shoes - the ones I bought in last year's January sale - but I shot back a suitable reply.[4] Back at the flat I sawed a bag of wood for the fire. Showered, ate tin beans and sausages, had a quiet TV watching evening.

Fri, 4 Jan - With John to Boulogne, using a cheap ticket I obtained from an offer in the *Folkestone Herald*. We left[5] at 7.40am on the *Stenna Cumbria*, a proper ship, with outside

---

[1] From her estate agency secretarial job.
[2] Bequeathed to diarist in grandmother's Will.
[3] Chinese restaurant in Tontine Street.
[4] *What about your dyed red hair?* the diarist had said.
[5] From Folkestone harbour.

113

promenades and a large open deck on top. We arrived in Boulogne about 10 am and wandered about along the harbour front and up to the Old Town, looking at restaurant menus. We went to a café off the ring road behind the Old Town, where we drank some local Boulogne *Christmas Ale*. We then went back to a restaurant called Le Cyrano, for a 48 franc meal of pate and a steak-frites and then cheese. It was good food and we had a quite good bottle of wine with it. Afterwards I left John in a cafe and revisited a stationery shop, where I hurriedly examined the fountain pens. I chose one quickly on the basis of appearances - a red Ville d'Argent pen, which I was told had been made in Lille. It cost £50 or £60 of Nanny's money. Another blast of channel air on the way home. We went to Cleggy's on arrival in Folkestone. Saw Chris later at the flat.

Sat, 5 Jan - Slept about ten hours. Porridge, boiled eggs, toast and jam and half a packet of Lincoln biscuits for breakfast. Walked to Sainsburys before eating to get some of these items, a lovely gale blowing on the Leas. Went into the town again in the morning, to visit a book sale at Folkestone library. Purchased slippers and a sale price pair of trousers. Also this journal.[6] Met Etelle in town and she later came to the flat with a chip making machine for me to give to Roy. Vincent arrived about the same time. Painted the joists holding the palm tree soil. John arrived 6 pm. Sawed a bag of wood and lit the fire at 6.30 pm. Peter Wagstaff phoned and while John remained stoking the fire I went to the Clifton hotel for a drink with him and his friend, Fraser - he with pretty eighteen year old girlfriend, Jane (or June) - plus Lindsay and a friend. I also greeted some bar regulars. Wagstaff called at the flat again at 11.45 pm.

Sun, 6 Jan - Walked to Bouverie Road newsagent and bought the *Sunday Telegraph* and the *News of the World*. Returned to the flat to enjoy my breakfast, though Chris visited half way

---

[6]   The blank paged hardback the diarist was writing in.

through it. Wrote in the journal then walked to the Metropole to visit the *Shepway Show*, where I verified that my work hadn't sold. I then walked to Sandgate and back along the seafront and undercliff path to Folkestone harbour. Purchased a 26p tin of tomatoes at the little grocery shop opposite the Salvation Army. In the evening John and Vincent visited the flat, then Chris. We were expecting Chris to provide a bar snack, but he didn't, so I later boiled some spaghetti and tipped in the tomatoes.

Mon, 7 Jan - Made my preparations for tomorrow's departure. In the morning I walked around the town. Purchased a £10 pair of shoes. Carried my few remaining groceries to John's flat. In the evening he arrived to sit by the fire and watch television, while I packed my suitcase. Have not been looking forward to returning to Spain.

Nerja, Wed, 6 March - Roy and I left the flat at 7.30 am and arrived in Gibraltar about11.30 am. I collected my GB Airways ticket and checked in. We then walked to a garage a little way along the road that goes round the Rock just short of the airport. The garage visit was something to do with Roy's brother's[7] car. We then walked into the town where Roy looked in the windows of jewellers' shops and then went in one to buy a new watch. We then walked back to the airport and my flight took off at 1.30 pm, arriving at Gatwick at 4.30 pm GMT. Complimentary wine with in-flight meal. Trains to Folkestone via Redhill and Tonbridge, arriving 6.30 pm. Was thrilled to see the crocuses in bloom on the walk to the flat. Returned to the Central Station area to shop and leave a note at John's flat. Return to Clifton Mansions to eat tinned ravioli and dig mattress out of cupboard. Felt happy, early to bed.

Tues, 7 March - Woke early, the sound of seagulls crying outside. Felt buoyant. After breakfast I embarked on a busy day, doing the necessary little tasks to do with the flat and my USA trip. I got my groceries from John's flat, on the way there

[7] Chris Johnson.

admiring the crocuses in Kingsnorth Gardens. I collected some mended shoes. I took a film roll with some shots of my pastels to be developed. I went to the bank. Lovely mild spring weather. Back at the flat I made some phone calls, including two to Phyllis. I spoke to Dan[8] and said I would be visiting on Tuesday or Wednesday. Sawed wood for the fire, showered, watched telly, ate tinned spaghetti bolognese in the evening. During the day Cathy Bagnell[9]noticed I was going a bit grey at the temples.

Fri, 8 March - A similar day to yesterday. Had an afternoon sleep for a couple of hours. At 9 pm I went for a short walk going down the Leas past the Clifton hotel, then past the Happy Frenchman pub and Castle Hill Avenue crocuses, and back to the flat via Trinity Crescent and past Nicola's restaurant.[10] I must have covered this territory thousand of times. John visited soon after my arrival back at the flat.

Sun, 10 March - Woke feeling gravely ill. Remembered walking slowly back from Cleggy's (now the Fox and Chicken) along the lower Sandgate road pathways, wanting badly to be sick but not deigning to do so. The journey seemed never ending. I should have been sick. To say it has ruined my breakfast is the least of my worries. I do not require any *severe insults to the brain*, thank you. I lay all day on my mattress. At 1 pm I ate some porridge, then two or three hours later some sausage and egg, Two hours after that I had some toast and later tea and biscuits. John visited in the evening and we watched *Lovejoy* on television.

Mon, 11 March - I don't feel right in the head again, yet. I did the US trip final preparations. I feel very anxious about this trip. I don't know what I hope to achieve, especially as I won't be taking any further work, new or old, with me. No doubt the people I see will wonder about this too. Also there is concern about how much it is going to cost, especially if I don't stay at

---

[8] Dan Chicorel, Weight Watchers Inc. executive, Phyllis Chicorel's son.
[9] Cathy Bagnell, Clifton Mansions neighbour, *theatrical* landlady.
[10] In the basement of the Lismore hotel.

Phyllis's house more than a night or two. I think I will try and keep in mind the attitude of it being a casual social visit to the people I know, rather than a carefully planned business trip. I think John visited this evening. Wrong! I left the flat at 10 am and caught the Chicago flight from Heathrow at 2 pm.

Folkestone, Thurs, 21 March - Woke with a thumping gin and lager headache. Gulped some British Airways orange juice with a couple of Anadins and went back to sleep, to wake after 11 am, having slept a total of ten hours, and then feeling very fit and refreshed I walked to Sainsbury's and back, and then to John's flat and to the bank, where I paid in Phyllis's cheque. After lunch I looked at my *Sun* newspaper Boulogne trip ticket[11] and saw that it was dated for today, not as expected for tomorrow. I walked to the harbour, but failed to get the date changed. I considered whether to go solo on the 5.30 pm boat, but finally I scrapped the ticket. In the evening Peter Wagstaff visited, then John arrived to hear my bad news about Boulogne.

Sat, 23 March - Cooked a fried breakfast at midday. Sawed firewood. A 3 pm walk to the Metropole to visit a book fair, then I continued up the Leas and down the steps to Riviera Road and came back along the beach, on the way collecting an armful of driftwood, which I sawed up on return to the flat. Sunny afternoon. I thought I would spend an evening reading, but John arrived and we sampled my new lager which, though still cloudy, seems to be alright after all, thank goodness.

Sun, 24 March - John arrived to have breakfast with me at about 11 am. He had to wake me with the doorbell, as I'd overslept. Walked with him afterwards down to the harbour. In the evening Chris arrived with a rice dish. We may have gone out afterwards for a drink.

[11] £1 day trip to France offer.

117

Wed, 27 March - Tried to chase Chris up about some firewood he has been saying he can get for me from his college. Tried to find him at Brockman Road and Broadmead Road this morning; saw Paul at the latter. At Clifton Mansions workmen are finishing painting the exterior by doing the walls of the flat, which is the basement of the building. Chris arrived in the evening and, I think, John. Drank three pints of home made lager. In the morning, after trying to find Chris, I sat in Kingsnorth Gardens before lunch, reading a local paper - warm sunny day.

Thurs, 28 March - At 9.45 am I walked from the flat to South Kent College, carrying six empty plastic fertilizer bags. At the college I met Chris and we filled the bags with offcuts of waste wood left by some of his college students. We brought the wood back to the flat to use as firewood. I then went shopping and to the bank. In the afternoon I sorted out some more timber to be sawn up for firewood, from a pile of stuff in the garden left from one of Mike Goody's Clifton Mansions flat conversions. In the evening John arrived and I left him stoking the fire, while I went to the Metropole exhibition opening. When I returned Chris was at the flat and he and I went to see Bob Bartell[12]playing country music, as Chris had got free tickets, this also at the Metropole.

Fri, 29 March - Good Friday. John arrived by invitation for breakfast. I cooked fried egg, bacon and fried bread. I spent the day reading one week old newspapers and doing domestic things, like putting the wood acquired yesterday into the store. About midday I went for a walk down the Zig-Zag path, to sniff the hyacinths blossoming along it now and see the daffodils growing at the bottom. I walked back to the town, then to the Central Station grocery shop, then back to the flat. Chris visited. John and I went for a drink at the Leas Pavilion Theatre.[13]

[12] Bob Bartell, Folkestone Country & Weston singer and band leader.
[13] Now the Leas Club bar.

Studley, Fri, 5 April - A wet day. Pasty, chips and curry sauce for lunch. Read in the afternoon and ate chocolate. Kim returned from a couple of days doing his job in London.[14] In the evening he went to the pub with Dad. I stayed at the house and wrote in this diary. Before I left Folkestone John mentioned that early one morning he had seen a council worker with a shovel and hand cart on the Leas, collecting dog excreta. I had previously thought that the Leas was looking strangely clean, so it seems that although I did not get any official response to my report from anyone, it was nevertheless not made and sent off in vain.[15]

Folkestone, Tues, 9 April - Unpacked after breakfast then went to the Marton agency, but there's no work available at the moment. To John's flat to leave a note, and at lunchtime he arrived at Clifton Mansions with the telephones. In the afternoon I worked out my finances. Slept an hour. In the evening Chris arrived and we went across to the Tavern Bar - newly installed in the basement of the Testwood hotel - then to the Salisbury hotel. Back at the flat I began brewing a further five gallons of lager.

Sat, 13 April - After having the weekend breakfast, I weeded the path going along the wall from the road to the flat. While I did this a couple of flat viewers sent by Seekers estate agency arrived. I showed them the flat and finished the weeding, then drank a pint of beer. I phoned Phyllis's house and spoke to Dan. Went for a walk to the harbour, drank home brew in the evening with John.

Thurs, 18 April - Was late arriving at the factory, due to a mix up about me getting a lift from Maggie.[16]Walked there in about half an hour, arriving at 8.30 am. Made some more Nair,[17] with the help of Graham, the foreman. John visited in the evening.

---

[14]   Acting in a touring theatrical production.
[15]   Diarist had sent a report to the council, after his voluntary work cleaning the Leas of canine excrement.
[16]   Maggie, co-director of the Marton employment agency.
[17]   Depilatory skin cream, made by Carter Wallace Ltd.

Sat, 20 April - A fried breakfast. Spent the day relaxing and doing domestic chores. Before breakfast I took some photographs for the benefit of the estate agent of the newly repainted exterior of Clifton Mansions. In the evening John visited and we drank lager at the bar. I left him stoking the fire and went for a walk, on the way having a drink at the Victoria hotel and the Garden House hotel

Sun, 21 April - A fried breakfast. Afterwards I lugged a step ladder from the garden shed to John's flat, then made another journey carrying paint and brushes. At John's flat I retouched some stains on the ceiling, caused by a water flood from the flat above. It took all afternoon - three hours. I would rather have rested, but I had for a week or two been promising John I would do the job for him for a couple of quid. In the evening John and I went to Bottoms gay disco.

Wed, 24 April - Am more or less left on my own now, to make the beer shampoo.[18] I quite enjoy the work. The day is broken up by the various steps in the procedure. You just follow the steps, as written down on a time sheet. Got paid £79 today from the agency for the three days last week. Carter Wallace say they will only need me until the end of the week, which is just right for me. John visited in the evening.

Sun, 28 April - After breakfast Etelle rang and invited me to lunch. Did some washing, wrote a letter then walked to her parents' house in Alder Road. A sunny day of tulips and wallflowers. Etelle cooked a spinach pasta dish. Afterwards I called at John's flat to retrieve the step ladder, which I carried back to Clifton Mansions. In the evening John visited and, I think, Chris, and possibly Peter Wagstaff.

Wed, 1 May - I finished cleaning the windows in the morning. John visited and we decided to celebrate May Day. At 1 pm we met in the Garden House hotel. I had just collected £135 wages from Marton. We went to the Burlington hotel where Julian

---

[18] Linco Beer Shampoo.

was behind the bar, then to the Leas Club. I left John there to walk back to the flat via Fads,[19] where I bought bags of cement and plaster. At the flat I used the cement to replace some broken tiles on the path leading to the main Clifton Mansions door. Worked at this til almost dark, skinning the tips of my fingers in my tipsy hurry. Keep thinking about a girl I saw yesterday at Marton.

Fri, 3 May - Took the beer making equipment and some groceries to John's flat. Returned with his hoover, having rented it from him for a fiver. Finished painting the damp corner and the wall in the bedrooms. At 4 pm I collected some photo enlargements of the repainted Clifton Mansions and took them round half a dozen estate agents in Bouverie Square. I also told them the asking price was now £52,500. Back at the flat Chris arrived with a chicken curry to be heated up. I provided the rice. Vincent came with a bottle of wine. John arrived and Peter Wagstaff. Adder and Wagstaff bickered with each other. Chris's curry was very good. I went to the Off-License and bought more lager, having run out of home brew.

Gatwick Airport, Fri, 28 June - Wandered the airport dazedly wondering what to do next. I took a train to Victoria station and left my luggage in a locker. Walked along The Mall to Trafalgar Square, where I phoned Pam regarding Jack's birthday present. On the way, in a pedestrian underpass in Buckingham Palace Road, I passed a boy in a sleeping bag just waking up. He looked pretty wretched. To Foyle's bookshop to find a few recent books I'd noted: biographies of David Tennant, John Minton and Baroness de Stempel - drunks, failures and criminals. Also diaries by Elizabeth Smart. I purchased the de Stempel book. Continued walking about, visiting the *John Player Portrait Award* exhibition at the National Portrait Gallery, the adjacent Central Reference Library, the Groucho Club for an application form, Christie's to

---

[19] DIY/home decorating shop.

look at the latest art auction catalogue, and the Fisher Gallery. Felt in abject misery throughout. Tube to Kings Road for Jack's present. Trains to Ashford and Folkestone. Arrived flat 6 pm, visited John.

Sat, 29 June - Was woken 5 am by the couple in the basement flat next door having a row. Moved my bedding into the hall. Beans on toast for breakfast, tea with no milk. To bank, to find that the cheque had come through,[20] but was unable to get more money from the cash point. To NatWest bank in Sandgate Road, which was open. Got some cash using my Servicecard, Access Card and Barclaycard. To the post office. Met Etelle. Did gardening back at the flat. Sunny today, but the garden looks like a rain forest, after a very wet June in England. To Chris's flat to leave a note. Returned to 2A for a shower (or shallow bath, as shower not working well), then gin & lemonade while reading the de Stempel book. John arrived, then elderly neighbour, Arthur. Cooked some rice and a tin of chilli con carne for John and myself.

Sun, 30 June - John came for breakfast - my usual fry-up. I went for a walk to Sandgate, then returned to read and write in this journal. In the evening Peter Wagstaff visited, and John came to take a telephone call from his mother, then he also accepted some more of my rice and chilli con carne.

Studley, Fri, 5 July - After breakfast I realised that what I had thought was a hangover was, in fact, probably the result of drinking a bad pint of beer. I had a queasy stomach and a headache that was made worse by looking out of the window at the bright sunlight. Had to cancel my walk, to be sick and swallow aspirins. I slowly packed and began to recover. I ate a tin of spaghetti, then left Dad to catch the bus to Alcester and the 4 pm London National Express coach. At Victoria my suitcase was not in the boot. I thought it had been stolen, but it had been accidentally taken off at the Heathrow stop and arrived on the next coach. Train from Victoria station to

---

[20] From the USA sale of the diarist's painting, *Where are all the moments that are here and are no more? (Members of the German Wine Academy).*

Ashford, thence to Folkestone, arriving at the flat 11.30 pm. John visited soon afterwards, to see about a proposed visit to Henley tomorrow.

Sat, 6 July - To Henley Regatta with John. I financed the outing, as John is broke. We took the 9.45 am London train then joined crowds going to the regatta at Paddington. Arrived Henley about 12.30 pm. We walked over the bridge then along past the Leander Club to the Regatta Enclosure. We successfully walked into it via an entrance by the river bank. We sat watching the races drinking half pints of Pimms, reasonably priced at £2.25, laced with my gin. Very hot. Did not chance braving more stewards to advance further into the enclosure, but our part of it looked the most pleasant anyway, with a relaxed cheerful crowd. The soviet army won the *Grand Challenge Cup*. We left about 5.30 pm, to walk the other bank in front of the corporate tents. A drink at the Brief Encounter,[21] where I left John to catch the 9 pm Folkestone train.

Sun, 7 July - Felt pretty fit after a long sound sleep. After breakfast I phoned Roundwood Farm. As expected they have hardly begun harvesting their strawberries because of all the wet weather. I will spend the mornings this week on my drawing. Had a walk down to Sandgate and along the promenade as far as Beachcombers. It was one of this year's rare summer days. Wrote my journal back at the flat. Chris and Adder visited. A 10 pm walk to a grocery shop, meeting John on the Leas.

Tues, 9 July - Began to work carefully on the drawing. After lunch John visited, bearing my acoustic guitar. At 4 pm we walked down the Leas and I went to the library, where I spent a couple of hours studying recent *Which* magazines on SLR cameras. I have got £200 from the insurance payout on the stolen one.[22]

---

[21] Gay bar in St. Martin's Lane.
[22] After a burglary at *Casa Don Miguel*.

Wed, 10 July - A studio morning.[23] Went to see Tom Green after lunch for a dental check-up. In the evening, feeling seedy and restless after three no-alcohol days, I drank the last of my Malaga airport gin and some lager. John visited.

Fri, 12 July - Studio morning. At lunchtime I walked to the nearest petrol station and then into the town in search of a bag of charcoal, which I eventually found at Woolworths. Went back to the flat for lunch. Transferred lager from the brewing bin to the polypin.[24] Did more shopping in town, had a 6.30pm bath then Vincent arrived as I was getting the barbecue going. He had some sausages, bread rolls and two packets of chicken pieces. We went to the Salisbury hotel, to find Chris at the bar. Chris declined to come with us for a drink at Bonkers,[25] so we left him and went there, picking John up on the way on the Leas. At Bonkers there was, at 8 pm, a loud disco and DJ and frenetic dancing by some of the staff.[26] The DJ fired a water pistol at Vincent's balding head. Back at the flat the barbecue was attended by the three of us, plus Charles Sturgis.

On his 40th birthday the author was going to stop writing his journal, but then he continued it in an abbreviated form.

Sun, 14 July - Wagstaff visited with John, then John and I went to Bottoms, where I spent fifteen quid and had an unenjoyable time. Was followed back to flat by someone from Liverpool.

Thurs, 18 July - Adder visited in the evening and John.

Fri, 19 July - Had an evening barbecue, attended by Chris, Adder and John. Chris and Adder in foolish mood. Went solo to the Harvey Wine Bar afterwards, where I met Tamsin.

---

[23] Diarist was using a bedroom for his studio.
[24] Thick polythene bag with a liquid dispensing tap.
[25] Basement bar in the Living Language School.
[26] English language tutors.

Fri, 26 July - Last day.[27] Did the left hand foliage and one or two corrections. Chris and John visited. The news is full of a queer in Milwaukee, who murdered and ate up to twenty Negro youths.

Thurs, 8 Aug - Dad sat on the Leas while I did decorating and shopping.[28] We had lamb chops with new potatoes and mint sauce for dinner. We were joined by John, who brought news of the pastel's acceptance.[29]

Tues, 20 Aug - Did routine jobs, accomplished at the flat and in the town. Am wallpapering the corners of the main bedroom that had looked damp. Chris and John visited. Gorbachev has been overthrown by a right wing coup.

Thurs, 23 Aug - Went into the town to the bank and such. Did wallpapering in the afternoon. Saw John at the flat and Chris at the Salisbury hotel. Gorbachev is back as soviet President, after the coup against him failed.

Fri, 23 Aug - A similar day to yesterday. John visited in the evening. He drank beer, I drank tea and went for periodic walks, peering in bar and restaurant windows.

Sat. 24 Aug - To the Metropole book fair. With John to the Testwood hotel bar in the evening. Gorbachev has resigned as General Secretary of the Communist Party. In reality, Russia has ceased to be communist.

Sun, 25 Aug - To the Sunday market after breakfast, seeking a kettle whistle. In the evening Vincent visited with a boy named Stephen. John and I followed them to a barbecue at Bottoms.

Mon, 26 Aug - Made departure preparations, trying to do everything in good time to avoid a rush tomorrow. John and Chris visited in the evening.

---

[27] Last day working on the pastel or doing any other art work.
[28] Diarist's father was on holiday in Folkestone.
[29] For the Mall Galleries *Pastel Society Open Exhibition.*

Tues, 27 Aug - Saw Chris, John and Peter Wagstaff before leaving the flat at 3.45 pm. Wagstaff drove me to the station. Got my 9.40 pm Dan Air flight from Gatwick, arrived *Casa Don Miguel* with Roy about 3 am.

Folkestone, Tues, 5 Nov - To John's flat for my bag of groceries and a fan cooler he has been keeping for me. Sawed wood back at flat. In the evening I barbecued a few sausages. John was present, also Chris and Venetia, who arrived with a few fireworks.

Wed, 6 Nov - To the Marton agency to find the prospects for any work from them not looking too hopeful. Unpacked, sawed wood and did admin. John visited in the evening and we decided, for a joke, to share a paper round, delivering the local free newspapers.

Fri, 8 Nov - To the Marton agency, to be asked to return at 4pm. When I did so, Maggie informed me that I would be driving to Brake Brothers[30]and working there. John and I now have an *Adscene* and *Citizen* paper round in the West End.[30]

Sat, 9 Nov - To the Metropole at 10 am for a *Folkestone Film Festival* talk by Derek Jarman,[32]but he did not turn up. Returned to the flat for breakfast. Bought some army trousers and a hat. John visited in the evening. I had a drink with film festival people in the Glanmoor Club.[33]

Tues, 12 Nov - Woke 5am. Drove two girls to Brake Brothers, where we packed some Mousaka and Lancashire Hot Pot. Back at the flat I found John awaiting the *Citizen* newspapers, which we found by the front door.[34] Spent two hours doing my round in a wet gale, with the help of the van.[35]

---

[30]   Farm producing frozen oven-ready meals.
[31]   Edwardian area of Folkestone.
[32]   Derek Jarman, film maker, lived near Folkestone at Dungeness.
[33]   Private club for Metropole residents.
[34]   The flat had a 2nd entrance door.
[35]   Marton employment agency van.
[36]   Home brewing kit bought at Boots.
[37]   Etelle de Baere, teaching assistant to children with special needs.

Fri, 15 Nov - No factory work today. Prepared a room to use as a studio. Did shopping in town. Did admin. John visited in the evening. We drank some Boots bitter.[36] I went solo to the Clifton hotel. Talked to Etelle.[37] Was drunk.

Sat, 23 Nov - Worked at Highland Court Farm for four hours until noon. Breakfast back at flat, then I slept two or three hours. John visited in the evening. I had a glass of Beaujolais at the Burlington hotel. Civil war in Yugoslavia is continuing.

Sun, 24 Nov - Met Etelle and her friend, Jessica, at 10.30am, for a walk to Folkestone Yacht Club, for a *Beaujolais Breakfast*, cooked by Bibby and Biddy. There was no sign, though, of any Beaujolais. Felt fed up. In the evening John and I shared a bottle of Beaujolais and a cooked pheasant, bought off Chris.

Mon, 25 Nov - Did Highland Court Farm work, including driving a lively bunch of women and girls there and back, picking some up and dropping some off at Dover.

Thurs, 28 Nov - My final day at Highland Court Farm, doing hectic unstacking and restacking of lemon cartons. Finished my paper round in the evening. John arrived at 9 pm and we drank some beer.

Studley, Mon 2 Dec - Got a 7.30 am bus to Birmingham, collected a hired Vauxhall *Nova* and drove to Folkestone, thence with John and three oil paintings to Brighton to hand them in for the Gardner Arts Centre's *Artists' Market* exhibition. We had a drink in a gay pub, then came back along the coast. Packed suitcase. Etelle bought the watercolour for £20.[38]

What's happening in the news? The Ukraine is Europe's newest and largest state. The independent states of the old Soviet Union are forming a Commonwealth. Gorbachev might be president of this or he might retire. News of Robert Maxwell's death and subsequent financial scandal.

---

[38] A landscape featuring poppies that she had requested.

Studley, Thurs , 2 Jan - Met Mr Harrison of Studley Parish Council at 11am and began renting an allotment off the Redditch Road, for £6.50 a year. I left Dad at 2.45 pm for bus and coach to Oxford and trains to Folkestone. John was at the station, so I bought some shop milk and got my tea from his flat.

Folkestone, Fri, 3 Jan - Slept til 11 am, then spent the day delivering *Adscenes* and *Kent Messenger 'Extras.'* Went with John in the evening to Nicolas's restaurant bar. The atmosphere there was frosty, as John is not really *persona grata* these days, with Nicola and his wife.

Sat, 4 Jan - John visited for a fried egg, bacon and bread breakfast. Walked into the town, where I bought two shirts and a pair of pumps in the sales. Saw John again in the evening and Chris. Went solo to the Clifton hotel, where I talked to Torrence[1]and Clive Botting. Unenjoyable, though Clive is always friendly.

Sun, 5 Jan - A fried breakfast. Pruned the cherry tree.[2] Had a walk to Sandgate. Sawed wood. John visited. Ate beans on toast and drank tap water.

Mon, 6 Jan - With John to the railway station, having got him to go and collect my Gardner Arts Centre *Artists' Market* painting at Brighton. Met Charles Sturgis and had a cup of tea back at the flat with him. Brushed the carpets and packed. In the evening I drank home made beer with John.

Folkestone, Wed, 11 March - Sunny day. Lovely to leave the flat and see crocuses, hyacinths and daffodils all out.[3] Also beds of polyanthus. Began the tasks on a *things to do* list, like going to John's flat for my bag of groceries. He visited in the evening. Met Chris in the street. Delivered my *Citizens* in the afternoon.[4]

---

[1] Torrence (or Henry), eccentric character living alone in neglected Folkestone house.
[2] In Clifton Mansions communal garden.
[3] Diarist had just returned from Spain.
[4] Diarist's newspaper round.

Fri, 13 March - Retrieved my home brewing equipment from John and began brewing some Boots *Continental Lager*. Sawed wood after lunch. To the Garden House hotel's half price *happy hour* at 6pm, later to the Harvey Wine Bar, then to another hotel bar, where Bob Bartell's Country & Weston group was playing. Spoke to nobody I knew during the evening.

Wed, 18 March - Drove a van taking seven or eight people to East Kent Packers, Faversham, where I spent the day stacking apple and pear cartons onto pallets, at a very easy pace. Chris and John visited in the evening.

Sat, 28 March - After breakfast I had a walk to Tontine Street, to buy a pair of braces for my work trousers. In the evening Chris arrived with a rice dish, with mussels and chilli pepper sauce. John and Vincent also partook of this, and we all drank my home brewed lager.

Thurs, 2 April - No agency work today. Spent it doing newspaper deliveries. There are also leaflets and heavy brochures to deliver - strained myself carrying too many at once. Saw John from time to time working on his round. I went to the Film Club to see *Prosperous Wind*, an incredibly tedious film with John Guilgud.

Sat 4 April - Hangover. Had an unenjoyable breakfast. Charles Sturgis arrived and we drove in his car to Elmstead, where we sought and found a little cottage where Cryril Connolly[5] and Barbara Skelton lived.[6] Back in Folkestone I went to a book fair at the Metropole, and delivered some brochures. Chris and John visited in the evening, Chris bearing a chicken curry. Boat Race and Grand National day. Had three ejaculations during the course of the day.

---

[5] Cyril Connolly, author, literary critic.
[6] Barbara Skelton, author, married to Cyril Connolly.

Fri, 10 April - Lovely sunshine. No work, thank God. Walked to the bank[7]and into town to shop. Did some newspaper deliveries. Picked the Marton van up for use on Monday. To the Garden House hotel *happy hour.* Chris and John visited in the evening. Chris brought with him a chicken curry. Drunk to bed, woke in night with cough and hangover. The Tories won again.[8]

Sun, 12 April - John visited at breakfast time, so I cooked some breakfast for him. Did some administrative paper work. Drank two pints of home brewed lager and had a walk down to the harbour. Drank some more in the evening.

Mon, 13 April - I did some driving for Marton in the morning and the afternoon, taking some girls to McCloud's fruit packing farm near Bridge. In between, I shopped in the morning and slept in the afternoon. John visited in the evening, with a gay Greek music teacher, called Nick.

Thurs, 16 April - To East Kent Packers. At 1.30 pm we were told to stop work for the day, a welcome surprise. Finished my newspaper and leaflet delivering in the afternoon. John visited in the evening. I am letting him do all the papers himself from now on, as he needs the money. I packed[9] after his departure, feeling exhausted.

Folkestone, Sat, 2 May - Did gardening. To John's flat. Sawed firewood. Walked into the town. Chris and John visited in the evening. Drank lager and ate some baked beans. A satellite has detected distortions in the radiation coming from the furthest reaches of the universe, which is supposed to prove the *big bang* theory about its birth.

Sun, 3 May - It was sunny and warm and I considered taking a bus ride and walk to Bilsington, to look at the bluebells. Instead, I stayed in the flat and thought about the bluebells

---

[7] In Bouverie Road West.
[8] Thursday's General Election.
[9] To go to Studley.

while I drank many pints of home made lager. Had a drunken walk to visit Venetia, but she was out. John visited in the evening. I cooked up some spaghetti which we shared.

Tues, 6 May - Made an unhurried departure from the flat at 12.15 pm, though I had no time to brush the carpets. John called, to collect my bag of groceries. Trains to Gatwick for 6 pm Dan Air flight to Malaga. Roy and I stopped for some fried sardines at a Torre del Mar *marisqueria* on the way to *Casa Don Miguel.*

Nerja, Sun, 31 May - Mopped the floor. A 5 pm drive to the airport to collect Lesley. I found no visible exit from the new airport car park, so I used the pedestrian pathway. Café stops on the way to Nerja. Phoned John at Clifton Mansions.[10] Roy cooked pork chops of that same name. Civil war in Yugoslavia still raging.

Folkestone, Wed 8 July - A sunny walk down the Leas into the town, for a 10.30 am dental appointment. Tom replaced a large loose filling. To John's flat to get some bottles of beer and beer making equipment out of storage. Chris visited in the evening. A cheerful day.

Seabrook, Sat, 11 July - A 10 am walk back to Folkestone.[11] Had breakfast. Walked into Folkestone to post a letter to Pam. Returned to the flat to position one or two more figures.[12] An evening visit from John. We sat at the bar discussing ways to make money. As another joke activity I will be paying John one penny each for any old magazines he can find, which I am then proposing to resell in Spain.

Sun, 12 July - A noon walk to Seabrook, to go with Margot to the Fountain hotel's *Fun Day*. We sat drinking lager in the garden, likewise at the Britannia Inn, before we returned to the Fountain to play pool. I walked back along the sea front to

---

[10] John was collecting the newspapers from there.
[11] Diarist had stayed overnight at Margo's house.
[12] In diarist's current pastel work.

the flat, to do gardening and drink home brewed beer. Continued drinking beer with John, but did no feel drunk at all.

Mon, 13 July - Had no hangover at all to begin with, though one seemed to develop as the day went on. Did studio work; was in and out of it every five minutes. A lunchtime walk to Sainsbury's - overcast and windy weather, not unpleasant. A 6 pm. walk to Sandgate and back along the beach. Chris visited. John came with a birthday card earlier, and some magazines for me to buy.

Sat, 18 July - John had some fried breakfast with me. Walked into the town to shop. Did an hour or two studio work. Held a barbecue in the evening, attended by John and Chris and Adder. Drank a large quantity of home brew.

Sun, 19 July - Hangover. Had a boiled egg breakfast. Walked up the Leas and back along the sea front to the harbour, going out on the harbour arm to look at the new Seacat ferry.[13] Did two hours studio work on return. Chris and John visited, also Clive Pratt, who is taking his family to Nerja for a holiday. John and I went to Nicola's restaurant, to hear Bob Bartell's band.

Thurs, 23 July - I ironed my shirts at John's flat. Chris and I met Margo and her friend, Claire, in the evening at the Portland hotel. Vincent also appeared. Margo, Claire and I then walked to Tonites disco's *Over 26* evening. Felt unenthusiastic and eventually left them, to shamble back along Tontine Street eating a bag of chips.

Sat, 25 July - After breakfast I did two hours studio work. Drank some beer before walking to the Albion bookshop, then Allcrafts, to purchase some frame moulding. Sat on the Leas to hear a band stand performance by the Maroondogs.[14] John and

---

[13] Catamaran ferry service to Boulogne.
[14] Folkestone pop/rock band.

Chris came to a barbecue I held in the evening. Four thirteen or fourteen year old French language schoolgirls, who had waved from the Rhodesia hotel,[15]came and did the cooking – magic.

Thurs, 30 July - The frame joints are not good - I will have to hope to improve them with sandpaper and wood filler. Got the glass today. Used Steven's[16] camera to take some slides of the picture. Did more corrections. John visited in the evening and drank beer at the bar, while I cooked some beans and hamburgers and drank beer also.

Fri, 31 July - In the morning some Seaboard electricians came to install new mains cut-out wiring in the flat. While this went on I went to Doves garage and hired a car for tomorrow. Visited John's flat, Chris's flat and Sainsbury's. Made final touches to the picture in the afternoon, before an inconvenient return of a Seaboard electrician, however this unforeseen event prompted some new energy in me. Finished the frame and drank beer, to blissful relief.

Sat, 1 Aug - Walked to Doves to collect the hire car. With John to London, to submit the picture to the Mall Galleries Pastel Society exhibition. Felt enormous elation at getting it safely off my hands. In marvellous sunshine we drove to Goodwood races, going into the cheap enclosure for the last three or four races. There was a good-natured happy atmosphere. We then went on, via Chichester, to Winchester, to visit Douglas, who's feeling isolated in his British Legion flat. Motorway return to Gatwick, then through Tonbridge Wells and Tenterden.

---

[15] Hotel next door to Clifton Mansions, accommodated foreign language students in the summer.
[16] Steven Johnson, Margo's son.

Sun, 2 Aug - John and Chris visited in the evening, for a little barbecue. John and I then went to Nicola's restaurants, to hear Bob Bartell.

Seabrook, Thurs, 6 Aug - Margot and I produced a leaflet advertising Mike and Caroline's[17] house for rent - too late, really, to do any good this summer. We went to the Fountain hotel, then I returned to Folkestone, to photocopy and send the leaflet to twenty three of Margo's contacts. It was probably a waste of time, but fun. John visited in the evening.

Sun, 9 Aug - A walk with Dad[18]down to the Sunday market and the harbour. Barbecued some sausages and hamburgers in the evening. John and Chris and Vincent were the visitors. With Dad afterwards to see Bob Bartell at Nicola's restaurant bar.

Sat, 15 Aug - A fried breakfast. Sunny warm day. Did a few domestic jobs and some admin. Had a barbecue in the evening, to which came John and Chris. Dad and I then went to the Portland hotel and Dukes Bar.

Sat, 29 July - I was woken by the alarm, feeling sick and ill as a dog. I blame a drop of months old black current juice that I drank last night. I put it in some home brew, as the beer wasn't as good as usual. Vomited, then had a feeble walk to the bus station. Picked eight trays of strawberries. Still felt feeble until I returned to the flat to drink tea and have a shit. John visited and we watched the Shepway Festival fireworks on the Leas.

Tues, 1 Sept - Went strawberry picking at Etchinghill. I was back in Folkestone at 3.30 pm on the bus. In the evening I did a barbecue, but only John came. Saw Chris and Adder across at the Salisbury hotel.

---

[17] Mike and Caroline, tenants of Las Mariposas bar, Nerja, opposite the Fontainebleau hotel.
[18] Diarist's father was on holiday in Folkestone.

Sat, 5 Sept - Spent an hour field mushrooming before arriving at the strawberry field at 9 am. I only picked five trays. I looked unsuccessfully for ceps in the wood near Newbarn afterwards. John visited in the evening and drank beer, while I ironed and drank tea.

Sun, 6 Sept - The Shepway Festival Airshow was held this afternoon on the Leas. Unfortunately, it was ruined by pouring rain. John arrived at lunchtime and we drank some gin. We went to the Burlington hotel, returned to the flat, then went out again to La Galleria restaurant bar, where we drank wine and talked to a gay couple from Deal, called Anthony and Allen. We heard a few 'planes roaring over our head. The four of us came back to the flat for a drink. I felt pretty drunk.

Sat, 12 Sept - Am feeling cheerful. After breakfast I had a walk to the harbour, where I bought some herrings and some squid. The carnival procession took place in the evening, after which I did a barbecue, to which only John came. Barbecued the squid and herrings, not very successfully. Went solo to the Clifton hotel and Dukes Bar.

Mon, 14 Sept - Have a couple of days for departure preparations. Oiled the old garden seat and table[19] and tidied the patio. Cold herring and rice to eat. John visited. Took some stuff round to his flat this morning.

Tues, 15 Sept - Began to pack and tidy the flat. Took a bag of remaining groceries to John's flat at 5 pm. More cold herring to eat. Had a visit from Chris. Lovely September weather. There is a heavy speculative run on the pound.

Nerja, 4 Oct - Felt pretty rotten all day. Had a late afternoon walk down to the beach. Before dinner I phoned John at the flat, and also Dad.

---

[19] Garden furniture made at Chilham Saw Mills.

Sun, 25 Oct - In the evening I phoned John, who told me the pastel he'd taken to London had been accepted for an exhibition at the Westminster Galleries, called *Britain's Painters '92* - not a prestigious event, but I feel pleased. Had a classic hangover to begin the day. Roy cooked a Robert Carrier dish with a cucumber and cream sauce for dinner.

Folkestone, Sat, 7 Nov - Sound sleep. To Sainsbury's, using a cheque card to spend the last few pounds (nine) in my bank account. Have no cash, not even to buy a poppy. A boiled eggs & Lincoln biscuit breakfast. Sawed up a bag of wood and got the flat organised for use. At 6.30 pm I walked down to Sandgate and back via Pelham Gardens, enjoying the occasional glow of a bonfire and noise of fireworks. Barbecued some hamburgers and drank gin with John. An owl is hooting on the Leas.

Sun, 8 Nov - Yesterday John went to London, as previously arranged, to get back my pastel after the close of the exhibition. Prepared a room for use as a studio. In the evening John visited and we ate some more hamburgers and finished my Spanish gin. In the morning I made three walking trips to John's flat, to get my groceries and beer. Found a fiver on the pathway.

Tues, 10 Nov - I do studio work from, say, 10 am to 2 pm, when it gets too dark. I then have some food and then a sleep, from 3pm to 4pm, when I go beachcombing for firewood. John visited this evening. He is still doing the paper rounds, and we have fixed up a temporary one for me to do in Sandgate.

Fri, 13 Nov - I walked down the Leas at 6.50 am to the Marton office - lovely sunrise. A van load of us - mostly cheerful women, also with hangovers - went to Brake Brothers, just for the morning. I was cutting Christmas puddings in half, to make them into some other sweet. Was back at the flat at 1.30 pm, to collect and saw firewood. John visited. I drank tea and heated tinned chilli con carne and boiled some rice.

Sat, 14 Nov - A fried breakfast. Visited Arthur next door, then returned to spend an hour on the picture. Went beachcombing for fire wood and sawed it up. Had another walk, going into the town as the shops were closing. John visited and we drank some beer. The Church of England has voted to allow women priests.

Sun, 15 Nov - John came for breakfast. Did an hour on the picture before going for a walk. Tried unsuccessfully to find Etelle's flat in Harbour Way. An afternoon visit from the Adder.

Thurs, 19 Nov - Worked in the studio until noon, when I showered and drank some beer. I visited John, then went to the Clifton hotel, where I saw Edna again[20] and drank a glass of Beaujolais Nouveau. Drank beer, cheerfully, back at the flat and packed suitcase. Slept, then had a walk to purchase a bottle of Beaujolais, which I shared with John.

Thurs, 26 Nov - I worked at Brake Brothers, on a line producing a Christmas pudding-in-brandy-sauce sweet. John visited in the evening with news of the suicide of Vincent's friend, Philip Flecture.[21]

Sat, 28 Nov - Slept poorly, just from 3 am to 8 am. Am feeling dispirited about life. Had a fried breakfast. Sent a note to Pam. Walked to the Girl's Grammar School in Coolinge Lane, for a book fair, then back along the Leas into the town, to shop. Visited Charles Sturgis's flat. Sawed a bag of wood. John visited and we barbecued some sausages.

---

[20] Edna, a retired woman the diarist met there the previous evening and walked home.
[21] Philip Flecture, Oxford graduate, had visited the Clifton Mansions flat with Vincent.

Sun, 29 Nov - My usual Sunday, having breakfast, writing my journal, going for a walk and sawing some firewood. In the evening I have a shower before beer drinking and something to eat - today a packet of Ross Chinese Chicken, £1.20 and seven minutes to fry up. John came for some breakfast.

Sat, 5 Dec - Sawed a bag of firewood after breakfast and did one or two domestic jobs in the flat. Sunny lunchtime walk into the town and there again in the afternoon, after a couple of pints. Went to the library and went into the Masonic Hall where a Peruvian folk group were performing at some occult fair. John visited in the evening.

Sat, 12 Dec - Slept deeply, about nine hours. Had a fried egg and bacon breakfast, then a walk to Sandgate, where I bought a bottle of wine at a shop's closing down sale. Bright sunny day. Drank some beer on return to the flat, then had an afternoon walk into town, to shop. Visited Venetia. In the evening John visited and we barbecued some hamburgers. The Prince and Princess of Wales are separating. How unthinkable this would have seemed until not so long ago! It seems like the institution of life long marriage is becoming untenable.

Sun, 13 Dec - Had an outing to Deal with John. We visited Darryl and Anthony at their flat in Adelaide House on the sea front. They are likeable, hospitable hosts. After several drinks we all went to the Star and Garter pub, where John and I stayed til closing time. I also went to the Royal hotel. There was a nasty lesbian feminist on train back.[22] I had drink at the Salisbury hotel, where I saw Chris. With John to Bottoms gay disco, was very drunk.

---

[22] Diarist recalls that he and John were sitting in a near empty carriage with their feet up when a woman and a man got on at Dover and insisted on sitting in the seats opposite them, where their feet had been, instead of in any other empty seats.

Fri, 8 Jan - Sound sleep. Sunny mild morning, to John's for my groceries and beer making equipment. To Sainsbury's, to shop with credit card money. Began brewing some beer after lunch, using a *Studley Bitter* kit.[1] Sawed a bag of firewood. An evening walk to the harbour and through the town. In the evening Chris visited, and John, and I felt calm and happy.

Sun, 10 Jan - After a fried breakfast I went out in a very strong gale to collect some driftwood. Dramatic waves. In the evening Vincent and John visited. Vincent left, then Chris arrived, as promised with a few slices of venison from a large joint he has. I had cooked some potatoes, swede and parsnips and made some gravy. Chris left John and me to share the food.

Mon, 11 Jan - Made a visit to the Crofts family household. Saw Paul, Mrs Crofts, Vincent, Denis and Bernadette.[2] Paul made me a cup of coffee. Vincent showed me his *condominium* upstairs. To John's flat afterwards to get my guitar. Phoned Mrs Sharman,[3] to ask to do a temporary paper round. Have also been to the Marton agency. Watched telly at Arthur's flat this evening.

Fri, 15 Jan - To Sainsbury's, some money from Roy having just come through. John arrived after lunch and sat at the bar reading and drinking brandy, while I did one or two jobs in the flat. Two parties of viewers came.[4] Before my shower I got some oily fire wood from the beach in front of the Rotunda.[5] Cooked a packet of Ross *Indian Fried Chicken*. Chris visited.

Sun, 17 Jan - Had a fried breakfast. Walked to the bus and railway stations to compare the cost of travel to London. Sawed firewood and went beach-combing at dusk for more - as long as I have my beer and a fire in the evenings! John visited.

---

[1] From Studley Home Brew Shop.
[2] Bernadette, daughter in the Crofts family.
[3] Mrs Sharman, newspaper distributor.
[4] Including subsequent purchaser, Mr Gooding.
[5] Circular building, now an amusement arcade.

Sun, 24 Jan - John visited in the afternoon and sat at the bar reading a pile of newspapers, while I did the washing up and went beach-combing for firewood. After a shower I lit the fire at 7.30 pm. John took a phone call from his mother. Chris arrived with some pieces of cooked chicken, and I had boiled some potatoes and swede. John complained of some youth who had been harassing him in the street.

Sun, 31 Jan - A fried breakfast. Met Margot in Sandgate and we played pool at the Sandgate hotel. Wore the suit.[6] Purchased a book in the window of Antiques Etc. (Mostly Etcetera). Drank more beer back at the flat with John. Cooked some potatoes and a swede and some gravy which we shared.

Fri, 5 Feb -Collected the hire van 8am. Loaded it with the fridge and freezer and other things with John's help. Drove to Leamington Spa and put all of it in my garage, apart from a few items to do with gardening. Drove to the allotment and put these items in my shed. It felt peculiar going there.[7] There was a beautiful wan, misty sunset and nearly full moon. Had a walk in Oxford, visited the Victoria casino in London, losing £15. In Folkestone I left the van, with broken exhaust pipe, at the hire depot and walked back to the flat at 2.30 am.

Sat, 6 Feb - I walked to Direct Leasing after breakfast, where my £75 deposit cheque was returned - no problem about the broken exhaust. I put the door from the patio to the passageway back on its hinges. Took some things to John's flat. Chris and Vincent visited in the evening and I saw them across at the Salisbury, together with Venetia and her mother. Returned to the flat to drink more beer and pack and tidy up.

Sun, 7 Feb - Was woken 5 am by the alarm clock, to stagger out of the flat at 6 am with rolled mattress and blankets, which I could hardly carry to John's flat. I returned for my suitcase

---

[6] Brown pin stripe, bought from charity shop.
[7] i.e. without the diarist being in Studley to see his father.

and hurried to station for the 7.13 am Victoria train. Got the 12.40 pm Monarch flight to Malaga, where Roy met me and we arrived at *Casa Don Miguel* at 7pm. Roy cooked a lasagne and we drank red wine.

Studley, Wed, 14 April - Planted the gooseberry bush and a few shallots. A walk with Dad in the afternoon across fields nearby and back along Castle Lane. With him to the Barley Mow and Swan Inn. Have arranged to spend tomorrow night at John's flat, then two nights with Margot. The U.N. is considering helping the Muslims in Bosnia to defend themselves against the attacking Serbs.

Nerja, 15 June - Worked on the picture[8] in my bedroom in the morning, followed by lunch with Roy and Lesley at a table out by the pool, then sunbathing. We had a fish soup dish in the evening. Had a letter from John's mother saying he is ill with schizophrenia. I will have to move my paintings.[9]

Folkestone, Sun, 18 July - A wash in the toilets opposite the Stade Court hotel.[10] Had a milk and peanut breakfast, parked in front of Sandgate Rowing Club. Called at John's flat at 10.30 am, to find him ill and shaky and like an invalid. He's been on medication for schizophrenia since May. He and his mother asked me to move my paintings today, as they were about to leave for Salisbury.[11] Found Chris and Venetia, who said I could bring everything to Brockman Road, which I did in two van loads. They have also put me up in the basement of their house. Had a kitchen drink with them, after a walk on the Leas.

Tues, 20 July - Had breakfast with Venetia, during which John arrived with a couple of letters for me. Wrote this diary in my room, then walked into the town for a key duplicate and down to the harbour for a dish of whelks. A drink later with Venetia in her kitchen, then one or two with Chris at the Salisbury hotel. To the chip shop in Tontine Street. A rest day.[12]

---

[8] Diarist's current pastel work, a beach scene.
[9] Diarist's paintings were currently stored at John's flat.
[10] After sleeping in a hired van.
[11] Mrs Heal's home.
[12] After taking another load of domestic things to the Leamington garage the previous day.

141

Wed, 21 July - Took the three pastels which John had been storing to London, to show to Mrs Woods, of the Medici Gallery in Grafton Street. She said I could leave several, on sale or return, if I reframed them. Drove to the British Newspaper Library at Colindale, to try and find anything about Philip Flecture's inquest. Saw Chris and Venetia and Tamsin on my return. Had a takeaway hamburger. The government has won a vote of confidence in the Commons following its attempts to ratify the Maastricht Treaty without the Social Contract (or Charter).

Tues, 27 July - Visited John, who was expecting the arrival of a woman from the Social Services to give him some therapy. Rang Mrs Sharman, to see if she wanted any *Citizen* newspapers delivered.[13] Began making some beer, having left the beer making equipment in Venetia's room. Had sausage and chips from the Tontine Street chip shop.

Wed, 4 Aug - Spent the morning visiting. Called on John, who looked better, as he had not taken the drugs for a few days. Called at the Crofts' household. Mrs Crofts answered the door, but didn't invite me in.[14] Called on Arthur and then Mrs Weston at Clifton Mansions. When it was dark, at 10 am, I crept into the garden at Clifton Mansions and lugged the palm tree back, which weighed a ton.[15]

Tues, 17 Aug - Called on John, who seemed quite his old self again. His breakdown was partly caused by debts, which his mother has now paid off. Also he lived an isolated life, made worse, as he acknowledges, by the fact that I was no longer here. Made arrangements to hire a car, which Dad is paying for, to enable me to bring Dad down here for a few days.

Sun, 22 Aug - Heavy rain on waking, so I finished delivering this week's *Citizens* instead of going strawberry picking. Went to Dad's hotel to find him hankering after going on a trip to

---

[13] John had had to stop all the newspaper round deliveries after his breakdown.
[14] This proved to be the diarist's last visit there.
[15] The palm tree had been uprooted by the flat's new owners and dumped in the communal garden.

France, but as the weather was bad and we spent the afternoon resting in his room. We had a Sunday roast meal at the Windsor restaurant in Tontine Street. We me John at the Mikado bar[16]*happy hour*, then we had a final drink at Dad's hotel.[17]

Studley, 24 Aug - Watered the allotment fruit trees. Left Studley at 10.30 am to return the car in Folkestone at 3.30 pm. Had a walk on the Leas, where I met John. Returned to Venetia's room to eat bread and jam without margarine and tea with sugar and no milk. Wrote in this diary.

Thurs, 2 Sept - Went strawberry picking, earning £12.60. In the evening I went to the Shepway Festival beer festival, put on by the Ship Inn at the Chichester Hall, Sandgate, and also in the Sea Cadet hut, where there was a marquee extension facing the sea. Met John there and we drank Green King *Abbot Ale.*

Tues, 7 Sept - Arrived at the train station with the picture to find John, who had decided to come with me to Bexhill. We arrived there about midday and walked to Terminus Road, where I left the picture with the removal company.[18] We then walked around Bexhill and went to a couple of pubs. We also walked around Rye and had several more halves, though I hadn't planned to spend the money.

Tues, 14 Sept - I also felt annoyed during yesterday's return journey,[19] as I had been told that I wasn't needed, as too many pickers had turned up. However, I phoned again today and was rehired. Made other futile phone calls in the morning regarding employment. Began making more beer. Met John on the Leas. Israel is signing a peace agreement with the P.L.O.

Sun, 19 Sept - Woke with a nasty unexpected hangover, after my three and a half pints last night. Must be because of my tiredness. Delivered another bag of papers before returning to the flat for breakfast, after which I felt recovered. Sunny day

---

[16] At the Metropole.
[17] Langhorne Gardens hotel.
[18] Prima European Removals Ltd.
[19] After the previous day's apple picking the diarist had cycled happily back through the lanes.

Visited Peter Wagstaff at his flat, then had a drink with John at the Mikado bar.

Fri, 25 Sept - My last day.[20] There was a golden sunrise, cycling past the Cheriton motorway roundabout, but it was misty further inland. Picked four bins of Coxes, to earn £24 - my best day. Returned to Folkestone to send a cheque off for the quarterly garage rental. Cycled to Seabrook, to return the bicycle to Steven. Met John on the Leas walking back.

Tues, 28 Sept - With John to Calais on a *Sunday Express* £4.50 day trip offer. We went to the P&O office in Snargate Street, Dover, to get the tickets. We went over on the *Pride of Calais*, sitting in the forward viewing lounge. We walked around Calais in dripping rain, visiting one or two cafés and me swigging from a bottle of red wine between times. Felt cheerful. Folkestone 10.10 pm. Walk to Seabrook to return Margot's bicycle cape.

Wed, 29 Sept - A toast and marmalade breakfast. Walked down the Leas and made an Albion bookshop purchase. Visited John, then went to Arthur's flat with the remaining beer and some empty beer bottles which he will keep for me. Drank with him until 5 pm, with interludes to pack suitcase and to make a small betting shop wager from a tip overheard yesterday, which lost. Got 6.55 pm train from Folkestone, then went via Redhill to Gatwick for the 10.20 pm flight. Diehard communists attacked in Russian parliament.

[20] Apple picking at Leigh Barton Farm, Stone Street.

Studley, Fri, 7 Jan - A 8.55 am suitcase walk to Alcester, for the 10.05am London coach, which I only just managed to catch. Victoria station phone calls to Prima European Removals, then trains to Ashford and Folkestone, arriving about 5 pm. Called on John then walked to Seabrook. Was given a meal by Margot, who was there with her son, Steven, and his girlfriend, Tanya. Watched TV sitting by Margot's cosy fire, then fell exhausted to sleep on the sofa.

Sat, 8 Jan - Walked to Folkestone, getting a good blast of channel air. Visited the current Metropole exhibition, featuring some work by Tamsin. Went into the town then to Venetia's house, finding her at home with Tamsin. Made another visit to John, then I called on Cathy Bagnell, who gave me the details of Arthur's death. Went back up the Leas and through Sandgate to Seabrook, to be given liver and onions by Margot. At 7.15 pm her daughter took me to the station, for a British Rail bus to Ashford and trains to Gatwick.

Nerja, Wed, 16 Feb - Studio work. A phone call from John. He has been ill again and has been in hospital. I wrote to him in the evening and had a 9.30 pm walk to the post office letter box. Cooked, or heated, tinned chilli con carne for Roy's return from the radio station.[1]

Sun, 20 March - Completed the pastel ground work on the picture.[2] I could do further work on the picture in England. Phoned John, who will put me up next Sunday. Roy cooked Chicken Kiev, or *Pollo Supresa*,[3] with Spanish fried potatoes and spinach, all greatly enjoyable. A walk down to the beach earlier.

Folkestone, Sun, 27 March - Roy and I left the house at 9.45 am for my 12.15 pm flight, a French charter, which arrived at Gatwick at 3.30 pm, about an hour late. The clocks went forward today. Had an enjoyable British Rail *replacement*

---

[1] Roy hosted a weekly *Easy Listening with Roy Johnson* show on Coastline Radio, Nerja, playing music from his collection of dance music from the '30s, '40s and '50s.
[2] Diarist's current pastel work.
[3] As named in Emilio's *Portofino* Italian restaurant, Folkestone.

service bus ride through the countryside between Redhill and Tonbridge. Folkestone 8.30 pm, to be met at the station by John, went early to bed at his flat.

Mon, 28 March - Visited Venetia, who said I can use her room after Easter. I walked through the town to the harbour, where I changed some *pesetas*, then up the Leas to visit Cathy Bagnell. Alexander plants are flowering, as well as the daffodils and also flowering red current. Walk to Seabrook to visit Margot, then back to Venetia's house to see Chris. Cooked hamburgers for John and myself, then we went to the Burlington and Harvey's Wine Bar.

Horn Street, Seabrook, Wed, 30 March - A happy morning, doing more sweetcorn planting for Margot and rebuilding a rockery. I departed after lunch for a sea front walk to Folkestone. Had a wash and a change of socks in the harbour ferry toilets, ate half a pound of nuts and raisins sitting watching the fishing boats. Walked to the Salisbury hotel, on the way sniffing daffs, redcurrants and Alexander plants. Pints of spring lager,[4] one with Chris. To the Burlington to meet John and with him from the Bay Tree bar to Harvy's Wine Bar.

Studley, Thurs, 31 March - With John on the 10.20 am London train, he on his way to visit his parents in Hampshire. I walked from Waterloo across Westminster bridge and on to Victoria coach station - blustery Spring wind and a sparkling 11.30 am blue-sky sunshine on the Houses of Parliament. Coach to Alcester, walk to Studley. My suitcase wheels broke at Spernall. Went to bed early, while Dad was at the pub.

Folkestone, Tues, 19 April - To the Marton agency, Job Centre, and the library to look at temporary vacancies in the local paper. Visited John. Ate peanut butter sandwich lunch, after which I wrote in this diary. Had 5 pm walk up the Leas and along the lower road pathways, sniffing at the Alexander plants. A tea with Venetia, then did admin and ate baked beans. Serbs attacking UN safe havens in Bosnia   .

[4] Diarist's personal annual lager-drinking ritual.

The John Diaries - 1994

Thurs, 21 April - With John to Calais on *Daily Express* £1 day trip tickets. We went to the Continental supermarket in the middle of the town, then had a picnic of bead and Camembert and wine in the park by the Museum of Art. We then walked to the Calais Wine and Beer Company, for free bottles of wine,[5] then back to the harbour for the 8.15pm ferry. Drank the wine on the boat - John drunk. We had chips awaiting train at Dover.

Fri, 22 April - A visit to the Marton agency, where Tony[6] offered me some Carter Wallace work next week. Later he rang to also offer me work to do with the catering for the Channel Tunnel opening parties. Venetia bought some furniture from the Salvation Army and I went with her to view it. Visited John and booked him a hire car, after he decided on doing this for a trip tomorrow. Walked up the Leas, enjoying Alexander scent in warm sunshine.

Sat 23 April - St. George's Day. Collected John's hire car - a Fiat *Uno* - and we drove to Ely, via Greenwich, where I had a brief argument with a resident about parking in a private road. We visited Ely Cathedral and walked in the town. After a fenland drive to Huntingdon, where we had another stroll, we had a B road meander to Cambridge, where we went to two Green King pubs and a pizza restaurant. Sparkling sunshine all afternoon and a mild evening. 1.15 am Folkestone return.

Fri, 6 May - Slept til 1 pm. Visited John. Am getting meals and eating unused food at work.[7] We provide a choice of four courses at lunchtime and five in the evening and they're changed every day.[8] Started work 6pm, so I missed the Queen and President Mitterrand. I held the fort with another Martin agency worker til 5 am. Ate breakfast before departing for the taxi.[9] Mandela elected President of South Africa.

---

[5] Included in the £1 Daily Express ticket offer.
[6] Tony, co-director of agency with wife, Maggie.
[7] Staffing at canteen, with some night shifts, for workers preparing a marquee for the Channel Tunnel's official opening ceremony on 6 May.
[8] Diarist was working with Woodhall Caterers, of Suffolk, run by Barry.
[9] Paid for by Barry.

Sat, 7 May - Had two pints of home brew on waking at 12.30 pm. Had more at John's flat, then we had a walk to see a children's carnival procession on the Leas - part of the tunnel opening celebrations - which had effective home made costumes and floats on a nautical theme. Crowds of people there, many French. We had a drink at the Mikado bar before I went to work. Fortunately for me it poured with rain and we all stopped at 9 pm. Got a lift from work mates and had a Burlington hotel drink with them and played pool there 'til 3 am.

Thurs, 12 May - To Calais with John on *Daily Express* offer tickets - a repeat of our last visit, except after our picnic we went to several cafés instead of going out to the Calais Wine and Beer Company.[10] We were both not as drunk as last time.

Fri, 20 May - To Calais with John, beginning with a visit to the Travel Market Company, off Snargate Street, to collect our £1 tickets. A Camembert and wine picnic in the park opposite the Town Hall. Café visits, to the station to make trains to Malaga enquiries. To the casino, where I bet 100 francs on the roulette table twice, winning once and losing once. Met a lovely girl on return boat, called Nathalie, prettier than Nathalie Wood; me a drunk buffoon. Had a row with Dover coach driver.[11] Labour leader John Smith dead.

Sun, 22 May - Cereal, toast & jam and Lincoln biscuit breakfast. Walked on the Leas and along the seafront to the Sunday market and harbour. Had a drink in the Salisbury hotel before dusk, and was joined there by John and then Chris. During the afternoon walk I visited Etelle in Harbour Way and sat in her garden drinking tea and reading the *Sunday Times*. Sunny all day.

Tues, 24 May - To London with John. Visited the Francis Kyle gallery off Regent Street, on the recommendation of someone Roy had been speaking to in Nerja. Saw Warhol portraits at Anthony D'Offay, and Damian Hurst dead sheep at the

---

[10] For free bottles of beer or wine.
[11] The port railway station courtesy bus driver wouldn't let the intoxicated diarist on the bus.

Serpentine Gallery. Made a Film Artists' Association office visit. Joined the new Sportsman casino. Had a brief visit to the British Museum. We had a £3 all-you-can-eat pizza & pasta in Charing Cross Road, and a drink in the Brief Encounter, before getting the 8 pm train.

Thurs, 26 May - Looked at the Basis Food Hygiene course booklet. Had the last of the four afternoon classes, during which there was a little tick-the-right-answer test. I thought I would get them all right, but the result was twenty eight out of thirty. Went Sainsbury's shopping, walked on the Leas in fine drizzle. John visited my room and we drank some home brew. Walked to the Salisbury hotel to see Chris, re Venetia's pottery exhibition tomorrow.

Fri, 27 May - With John to Canterbury on lunchtime trains via Ashford. Crowded streets. We had a drink in the County hotel then went to the cinema, to see *Four Weddings and a Funeral*. Met Henry, from Folkestone, while we were drinking home brew on a park seat in front of the Chaucer hotel. To the Pizzaland restaurant beside the Cathedral gateway. To Crotchets wine bar. To Venetia's degree exhibition of her pottery at Christchurch college, her family there in force. We got a lift back from Chris. A dusk walk with John to the beach, down the newly lit Zig Zag Path

Studley, 16 July - Got the 7.55 am bus to Stratford, where I sat opposite the Encore pub writing up this diary while awaiting the coach to Oxford. It was sunny and quiet, then there were shoppers and tourists. Got Oxford train to London, where I passed time walking with my luggage from Charing Cross to Bryanstone Street, where I collected my Sportsman casino membership card. Hot walk back, stopping for mini picnic in Green Park. John was at Folkestone station, as arranged.

Folkestone, 17 July - Spent the night at John's flat, where I slept soundly. Visited Venetia and moved my luggage into the room in her basement. Rang Margot, who invited me to her house for lunch, her children, Steven and Jacky, were there with Jacky's husband, Tony, and Steven's girlfriend, Tania. We watched the World Cup football final. Rang Roy, to confirm that Margo was to visit *Casa Don Miguel* with Jacky and others.

Sat, 23 July - Awoke with headache and feeling nauseous. Have had too much sun. Decided I needed a rest from strawberry picking[12]and went back to sleep. Had cereal, toast, jam, Lincoln biscuit breakfast and slept again. To John's flat, to learn that the pastel has been accepted.[13] Did some admin and walked on the Leas, feeling fit again. Ate tinned spaghetti, was in bed reading by 8.30 pm. A comet has been observed striking Jupiter.

Sun, 24 July - Went strawberry picking for three hours, finishing at 11.30 am. Continued with my breakfast - toast, jam and biscuits - on return to my room. Wrote in this diary. A 6.30 pm walk up the Leas with John, to the Mikado bar *happy hour*, then to the Burlington and Salisbury hotels.

Fri, 29 July - Last night I went with John to the *happy hour* at Copperfield's wine bar, then we returned to my room and drank some strong John Bull home brew. Had a nasty hangover this morning and arrived late again for strawberry picking, my last day. Earned £9.70, making a total of £88.10. Saw Venetia and Chris upstairs this evening.

Fri, 5 Aug - With Dad to Littlestone for a game of golf at the eighteen hole Romney Warren course, formerly the nine hole course.[14]An overcast but mild day, with no breath of wind. We both hit some good shots. Beer and cockles and whelks afterwards at the Ocean Inn, Dymchurch. A drink with Chris and John at the Salisbury hotel. Fish and chips in Dad's hotel room.

Mon, 15 Aug - Visited John, then did Sainsburys shopping. To the Job Centre and the library - Ratling Court Farm are advertising again in the local paper for pickers. Walked to

---

[12] At Ratling Court Farm, Aylesham.
[13] For the Mall Galleries *Pastel Society Open Exhibition.*
[14] Diarist normally had only played on the presently situated nine hole course.

Margot's house in the evening to watch television. She gave me a meal prepared by Steven's girlfriend, Tania.

Sat, 27 Aug - Had my weekend breakfast, having decided last night not to bother waking early today, but to see if it was raining first. Spent the day writing another story in the scrap book.[15] At 8.30 pm I met John in the Burlington's Bay Tree bar and then we watched the firework display on the Leas, marking the start of this year's Shepway Festival. We then went back to the Bay Tree bar.

Sun, 28 Aug - A lunchtime walk with John to Sandgate, for beers at the Clarendon Inn and the Ship Inn. We then had a promenade walk to Tontine Street, where John paid for a café meal.

Tues,30 Aug - Went strawberry picking. John visited briefly in the evening. Drank two or three pints of home made cider and ate some curried beans. Before this I had a deep sleep for an hour or two, when I arrived back in my room.

Wed, 31 Aug - With John on the 10.20 am train to London, for the *Pastel Society Open Exhibition* opening. First we went to the Francis Kale gallery, where I gave one of its director one of my exhibition invitations.[16] We then went to the Mall Galleries to view the exhibition, then to a Deep Pan Pizza *all-you-can-eat-for-£2.99* restaurant, then back to the Mall Galleries, where I met Kim and his actress friend, Nicky. John and I had a Brief Encounter drink then caught an early train.

Sun, 4 Sept - To John's flat after breakfast, to drink some home brew cider. Actually, I had a sunny walk on the Leas after breakfast, to browse along the stalls there for the Shepway Airshow. John and I saw the air show in the afternoon from outside the Mikado bar. We bought cheap day trip-to-Boulogne tickets at a stall. John bought us a meal in the Sandgate Fish & Chip Shop, then we went to the Shepway Beer Festival. We were both drunk, me sick in the sea. Yugoslavs still yakking.[17]

---

[15] Diarist was writing some children's stories for his son.
[16] For the aforementioned exhibition.
[17] At peace talks.

Thurs, 8 Sept - Finished the last story I was writing and copied it into the scrap book. An evening visit from John. Heated some baked beans with curry paste and chopped onion.

Sat, 10 Sept - To the supermarket after breakfast, then a lunchtime expedition to Hythe with John. We caught a bus from the Metropole - or by Coolinge Lane - and went to what we thought would be the reopening day for the Butt of Sherry wine bar. The party was last night, though, so the place was quiet and subdued. John still enjoyed it. We then walked back, blown along by wind and sea spray, stopping on the way to sip home brewed lager in a wind shelter.

Tues, 13 Sept - Picked four boxes.[18] Got back to Folkestone in time to go to the post office and send the scrap book to Jack. John visited in the evening and we drank some lager.

Wed, 14 Sept - To London to collect the Pastel Society exhibition exhibit and to see Kim at his flat, to collect an anorak that he got for me from the allotment shed. John travelled up to London with me on the train, and he came back on an early train, as it was a signalmen's strike day.

Sun, 18 Sept - Had a weekend breakfast, shopped for food, rested from apple picking. John visited this evening.

Wed, 21 Sept - Arrived promptly at 8 am to pick as quickly as I could until 3.30 pm, to earn £32, my best result. Felt good bicycling back to my room. John visited. He had a day trip ticket to Boulogne for tomorrow, but is not now going there with me.

Sun, 25 Sept - Went apple picking. Not many pickers are left. Early autumn sunshine. On the way back I discovered a spot in the Lyminge forest where there were many ceps. Unfortunately they had all gone spongy or black, so I have missed the season again.

---

[18] Apple picking at Leigh Barton Farm, Stelling Minnis.

Wed, 28 Sept - Apple picking, expecting each day to be my last. Returned early to go to the bank. John visited and we ate some chicken and chips and drank lager. Began to brew some more after his departure.

Sat, 1 Oct - Phoned Pam, Dad and Roy. Pam tells me my stories went down very well. Walked up the Leas and through Sandgate and back through Folkestone, feeling buoyant. In the afternoon one of Venetia's nephews started burning some garden rubbish for her in a dust bin. I told him it wouldn't burn and was proved wrong. Walked to Hythe for a drink at the Butt of Sherry, where John is helping the landlord by writing all the restaurant bills. Got a bus back as far as Sandgate.

Sun, 2 Oct - After breakfast I had another walk to Sandgate, to visit the *Antiques* Etc. bric-a-brac/books shop, but the old boy running it wasn't there again. Had a sunny promenade walk back to the room to drink several pints of home brew and then fall asleep. Was woken by John's knock on the door. Drank some more home brew to wake up and cooked up some spaghetti and pasta sauce.

Tues 4 Oct - Made phone calls to the Polo Express Company,[19] regarding my making a courier trip to the States, so I can visit the Cissie Peltz Gallery,[20] whose cheque hasn't yet arrived. Felt much calmer than during yesterday's complaint day.[21] John visited this evening. Visited Cathy Bagnell today.

Studley, Wed 12 Oct - Walked to Redditch for the 9.50 am National Express coach to London. I left my suitcase at Victoria and walked to Cork Street, to see Michael Murfin's current exhibition, and to the Francis Kyle gallery, to enquire about my slides.[22] Train to Folkestone, to arrive in my room at the same time as John, with whom I drank some lager.

---

[19] Company offering discount price flight tickets in return for acting as a parcel courier.
[20] Milwaukee gallery selling oil paintings by the diarist.
[21] Diarist had been complaining to AVRO about a twelve hour Malaga to Gatwick flight delay.
[22] Diarist had sent slides of his work to the gallery.

Thurs, 5 Jan - Slept well. Visited Venetia. I would like to spend a week or two in Folkestone, but can't afford not to use my return flight. To Smith's, to spend a book token. Returned to John's then had a walk down to Seabrook to call on Margot, who had a lovely fire going and fed me ham sandwiches. Dusk return to Folkestone, enjoying a stormy sea and great blast of channel air. Made a small purchase from Antiques Etc (Mostly Etcetera), old boy owner there. Got 7.02 pm train for Gatwick.

Nerja, Sun, 5 March - Hangover. Phoned John, who tells me the crocuses and daffodils are out. The British and Irish governments last week published a framework document on their agreement for peace in Northern Ireland. Unionist politicians will have to do more than just stonewall it, if it has popular support. The situation is promising for peace.

Tues, 21 March - Roy and I have begun doing some cleaning[1]for Tony Bull and Margaret,[2] who are now managing property with Savoy Properties. This morning we cleaned furniture at a big country house off the Frigiliana Road. I had one pound newspaper offer day trip tickets to Calais for today - would have gone there with John.

Studley, Sun, 23 April - A walk to the Studley car boot fair on the Slough. A busy, sunny, car queuing morning. Purchased a garden folk for £1.50. Decided to stay in Studley until Thursday, rather than go to Folkestone tomorrow. Sipped gin and helped Dad prepare the roast beef dinner. Phoned Roy and John and felt happy with the decision. Roy says he may get planning permission for houses on the sawmill land.[3]

Thurs, 27 April - Made a 12.15 pm departure from the house for a bus to Stratford, Dad gloomy and me a little ratty with him, as he wanted to know where I was staying and I wasn't sure about it myself. Had a walk around Stratford awaiting the Oxford coach. Train to London, bought an art mag at the ICA bookstall. On train to Folketone I was still feeling anxious.

[1] Roy and the diarist had begun doing carpet and upholstery cleaning.
[2] Tony and Margaret Bull, former tenants of Tony's Inn, Nerja.
[3] Site of Chilham Saw Mills.

John wasn't at his flat at first, but he was there soon, and so I stayed the night as arranged.

Fri, 28 April - I'll stay two or three weeks, if Marton have any work, if not it's back to Spain after the weekend. To Venetia's, who said it would be quite alright to use her basement room as usual. To the Marton agency, where Tony said there could be work with the Council. A walk to the harbour for a plate of whelks. Returned to John's flat then I walked to Seabrook to visit Margot, who gave me a pork chop meal. Return to Folkestone for late drink with John at new Westbourne Gardens *Jake's Bar*.

Sat, 29 April - Rose at midday at John's flat. Tony has confirmed he has some work, so I phoned Venetia to say I'd like to stay. Had the dish of whelks down at the harbour. Moved my luggage to Venetia's. Delivered a few *Adscenes* for her in a nearby street.[4] Began brewing some lager, reusing the Boots portable brew bag.[5] Dusk walk in a light spring drizzle to Jakes Bar, for a game of pool and chat with John's new found friends there.

Thurs, 4 May - to Sapphir's, stacking cartons of fruit.[6] I felt very tired and sleepy indeed today and developed a blinding headache, bending down to handle the cartons. Aspirin and tea back in my room, then John visited and we had some home brew and shared some chicken curry that Margot gave me. It had turmeric in it and was really good. Early to bed.

Sat, 6 May - A Shredded Wheat, toast, jam and Lincoln biscuit breakfast. Strolled into the town then came back to my room to drink several pints of home brew. I then went back into the town to make a book token purchase at the Albion bookshop - a Paul Bowles novel. Slept back at the room. Met Venetia and her mother for a drink in the garden, then went for a walk up the Leas, the evening mild and scented. To Jakes Bar to play pool with John.

---

[4] Venetia had begun doing an *Adscene* newspaper round.
[5] Polythene bag with plastic tap, originally containing wine or beer.
[6] Sapphir's Fruit Packers Ltd, Faversham.

Sat, 13 May - To Ashford, to fruit packers, Griffin & Brand, unpacking, examining and repacking grapes from 7.30 am to 1 pm - chilly, tedious hours. Had toast, jam and biscuits back in my room. Walked to Folkestone West railway station to take a train to the Central station, so I could walk through the train looking for free London mags that advertise one way flight tickets. Did this twice, but no luck.[7] Played pool with John at Jake's Bar.

Sun, 14 May - Had hangover. Rested and read, went for a harbour stroll? Have begun making some more lager, using a Boots/Unicorn kit that was past its sell-by date. Sat in the garden a while with Venetia. Think I played pool with John this evening. Went to Margot's last night.

Wed, 17 May - Worked at Griffin & Brand from 7.30 am to 4.15 pm. Went to bed at 8.30 pm, after a visit from John.

Sat, 20 May - Had a fried £2.65 breakfast in the café by the railway bridge. I then walked into the town to get some shoes mended. Packed and tidied room. John visited and we finished up my lager. Collected shoes. With John to Jakes Bar, then solo to the Salisbury hotel, for a drink with Chris. Missed the 9.02 pm train, took one later going to Charing Cross instead of Victoria. A midnight suitcase walk up The Mall to Victoria, Gatwick 2 am, to sleep until 5 am.

Folkestone, Sun, 23 July - Dad is in the Langhorne Gardens hotel and I am in Venetia's basement room, God bless her. An afternoon drive[8] to Ramsgate, where we had a café Sunday lunch - Dad steak & kidney pie, me liver & bacon. We preceded the drive with a visit to the clifftop café in Capel. Back in Folkestone I met Dad in the Salisbury hotel, then we went to Jakes Bar for a brief drink with John. We then went to the Leas Cliff Hall and got in free for the end of a ballroom dance.

Tues, 8 Aug - Saw Venetia upstairs. Called on John. Did Sainsburys shopping, wrote in this diary. Drank a couple of pints of *Studley Bitter*, then had an evening walk to Margot's

---

[7] Diarist does not recall whether he bought a ticket.
[8] In a car rented by the diarist's father.

156

house to borrow Steven's bicycle, which I walked back, as it had a puncture. Margot not there. Marton agency is either on holiday or closed down.

Fri, 11 Aug - Was woken 4 am by alarm. Had a dawn ride to Addisham Farm, to arrive soon after 7 am. Picked strawberries til 1 pm, to earn £10.50. Hot sun, aching back. Finished sandwiches and slept on the way back, near Denne Hill. Arrived room 4 pm. Called on John, who was out, so had a walk on the Leas. Drank two pints home brew and went early to bed, very exhausted. Had a swim with Venetia by the Rotunda yesterday.

Sat 12 Aug - Gave the £10 to Venetia, which she reluctantly accepted.. To Boots, buying a beer kit with credit card and returning to my room to start brewing in the (most convenient) Boots brewbag. Visited John and later saw him again to borrow £2, to buy an old Rima grill at the Radnor Park Donkey Derby boot fair. Drink upstairs with Chris and Venetia and I had a meal from her, then I drank beer and read in my room. Spoke to pretty girl walking nearby, but later saw her with her boyfriend.

Thurs 17 Aug - Went strawberry picking from 8.30 am to 12.30 pm. Am not needed again until Monday. Drank tea, read and dozed back in my room, away from the heat outside. John visited in the evening and drank water, while I drank home brew. Found bike with a puncture this morning at 5 am.

Thurs, 24 Aug - Shopped for food and a beer kit. Began brewing, slept, tidied the room. An evening visit from John, ending with us drinking home brew til nearly 1 am. Wrote to Roy. Oh, this morning I went to see Tom Green, on the strength of £40 Roy sent me. Realised, sitting in his chair, that a mercury filling had fallen out, not the gold one.[9]

Sat, 26 Aug - Shredded Wheat, toast, jam breakfast, no biscuits. Shopped for food, did some washing, read and rested. An evening visit from John and another fairly late night for me.

---

[9] Tooth with gold inlay filling.

.Thurs, 31 Aug - Woke after a good sleep and remembered I had been supposed to go picking. Had thought it was Wednesday, due to Monday's bank holiday. Began typing the last chapter of the children's story[10]which I didn't have time to do in Nerja. It was raining this morning anyway. An evening visit from John.

Sat, 2 Sept - Photocopied the last chapter and got the whole story (this time) prepared to send to two publishers. Spent my last coins on postage for one of the publishers. Rain storm on return from the post office. A surprise visit from Paul and Denis. Walked to Boots, to buy a beer kit with credit card. A visit from John and we went and watched the Shepway Festival fireworks and made a brief visit to Nicola's restaurant bar. UN/NATO have gone to war against Serbs, to protect Sarajevo safe haven.

Sun, 3 Sept - A walk after breakfast up the Leas to see if the Shepway Festival Airshow Day Hoverspeed stand were doing £5 day trip offer tickets, like last year, which they were. I found John and we booked a couple of tickets. Saw Chris. Spent the afternoon in my room drinking home brew. Slept. It's 8 pm and I'm writing this.

Thurs, 7 Sept - I woke at 4 am, as usual, but did not leave 'til 7 am, as rain was threatening. I had to go, to get the last two day's money (paid daily, usually). Had a puncture on the lane to Wootton, so didn't arrive til 10 am. Picked a couple of trays before we were rained off at 11.30 am. It was sunny again approaching Folkestone. Slept then shopped for food and went to the library. An evening visit from John.

Tues, 12 Sept - John was due to call at 10 am for our day trip to Boulogne, but he arrived soon after 8 am to say he was going instead with some of his new Jake's Bar friends. Feeling annoyed and let down, I went to Boulogne by myself. I had another pork paté/vin moelleux picnic and visited the tourist office, railway station and the library, to research the possibility of strawberry picking at Samer next time.

---

[10] Diarist was writing some children's stories for his son,

Seabrook, Tues, 26 Sept - I typed the review on Margot's computer.[11] Walked back to Folkestone at 2.30 pm to send it to Tony. Called on John, still feeling annoyed with him, though I found him a bit contrite.[12]

Wed, 27 Sept - Am enjoying having a few days of leisure. Did Venetia's paper round for her today. At lunchtime I went to the Hi Tin Chinese restaurant in Tontine Street, thinking Chris might be there, but he didn't show. Had a shrimp curry, then a walk along the sea front and back to my room to sleep. A drink with Chris at the Salisbury hotel, and one with John at Jake's Bar, where I won £5 on a scratch card.

Thurs, 28 Sept - Have bought a one way flight to Malaga, for £49. Today I mended the bicycle slow puncture then took it back to Margot's house, where I also fitted a new brake cable. An evening visit from John and we had a drink at the Sandgate hotel, before I went to Margot's house again, to take her by taxi to Hythe, for a few drinks and a meal at a Chinese restaurant, for which neither of us was all that much in the mood.

Nerja, 5 Oct - To Folkestone post office and a sunny walk down to the East Cliff Sands. Sent my monthly contribution[13] to Pam. Packed suitcase, tidied room. John arrived at 5 pm and we finished up my cider. Got the 9.02 pm train to Tonbridge, for train to Gatwick and 1.55 am Viva charter flight to Malaga, where I arrived at 4 am GMT, with a hangover. Arrived *Casa Don Miguel* about 5.30 am with Roy. Net Book Agreement[14] Scrapped.

---

[11] Diarist was writing a review of Nerja friend, Tony Sharp's novel, *The Gov'nor.*
[12] John had taken Jake's Bar landlord's son, Jake, and his girlfriend, Beth, on an expensive trip to Le Touquet, as the diarist later learned.
[13] Diarist's modest financial contribution to his son's upbringing.
[14] Had fixed book shop retail price of new hardback books.

Studley, Thurs, 4 Jan - Woke feeling nervous and wishing I could stay in bed. Got up to have some porridge and pack suitcase. 2.45 pm departure from house, Dad upset saying goodbye. 4.10 pm London coach from Redditch, feeling worried about money, and Dad, and sentimental about Pam. A walk down the Mall, pulling the suitcase from Victoria to Charing Cross. Felt better on Folkestone train. Arrived John's flat about 10.30 pm.

Folkestone, Fri, 5 Jan - At 11 am I visited Venetia, finding her at home with granddaughter, Chantelle. Spent the rest of the day strolling around Folkestone, buying a couple of things and walking down to the East Cliff Sands. Bumped into Colin and Harold and in the evening I visited them at their new Manor Road flat, and had whisky and sandwiches there, then I had a last drink with John and his pals at Jake's Bar.

Sat, 6 Jan - Had a hangover, comprising of a headache and queasy stomach. Got up at 11 am, after John got a phone call from his Jake's Bar friend, Peter Simmons,[1] with whom we drank last night. Peter arrived in his Mercedes and took us to his flat, to view his collection of shaving mugs. He is consulted by the major auction houses and has a collection of mugs worth thousands. An evening walk to Margot's house, for telly and meal. Had a 2 am return.

Nerja, Sun, 18 Feb - Ate porridge. Wrote page.[2] Cleaned a sofa. Roy dropped me at the Punts Lara urbanisation on his way to the radio station, and I walked back along the beach - sunny and breezy, snow on one or two peaks behind the town. At 8.30 pm I picked Tony[3] up and returned to the house with him for a lasagne. Have phoned John, who told me that the *Two Doorways*, which I left with him to submit to the *Pastel Society Open Exhibition*, has been rejected.

---

[1] Peter Simmons, chartered accountant, businessman, collector.
[2] Of diarist's novel, *Vapour Trails in the Blue*.
[3] Tony Sharpe, pianist & writer, owner of *Sharpe's* piano bar, Nerja.

Sun, 31 March - After breakfast Roy and I visited the boot fair in the Echo Ahorro supermarket car park. Return to house to clean a very large square woollen carpet that we collected from customers in Maro on Thursday. Phoned John Heal and Lesley. A cannelloni for dinner, not Roy's best. EC ban on *Mad Cow* disease beef from Britain.

Folkestone, Tues, 30 April - Arrived at John's flat towards 11 pm last night, to sleep there pretty soundly. Made telephone box calls re a flight this morning, resulting in the purchase of a £59 Monarch charter[4] for Sunday, from Stansted to Malaga. Called on Venetia, who cooked me a fried breakfast. To the Marton agency, where Tony offered me three days work, but I changed my mind about it over a dish of whelks at the harbour. To Margot's house, where I did some weeding for her, watched telly and was given a meal.

Wed, 1 May - Had a lovely evening seaside walk late last night, from Margot's house to John's flat. Am going to just *potter*, as John calls it, doing nothing much apart from some writing. To the library reading room for this, but there were some distractions, so I shopped and returned to John's flat to write, he having gone to Canterbury. Had some of my *spring lager* in the evening and pints in the Metropole, the Salisbury and with John in Jake's Bar - had seven pints in all.

Thurs, 2 May - Had a severe hangover, lay abed til gone 11 am, then I walked through the town and on to The Warren, where I sat on the beach in the shelter of the concrete groynes to write. I continued in a shelter near the East Cliff Pavilion, as it had begun spotting with rain. Purchased some steak and a bottle of Frascati at Sainsbury's before returning to John's flat to cook and share a meal with him. Early to bed.

Sat 4 May - Wrote in room til 1pm, then had sunny walk with sandwiches to The Warren, to write there and then a bit more in the shelter near the East Cliff Pavilion. To Sainsbury's for

---

[4] At the time people could buy or sell an unused part of a return flight ticket.

steak and a bottle of Frascati, for a repeat of Thursday's meal with John. An evening walk on The Leas, then I returned to John's flat to pack suitcase and go early to bed.

Nerja, Sun, 5 May - I left John at 9.15 am, for trains to London and Stansted airport. Got the 3.15 pm Monarch flight to Malaga, arriving half an hour late, leaving me with just another half an hour or so to wait for Roy, who came to meet me after doing his radio programme. Drank beer in Torre del Mar and after showering at *Casa Don Miguel*.

Sat, 2 June - After breakfast I *hoovered* the pool (cleaned bottom tiles with suction tool) and did some gardening and cleaned the birdcage out,[5] bringing it indoors to let the Diamante Mandarin fly around. After Roy's return from the radio station I phoned John, who told me my entries had been rejected.[6] This news cast a pall of gloom over the evening, which was a shame, as dinner was an appetising bit of steak from Gibraltar.

Studley, Sat, 20 July - Failed to finish a page up at the allotment. Slept and shopped for food in the afternoon. Phoned John to ask if I could stay with him next weekend while Dad is at Folkestone, but it seems he could be just about to take in a female lodger. Hot sultry afternoon. Left the phone box and went for a walk across the field, past church and up the track towards the castle, feeling despondent. A dismal pint with Dad at the Needlemaker's Arms and Little Lark.

Thurs, 25 July - Collected Dad's hire car, a Nissan *Micra*, from Newtown Vehicles, Arthur Street, Redditch. To the allotment, to water things. At 3.30 pm I left with Dad for Folkestone, where he got installed at the Langhorne Gardens hotel, after which we went to Jake's Bar, where John is now at work on the other side of the bar. Dropped Dad at his hotel then John put me up at his place.

---

[5] Containing Zebra Finches.
[6] For Royal Academy Summer Exhibition.

Sun, 18 Aug - I arrived at Folkestone at 9.30 pm, to be met by John at the station. Slept at his flat, after slacking thirst with lots of tea. This morning I had a sunny walk to Sainsbury's. John was behind the bar at Jake's Bar this evening, where I had three pints during the 7 to 8pm *happy hour*.

Mon, 19 Aug - Resumed writing. To Margot's house this evening, to watch TV and be given a meal - corned beef and salad - prepared by Tania. It was another wonderful sunny afternoon and evening. Began brewing some beer in the brewbag on return to John's flat. He is working at the bar until very late each evening and sleeps all morning, so I can write then and we won't disturb each other   .

Tues, 20 Aug - A lunchtime visit to Venetia. Her basement was flooded by the torrential rain that fell here a week or two ago. Had a dish of whelks at the harbour and a swim near the Mermaid café. Returned to John's flat to cook a steak for us both, with peas and fried onions, chips from Tontine Street, and a bottle of Frascati to drink. I should note I had a swim yesterday with raw sewage - shit - floating in the sea.

Wed, 21 Aug - An afternoon walk to Sandgate to see an exhibition by Margot's ex husband, Derek Hedgecock. Had a beach and promenade walk back to the harbour in a light drizzle, with feet aching. Had a bag of chips at the flat, while John was working at Jake's Bar.

Fri, 23 Aug - Had a hangover, but was OK by 9.30 am, for an appointment with Tom Green, to have a small bit of a lost filling replaced. I then began walking towards the East Cliff, to write in a shelter, but heavy rain forced me to catch a bus and return to John's flat, to write there. A walk to Margot's again,[7]to enjoy a sedate evening watching TV, drinking tea, eating a stew and rocking asleep Margot's new grandson, Cameron.

---

[7] Like the previous night.

Sun, 25 Aug - John and I visited his friend, Peter, at his flat last night, to view the latest additions to his collection of shaving mugs. This morning, after writing a page, I drank some of the home brew, then had a couple of halves in Jake's Bar, where John was presiding. I then walked to the harbour for some whelks and had a short walk on The Warren beach, over the wooden groynes, the tide being out. Called on Etelle on the way back, and was given some curry while reading Sunday papers and watching TV.

Tues, 27 Aug - Had a pleasant afternoon with a sunbathe on the beach and walk to the harbour. Back at John's flat I ate some cold chicken from Margot's and shared a bottle of Frascati with John. Phoned Margot, as there was a possibility of two spare free seats on a coach trip tomorrow to Sluis, for which she is the courier, but no such luck.

Wed, 28 Aug - With John to Calais, at his expense, primarily so he could get some cigarettes for John,[8] the tenant at the bar, although I also got 200 cigarettes for Dad. I left him in a *brasserie* to have a meal, while I went to the beach to eat sandwiches and drink from a litre bottle of white. We went there and back on the *Fantasia*. Back at Dover station buffet I lost my temper with three kids who were poking fun at John.

Sat, 31 Aug - Wrote my usual daily page, then walked into the town and down to the East Cliff Sands. Returned to the flat to pack suitcase. Drank some gin and lemonade with John. Exchanged a glance with an attractive girl near Kingsnorth Gardens today, or yesterday. Have arranged with Pat[9] to stay at her St Albans house next Saturday evening before my flight.

Studley, Sun, 1 Sept - Departed John's flat 7 am for a train to London. Got taxi from Charing Cross to Victorian coach station, to succeed in catching the 9.30 am coach to Redditch. Bus to Studley, to arrive at Dad's house at 2 pm. Bought some additional vegetables from the Pioneer supermarket, which I

---

[8] John, Jake's Bar landlord.
[9] Pat Newton, Harpendon & Nerja resident.

left at the allotment (plumbs there ripe)[10]before walking to the bootfair, which was nearly over, so I went fungi hunting in Wirehill wood, in which I got lost. Retrieved vegetables for roast pork dinner.

Tues, 3 Sept - Finished another page in the greenhouse.[11] Finished packaging two pictures.[12] Finished duty free gin in the evening, while Dad was at the pub. John is going to collect the third pastel for me[13]after it is exhibited at the Royal Society of British Artists Mall Galleries exhibition.

Nerja, Mon, 23 Sept - I cleaned two mats after lunch. A phone call from John, who says he was knocked down by a cyclist on the pavement yesterday. He warned me he didn't expect to be well enough to collect my Mall Galleries picture. Am rereading my journal. Dear oh Law'! - some acutely embarrassing things about myself every other page or so. I see I voted conservative in '79, which I can hardly believe. I think it was because my system then was to vote automatically for whoever was in opposition.

Sat, 19 Oct - Wrote a page after breakfast. Cleaned a Chinese round carpet. In the evening Roy and I drank some rum then went to a back street café for a *racione* each - me mixed fried fish, Roy *boquerones*. A Spanish football match of the day was on telly in every café. Wonderful cloudless, warm sunshine every day. After some persuading, John collected my picture from the Mall Galleries after all.

---

[10] On diarist's young Victoria plumb tree.
[11] On diarist's allotment.
[12] To take to Spain.
[13] While the diarist was in Spain.

Seabrook, Wed, 8 Jan - After a sound, comfortable sleep on Margot's couch cushions, I had a slow but pleasant walk in powdery snow, icy underneath, to Folkestone, where I walked around the shops buying one or two things. Called on Venetia, but she a was out. Phoned John. Returned to Margot's house with a large bottle of wine to accompany the meal there, cooked by Tanya. Was tired but chatted with Margot til midnight.

Thurs, 9 Jan - Another sound sleep, waking to find it snowing outside. Had a pleasant morning chatting with Margot, then a lunchtime walk to Folkestone, not so pleasant, as snow had turned to fine rain and feet got soaked by slush. Collected the Pastel Society exhibition picture from John. To the library. To *happy hour* at Jake's Bar, John presiding, no one else there on my arrival. Bus to Seabrook and game of pool with Margot at the Fountain Inn.

Folkestone, Thurs, 24 April - Wrote a page then began doing Netia's[1] *Adscene* paper round for her, finishing 4 pm. At 6 pm I went to Jake's Bar *happy hour*, which was quite busy. I talked to a person who'd come from Norfolk to live in a Sandgate Undercliff house, who told me a tragic story about his five year old daughter having drowned in his swimming pool in Sandgate. At 7 pm John was relieved working behind the bar by Jo, the girl who lodges with him. I walked down to the harbour to buy and eat some chips. Phoned Colin and Harold and was invited to their Manor Road flat, where I went for a drink and chat til about 1 am.

Wed, 27 Aug - I seem to have lost heart with the book.[2] I've been dipping into one or two *how to write a novel* books in bookshops in the town and library, which hasn't encouraged me, as I can see I've made some of the most common mistakes, and have been going against much of the good advice given, especially in not producing a work of fictional art but instead

[1] Netia - Venetia Atkinson.
[2] *Vapour Trails in the Blue.*

indulging in some long winded confessional therapeutic thing. I seem to have ground to a halt with it, but I've got to carry on somehow, whether it's bad or not, as the thought of abandoning it just doesn't bear thinking about. At 5 pm this evening I drank some home brew, then went to Jake's Bar *happy hour*. I only had money for a couple of pints and felt fraught and uncomfortable with the other customers and Jo, John's erstwhile lodger behind the bar.

Wed, 3 Sept - I went down to The Warren this afternoon and wrote on the beach. To Jake's Bar *happy hour*. John was there. Had three pints, plus some tinned lager in my room before and afterwards. The whole world seems affected by the death of Diana. The news is still hard to believe.[3]

Sat, 6 Sept - Was awake before dawn, hearing the extra trains rumbling into the station taking people to the funeral. I dithered about whether to go myself, but I commenced writing and at 10.30 am I went to John's flat to watch the funeral on his lately acquired TV - a heart rendingly emotional event, with every moment of the services etherially beautiful . I walked afterwards through completely deserted streets and up the Leas. Wrote another page in my room, then in the evening, after a tin of lager, I went in search of Chris at the Salisbury hotel, but he wasn't there, so I moved to the Clifton hotel, and also visited the Executive Club. Got fairly drunk.

[3]   Diana, Princess of Wales, died on Sunday, the 31st of August.

Seabrook, Sat, 28 March - Hangover. With Margot and Steven both at work, I waited alone in the house for the arrival of Tom,[1] who delivered a Packard Bell computer (4 MB RAM), together with a mouse and a new keyboard, for which I paid him £120 in all. Walked to Folkestone (Alexanders fragrant along canal and Leas) to visit the library and try and take out a computer book, but found my ticket no longer valid, and I had no ID on me to rejoin. To Waterstones bookshop in the old Town Hall, but I resisted buying a new computer manual there. Met Etelle outside the shop. Had chips and a fish cake from Tontine Street chip shop, then walked back through town to Horn Street, where Steven had got my computer functioning and gave me a lesson. Got the computer and keyboard packed up ready to carry, then returned to Folkestone for a drink with John at his flat and one with him in the new *Kepples* bar in the basement of the Grand. We then had one in Nicola's restaurant bar. A midnight walk back to Margot's house.

Studley, Sun, 31 May - Typed and edited and continued getting accustomed to working on the computer.[2] An afternoon field walk, returning to prepare lunch. I did salad and boiled potatoes to go with some thinly sliced ham - the remainder of Lesley's boiled bacon from Wednesday. Phoned Roy and also John, who is sending a credit card I have acquired, using his address.

Sun, 7 June - This morning I spoke on the phone to First Direct, the bank I have just got an account with from John's address. Having given me a Visa card, I got them to transfer £600 of my outstanding Access card balance to them, as they have a 9.9% ARP six month introductory offer on credit taken on their card. With Kim and Meryl[3] visiting this weekend, I dismantled the computer and stored it in Dad's bedroom.

[1] Tom, computer expert friend of Margot's.
[2] The diarist had begun the first typed draft of his novel.
[3] Meryl, Kim's girlfriend, assistant stage manager.

Seabrook, Fri, 5 July - Used Margot's chainsaw to prune the top of the hedge in her garden. The palm tree from Clifton Mansions is flourishing.[4] A 3 pm walk to Folkestone to go to the bank, post office and John's flat at 5 pm, for some post and to have a drink together. A 7 pm return to Margot's house for some most delicious curry she's just cooked and had just had with her family. Drank lager,watched TV, washed up and talked. Felt weary at 1 am, when we finally said goodnight.

Sat, 6 July - Slept until 10 am, getting up to find no one else in the house. Have just spent the morning writing up this journal on Margot's kitchen table. Have a slight sore throat. A walk to Folkestone library (finding a huge dragonfly on the pavement at Sandgate and taking it to a green place) to rejoin. Called on Venetia, who was in and who gave me some cake and scrambled egg on toast. For years she's been trying to pass her driving test and I took her for a lesson, going round the block in the car she has at the moment. It was raining steadily. To Jake's Bar for a *happy hour* pint, then to Nicola's restaurant bar, to meet John for a drink. Walked back to Seabrook, against the wind and an unseasonal driving rain. Margot was there, having just returned from a Le Touquet courier trip. She didn't stay up for long, so neither did I.

In August the diarist decided to give up writing his journal, but then continued it in a very brief form.

Seabrook, Sat, 3 Oct - To Hythe with Margot, Jacky and Cameron.[5] Saw John and Venetia in Folkestone. Dinner with Margot and her family.

---

[4] Diarist had transplanted the palm tree.
[5] Cameron, Margot's grandson.

Seabrook, Sun, 10 Jan - Walk to Folkestone to visit Venetia and John. Roast chicken dinner with Margot.

Welford on Avon,Wed, 24 March - Departed 11 am for bus to Stratford. Coach to London and train to Folkestone. Saw John, Venetia and Margot. 9 pm trains to Gatwick via Tonbridge.

Welford on Avon, Mon, 9 Aug - Was given a lift by caravan[1]neighbour, Dave, to Stratford. Coach to London, train to Folkestone. Saw John. Bus to Seabrook, steak dinner with Margot and her family.

Folkestone, Wed, 8 Sept - A day trip to Boulogne with John and Colin Williams. We went there and back on the Seacat.[2] Hot day. In Boulogne we visited the antiques shop of a lady called Michelle, whom Colin knew.

---

[1] The diarist had started renting a caravan in Welford on Avon.
[2] Seacat catamaran ferry service between Folkestone and Boulogne.

Folkestone , Sun, 16 April - Slept 6 am to 9 am at Gatwick.[1] Trains to Canterbury, going there by mistake. Bus to Folkestone. Tea at Morelli's café on the Leas. At 5 pm I visited John, for my post, and Venetia. Lager at Salisbury hotel then 9 pm to Colin and Harold's flat, where they put me up. President Mugabe seizing white farmers' land in Zimbabwe.

Seabrook, Sun 28 May - 12.30 pm walk to Folkestone, where I visited Venetia then John. Went with John on bus to Canterbury, where we had a pizza and went to a Weatherspoons pub. To Salisbury hotel back in Folkestone, where I found Chris. Slept at Venetia's house on her bed-settee, a young couple nattering all night next door.

Seabrook, Fri, 8 Sept - Walked to Folkestone and had a drink at the Park Inn, thinking Paul might come in, but he didn't. To the library, then to Tontine Street for chips and the harbour for whelks, a lunch eaten on the East Cliff Sands. To John's flat for post and a drink with him. Jake's Bar has just closed down. Went to the bar at the Windsor hotel, a new gay bar? Walk to Seabrook, pint Britannia Inn, Horn Street.

[1] On airport seating.

171

Seabrook, Sat, 6 Jan - Margot cooked me a fried breakfast. A walk to Folkestone, went to the Park Inn (Paul not there),[1] the library (to fill in a credit card application form), and John's flat (for mail). Visited Venetia. Return to Seabrook for a meal and quiet telly evening with Margot.

Nerja, Mon, 11 June - Spent an hour on the book, then to Nerja, where we cleaned two sofas in the Fuentes de Nerja apartments, c/Malaga. To El Zoco PO Box, where I found some UK stamps had arrived, which I asked John to send. Chicken curry for me, chicken in wine sauce Roy.

Fri, 29 June - Worked on the book in the morning. Did some printing in the afternoon. Roy cooked a beef dish - planchared and flambéed filets in a cream sauce. John away until the 10th of July.[2]

Seabrook, Sat, 11 Aug - Did some gardening for Margot, then I got a lift from Jacky to Folkestone, where I visited John for some post, including a First Direct bank credit card. With John to Paul's restaurant for lunch - skate wings in cream and vermouth sauce me, breast of pheasant John. We had a good Burgundy wine. Seventy eight quid bill. To the Brevet Club afterwards and the new *Angels* bar, then we visited Venetia, who has some foreign language school children staying with her, including a delightful Russian girl. Walked back to Margot's house for some supper.

[1] Paul Crofts was a regular customer at the Park Inn.
[2] As diarist had previously noted.

Welford on Avon, Sun, 13 Jan - Got up early to pack flight bag and take a bus to Stratford, where I went to the library to look at a Sunday paper, and to Somerfield's supermarket to buy some cheese. I then got the 12.30 pm coach to London. Bought a girlie mag in the Victoria arcade porn shop. Got 5 pm coach to Folkestone where I visited John for some mail, then I walked to Margot's house, arriving 10 pm for a chat with her and bite to eat and early to bed.

Thurs, 6 June - Got the 11.29 am bus to Stratford and 12.30 pm coach to London. Walked from Victoria coach station via The Mall to Charing Cross. Folkestone 7 pm. Visited John at his flat then walked to Seabrook, where I had three pints at the Fountain Inn. Saw Margot at 11 pm, after she'd finished putting granddaughter, Katelyn, to bed. Gave Margot the manuscript to read.

Seabrook, Tues, 30 July - Margot was looking after her grandson, Cameron, and I did some gardening for her. Cameron and I cooked some bacon and eggs. Had a dip in Margot's inflatable children's pool. 5.30 pm walk to Folkestone, where I visited John and we went for pints at the Burlington and Clifton hotels. A pint at the Ship Inn, Sandgate, on the way back to Horn Street.

Wed, 1 Aug - Margot was doing an En Route[1] courier trip to Ostend and I got a lift on her 8 am coach to Dover, where I got another International Driving License from the AA. Walked in drizzling rain to the town centre for a bus back to Folkestone. Visited Tom Green re a large filling that fell out yesterday. To John's flat then with him by train to Rye, where we had pints at the Mermaid and George hotels and the Standard and Ypres pubs, then fish and chips in a café near the Standard.

---

[1] Hythe Travel Company.

Folkestone, Sat, 17 Aug - Made a prop for Netia's half blown down lilac tree. Called on John at Kingsnorth Gardens then on Colin and Harold at their Manor Road flat, where I ended up buying a flight ticket to Malaga on Colin's internet computer, for £65. Met John again for a couple of pints at the Clifton hotel, then I went for a walk along to the Warren beach. Talked to two young French girls sunbathing topless there. I met John again outside the Clifton hotel to watch the carnival procession, then we both came back to Netia's basement for a beer and a little barbecue in her garden. Some fireworks were going off in Radnor Park and Venetia came down to watch them with Chantelle and a friend of hers (both aged about ten, the same age as tragic Holly and Jessica, just found murdered in Cambridgeshire).

Seabrook, Wed, 8 Jan - Did gardening for Margot, then walked to Folkestone, where I saw John and then had a pint at the Park Inn. Cold day, early return to Horn Street to see Margot's grand children and have a meal.

Folkestone, Tues, 5 Aug - With John on a £1 *Daily Mail* offer day trip to Calais. I stood lunch at the restaurant Saint Malo - moules marinière & fish baked in foil me, herring salad & steak John. Eighty two euros plus tip. Both drunk. Sunny excellent day.

Tues, 11 Aug - Another £1 trip to Calais with John. This time we settled for wine, cheese, paté and bread picnics in the parks. Hot, but not unbearably so. A pint at the Priory hotel, Dover station, before catching the 10.03 pm train to Folkestone.

Seabrook, Thurs, 15 Jan - Porridge and a fried breakfast. Did gardening for Margot then walked with her to the Sandgate hotel and the Clarendon Inn for drinks. Visited John in Folkestone and drank some rum at his flat. Walked back in head-on rain to Horn Street for a shower, TV and ham sandwiches with Margot.

Fri, 16 Jan - A walk to Folkestone for a lunch of a bag of chips and a dish of mixed seafood, eaten on the East Cliff sands promenade. With John to the library, to help him get an email address. To a birthday party for Margot's son, Steven, at his Castle Hill Avenue flat. We played *Trivial Pursuits*, I felt tired, got a taxi back to Horn Street with Margot.

Folkestone, Sun, 19 Sept - With John on a £1 *Daily Mail* day trip to Calais. Sunny day. I stood us lunch at La Kabylie French/ Moroccan restaurant. We had a walk to the beach for a drink. I think I saw a seal on the way over to France.

Mon, 20 Sept - Weetabix and milk for breakfast. Spent an hour on a library computer. Chips and a dish of mixed seafood for lunch. Walked to Capel to visit caravan sites there.[1] Later I went to John's flat and I walked to Horn Street, but Margot wasn't there. Iraq is becoming chaotic, with suicide bombings and kidnapping of USA/UK hostages.

[1] Diarist was considering moving his caravan from Welford on Avon.

Welford on Avon, Wed, 12 Jan - A 5.30 am walk to Stratford, for National Express coaches to Folkestone (£9 each way Jan offer), arriving 2.15 pm. To the library to check discs again, which now seem OK on MS Word.[1] A glass of wine with John at his flat then a walk to Margot's house, to let myself in, shower, then go and wait for her (returning from a courier trip) at the Fountain Inn.

La Herradura, Tues, 22 Feb - To Nerja with Roy, posting some *Daily Mail* Free USA flight offer coupons to John for him to repost, as flight applicants are supposed to live in the UK. While I walked to the post office Roy went to a Torrox nursery and we met in a café by Nerja Medina urbanisation.

Seabrook, 27 April - Worked on Margot's computer, spell checking and printing. Fixed her sticky bathroom door, plus an outside wooden door. Had a sunny walk to Folkestone and went to John's flat, with some White Lightening strong cider, which I drank with him. A great walk back to Seabrook at 9.30 pm – Alexander scented evening, legs feeling weightless, going top speed.

'Little Switzerland' Camp Site, Folkestone, Thurs, 18 Aug - A Weetabix & milk breakfast. Got £2 *Day Ticket* buses to Folkestone and Seabrook. Had a problem printing two pages per sheet on Margot's computer. Returned to Folkestone where I bumped into John on the Leas and together we went to the Channel Business Centre, Ingles Court, where I got the MS printed from my floppy discs, though on one side only. Drank lager at John's flat, had a pint at the Britannia pub, Horn Street after getting off the bus. Michelle[2]cooked some fish. Slept on Margo's sofa.

Sun 21 Aug - A walk, via the Burstin-Grand hotel (for free *Independent* newspaper), to Horn Street, where I repaired Margot's wobbly kitchen table for her. 3 pm return to

---

[1] Diarist had changed his word processing software from WordPerfect to MS Word.
[2] Michelle, fiancée to Margot's son, Steven.

Folkestone, buying some cans of beer and having another drink with John at his flat. To the Clifton hotel afterwards for a drink with Chris and his old friend, Geoff Cannon. Ate chips and a cod roe while walking back to the camp site, via the East Cliff.

La Herradura, Sat, 14 Jan - Phoned John, also Egg and First Direct, re my internet credit cards. Cooked fried breakfasts, did domestic/gardening chores. Drank beer in the Rock Room.[1] Felt restless in bed, got up again and drank some brandy.

'Little Switzerland' Camp Site, Folkestone, Sat, 15 July - At lunchtime I went to John's flat, taking a three litre bottle of Frosty Jack cider, which I mostly drank, while he mixed it with some Strongbow cider. To the Warren afterwards, for a swim and shower.[2] Dusk return to tent, having to move with sleeping bag a little distance from it, due to a neighbouring heavy snorer.

Mon, 17 July - A morning visit to John's flat. To Lidl's supermarket. Had a lunchtime sardine and bread snack, sitting in Kingsnorth Gardens. Did daily editing stint at campsite,[3] splendid weather continuing. To Margot's house in the evening, had a pleasant walk back to the tent at dusk.

Thurs, 20 July - With John on a £4.50 *Go Anywhere* bus ticket to Rye, where we had a snack in a café and went to the Mermaid Inn for a pint. We had a pint in Hythe, at the Swan hotel, on the way back (now run by Nepalese).

Folkestone, Tues, 1 Aug - To the library to type and print some details for the NatWest bank, with whom I made an application to open a business account.[4] Got some Visa card cash, did Lidl supermarket shopping, drank cider with John at his flat. Bicycled to Margot's house in the evening, but she had just returned from a courier trip and was tired and fraught.

Thurs, 3 Aug - To a library computer, buying a Ryanair Stansted to Granada flight, for £40. To Lidl's supermarket for wine. In the evening John visited[5]and I fried some filets of steak that Netia had in her freezer. Arthur Lee[6]died today, 61.

---

[1] Extension to rented house, built by diarist.
[2] Under a spring water outlet on the beach.
[3] Diarist was working on *Vapour Trails in the Blue*.
[4] The diarist had started his publishing company, Cefas Productions Ltd.
[5] Diarist was in Netia's basement flat.
[6] Authur Lee, songwriter & lead singer with Love.

Syd Barrett[7]died recently, similar age.

Sun, 6 Aug - Walked to the hotel Burstin for a *Sunday Independent*.[8] To the Cheri-Stones café,[9] Cheriton, for some currant cakes, but it now closes on Sundays. To the Co-op supermarket, Cheriton. John visited in the evening and I made a stew with some freezer stewing steak and we drank a three litre bottle of cider each.

Wed, 9 Aug - Made departure preparations. Had a mid morning lemonade at the Park Inn, Paul there. and made a brief visit to John at his flat. Walked to the harbour and Tontine Street, had bag of chips lunch. Delivered Netia's newspapers. Had an evening Leas/Sandgate walk.

---

[7] Syd Barrett, songwriter, co-founder of Pink Floyd.
[8] Free copies of the *Sunday Independent* were currently being distributed.
[9] Long-standing café & bakery, run by Italian couple.

Folkestone, Sun, 7 Jan – A Sandgate toilets wash & shave.[1]Weetabix & milk breakfast. Visited Etelle at her Harbour Way home. With John to the Cat and Custard Pot pub, Paddlesworth. Drove to Harpenden, where I rang Pat and visited her in her new home at Fairfield Park, Bedfordshire. A midnight arrival at Stratford.[2]

La Herradura, Sat 24 Feb - Phoned John re a phone call about swimming pools from *Shaving Mug* Peter.[3] Walk to Zen II Net[4] to download some free software. Tinned herring lunch, in the evening wood stove oven cooked tortillas, pizza and a fried, home-filled Chinese spring roll.

Seabrook, Thurs, 26 July - A 9.30 am return to Folkestone, with a computer hour at Sandgate library. Stabilized the rickety wooden steps up to the loft[5]with some bricks and breeze blocks. A drink in the house with Chris and Venetia, John there too, having taken to making regular visits to Netia.

Sun, 29 July - Had a shit at the railway station toilets. To the library and the Burstin hotel, to read the Sunday papers. 5 pm to John's flat with two large bottles of cider, which we drank. A dusk walk to Sandgate, with a drink on the way at the Irish run Hamlet hotel, Shakespeare terrace.

Wed, 1 Aug - A Calais day trip with John was cancelled, due to a stomach upset of his. Instead, I had a long bike ride to Aylesham, Bekesbourne, Littlebourne, Wingham and Preston. Made strawberry picking enquiries. A sunny happy day, drank cider on return.

Thurs, 2 Aug - Had a sun/cycling/cider induced headache. Did loft tidying, walked to Wickes, Cheriton, for a tube of glue to fix a plastic jerry/water can found on ride yesterday. Saw Chris and Netia in the house this evening, John also visiting

---

[1]   After sleeping in rented car.
[2]   Stratford-upon-Avon, to return rented car.
[3]   Peter Simmons collected shaving mugs.
[4]   Internet shop, Almuñecar.
[5]   Upper floor of Venetia's outhouse, which the diarist was to buy in 2013.

Sun 5 Aug - 30° heat. Read newspapers at the Burstin hotel and library. Bought cider at Lidl and later some Morrisons roasted bits of chicken and pork, with which I went to John's flat at 5pm to share this fare with him. Dust walk on Leas and to Sandgate.

Thurs, 16 Aug - A 4 am bicycle ride,[6]wet clothes drying on the way.[7] The strawberries are grown under plastic - boo! No rain problem, though, and the weather is cool, so it's not hot either. An evening drink in the house with Chris, Venetia and John.

Seabrook, Sun, 19 Aug - Ate cornflakes, did gardening, cooked fried breakfasts, then had a promenade bicycle ride to Folkestone library. Four books[8]are on sale with Amazon - should I buy them back? To John's flat in the afternoon with some cider and a chip shop meal for him. I had some harbour stall dressed crab.   .

---

[6] To Mansfields Farm, Shatterling, for strawberry picking work.
[7] From previous day.
[8] Hardback first edition of Vapour Trails in the Blue.

Folkestone, Fri 1 Aug - Finished carpet laying.[1] Visited John, Morrison's supermarket and Margot's house. Returned with Margot for a barbecue in Netia's garden. Flo[2]and her son, Reme, Gorcam,[3] Chris and John were also there.

Sun, 3 Aug - An 8 am walk to the Burstin hotel for a free *Independent on Sunday* newspaper. To Morrison's, to Margot's, then with her and Steven and Michelle and their son, Thomas, to Jacky and Tony's[4] Golden Valley house, for Sunday lunch, with them and their children, Cameron and Katelyn. Drank cider with John at his flat.

Sun, 10 Aug - To the Burstin hotel before breakfast, for a free *Independent* newspaper. Finished garden pruning for Netia and fitting a garden gate for Margot, who cooked a steak meal. To John's later, to drink cider. Phoned Roy - Guapa[5]has died.

Sun, 17 Aug - A 9 am walk to the hotel Burstin, for an *Independent* newspaper. Phoned Margot, who more or less accused me of abusing her hospitality.[6] To Morrison's supermarket. To John's flat to drink cider with him.

Sun, 24 Aug - A ten hour sleep on my day off.[7] To the Burstin for a newspaper. Did Netia's paper round, to Morrison's, phoned Margot, still sounding frosty. Drank home-brew with John at his flat.

Sun, 7 Sept - To the Burstin for an *Independent*. Did Netia's paper round, had a toast & marmalade and custard cream biscuit breakfast. Returned Steven's bicycle to Margot's house, didn't see her. Drank home-brew with John at his flat.

---

[1] Diarist had been laying a stair carpet for Venetia.
[2] Florence, Venetia Atkinson's daughter.
[3] Gorcam, young language student lodging with Venetia.
[4] Jacky and Tony, Margot Johnson's daughter and son-in-law.
[5] *Guapa*, adopted street cat in Nerja.
[6] After a tiff on the diarist's previous visit.
[7] Diarist was strawberry picking at Middle Pett Farm, near Bridge.

Mon, 8 Sept - Finished Netia's paper round in the Radnor Park/ Cornwallis Avenue area. Went into town to the Vodafone shop, bank and library. Chips & dish mixed seafood lunch, eaten by East Cliff sands, then I had a swim and Warren spring water shower. Drank more home brew with John.

La Herradura, Sun, 14 Sept - Had a sound sleep. Am working on a leaflet for John and myself to provide a *post-your-mail-in-England* service for expats in Spain. I have put an ad in *Sur in English* newspaper. Drank beer, including one at the Alcazar hotel. Was drunk and late for dinner.

Sat, 4 Oct - Phoned John, who sounded glad to take over from Coastal Office Support,[8] receiving my mail again and providing the registered address for Cefas Productions Ltd. Pizza snack, drank beer in the Rock Room, walk to Alcazar hotel for a drink.

Sun, 5 Oct - Wrote to John about his take over from Coastal Office Support, which he's doing on the same terms. A walk to a Royal Mini-Arcade[9] computer. Roy cooked a meat pie[10]& veg dinner. Drank brandy and coke, plus a glass of wine.

Mon, 6 Oct - Posted the letter to John. Am feeling like an office managerial worker - where's the book in all this?

[8] Accommodation address providers.
[9] Almuñecar seafront amusement arcade which also had computers.
[10] From *Jim's Pie Shop*, Nerja.

Alcester, Wed, 7 Jan - An 8 am Sandgate toilets wash, where I had a contretemps with a cleaner, she saying *homeless people* aren't allowed here, etc. Walked into town, called on Venetia, saw Paul outside the Park Inn pub. With John to the Black Horse pub, Monks Horton.[1] Drove to Alcester, via Morton-in-the-Marsh and Chipping Camden, where I had a walk. Slept in the car near the public common.

Studley, Sun 29 March - An 8.30 am walk, via Green Lane, to the boot fair,[2] but it wasn't on. Walked on to B&Q, Redditch, to look at spades. Train and Megabus to Victoria. Sunny, fluffy white cloud weather, had a walk in Piccadilly and a daffodil strewn Green Park. National Express coach to Folkestone, arriving at John's flat at 9.30 pm, for a welcoming pint of cider.

Folkestone, Mon, 30 March - Slept OK, porridge with powdered milk breakfast. Phoned and visited Margot for coffee and chat. Met John on the Leas for a pint at Kepples bar, me with a lapel daffodil. I went to Morrison's for cider and a roast pork snack, shared back at John's flat. A dusk walk on the Leas and to Sandgate and back on the promenade to Folkestone harbour.

Studley, Sun, 2 Aug – Better weather, had a more relaxing day.[3] Completed the grass sawing.[4] Phoned Kim and John Heal. Venetia yesterday. Had a tinned meat ball and mushy peas *Sunday dinner.*

Northampton, Thurs, 6 Aug - Had a sound sleep.[5] Walked back into the city, phoned Roy, who is delivering my books[6]to the Bookworld España's Torre del Mar branch. Had a shave at the railway station, met Kim, who took me to an Indian restaurant, then I saw him play Douglas in Ayckbourn's *Men of the Moment* at the Royal Theatre. Train to Folkestone (£48). We

---

[1] Now run by Nicola, formerly of Nicola's restaurant, Folkestone.
[2] After sleeping at the allotment.
[3] Diarist had been at his allotment since Wednesday.
[4] Diarist had been cutting the overgrown allotment plot with a hand saw.
[5] In a tent near Barnes Meadow.
[6] From the paperback edition of *Vapour Trails in the Blue.*

weather, dry in Folkestone. Arrived John's flat 10.45 pm, was welcomed with some cider.

Folkestone, Fri, 7 Aug - Porridge breakfast. Called on Venetia (out), had an 11.15 am pint with Paul at the Park Inn. Walked to Little Switzerland camp site (full over the weekend). Called on Venetia again, her basement is occupied, but it's OK to use her outhouse. Had a swim below the Leas Cliff Hall. 8pm to John's flat with cider and peanuts.

Sun, 9 Aug - To the hotel Bustin for a free *Independent*. Had breakfast back at the outhouse (uncooked porridge and powdered milk and jam sandwiches). To the Leas Cliff Hall toilets, did Morrison's shopping and outhouse sweeping, had a swim. To John's flat at 6pm with cider and peanuts. Sunny weather, no rain here yet.[7]

Wed, 12 Aug - To the library, bought a Stansted - Granada flight on the 27th of August, for £38. Had a Warren swim and spring water shower. In the evening I went to John's flat with cider and peanuts.

Sun, 16 Aug - At 7.30 am I read the *Independent* at the Burstin, before going to Etelle's Harbour Way home for breakfast. To the library and to Wickes at Cheriton. A swim with Venetia, To John's flat with cider and peanuts, I also drank some home brew from last year and went for an after dark Leas and Sandgate walk, grass hoppers chirping.

Tues, 18 Aug - With John on a £5 *Rover* bus tickets to Margate, to visit Colin and Harold, now living at Dickens Court, Cliftonville. We had a sunny walk there past Margate beach. Colin took us to see their caravan near Deal, then we got buses to Dover and Canterbury, where we had drinks in the Parrot Inn and City Arms. We finished the home-brew back at John's flat.

---

[7] There had been wet weather while the diarist had been in Studley.

La Herradura, 27 Nov - Some dire news (yesterday) from John. I have received a £500 late payment fine, and a £3000 estimated tax bill, from the Inland Revenue. They must have been trying to contact me via the old Southampton registered address - fucking hell!

Wed, 2 Dec - Did after sales trip paperwork,[8] while Roy went to Velez Malaga for the leaking car radiator repair. Tax bill arrived from John.

---

[8] Diarist had been selling copies of his novel in Gibraltar.

Leigh on Sea, Mon, 4 Jan - Had walks into the town and to London Road, ordering an *Almera* maintenance manual.[1] Roast beef sandwich lunch, left house 3 pm, collected manual 4.30 pm, called at the house again to say goodbye to Kim, who'd made himself scarce earlier.[2] To Folkestone, arriving John's flat 8 pm.

Folkestone, Tues, 5 Jan - A walk into the town. Had a drive with John to book distributors, Aldington Books Ltd., then we had a couple of pints at the Farrier's Arms, Mersham. Drank home-brew back at John's flat, me having a break with a dusk Leas/Sandgate walk.

La Herradura, Sat 16 Jan - A walk to the village bakery for bread. Phoned John. Am printing pages, sticking them in and cutting the wrong ones out of about 20 books - desperate measures![3] The printer began playing up this evening - got very fraught and irritable.

Mon, 18 Jan - Was covering stickers[4]with sellotape, ready to cut out and stick on when John rang - bailiffs threatening to seize his goods, if Cefas tax bill not paid by Monday. Downloaded a postal tax return form.

Wed, 20 Jan - Phoned John to get an online tax return filing Activation Code posted to me. Walked to Zen II Net, but *system unavailable* was on the Revenue & Customs website - same problem back at village cyber shop.

Wed, 27 Jan - Phoned Brighton Revenue & Customs - my first tax return was received, but is not yet dealt with. I also phoned Kent Debt Management,[5] Maidstone, for John.

---

[1] For Nissan *Almera* in Spain.
[2] After a row on Sunday.
[3] To correct defective paperback copies of *Vapour Trails in the Blue*.
[4]   Diarist was sellotaping *...a rollicking tale of expat life in Spain* label on the front covers of the paperbacks.
[5] For John.

Wed, 10 Feb - We had a cheerful, boozy lunch at Jackie's[6]house. Little Hugh,[7] from Bristol, and Pam[8] the other guests. Wet day, drank beer back at house. John phoned - tax return accepted, penalty assessment discounted. Felt buoyant.

Thurs, 11 Feb - Had twelve hour's sleep. Phoned John, Nerja International Club, *Euro Weekly News* and *Ladies Primera* magazine - publicity campaign stalled again. Daily bookbinding and Lidl guillotine repair.[9]

Fri, 26 Feb - We cleaned two flood damaged sofas in urb. Capistrano, Nerja, treating mould patches with bleach solution. John phoned - the £200 late tax return filing penalty has been levied after all. Made an online application for a post office credit card, with a 0% balance transfer offer.

Sat, 13 March - Slept off hangover. Phoned John and Hugh. Finished monthly financial admin and credit card payments. Walked to the bakery. Did photocopying, guillotining and collating. Wood stove oven cooked pizza, drank fruit juice.

Sat, 20 March - Glued front cover labels.[10] Phoned John. Did some page clamping. Walked to the bakery, then began drinking beer while reheating some pasta. Continued drinking beer all day. We cooked pizzas in the wood stove oven. A 10 pm walk to the feria[11] and to the end of the beach.

Studley, Mon, 12 July - Made an 8 am departure for a walk via The Slough to Redditch, in a pleasant rain drizzle.[12] Train to Birmingham, 1.55 pm Megabus to Victoria. A walk to the Hotel InterContinental cloakrooms. Got National Express coach to Folkestone, had a welcoming pint of cider from John, who put me up.

---

[6] Jackie Claybourne, Nerja and Wivenhoe resident.
[7] Hugh Tulloch, retired university history lecturer.
[8] Pam Dan, Wivenhoe artist.
[9] Diarist had bought a plastic paper guillotine from Lidl supermarket, which had cracked with use.
[10] Diarist was now gluing the front cover labels instead of sellotaping them.
[11] Annual fair in La Herradura.
[12] From the allotment.

Tues, 13 July - Visited Venetia, at home with her granddaughters, Charlotte and Chantelle. Got installed in her outhouse. To Morrison's. To John's flat in the evening and he stood me a birthday meal, which I got from Mario's fish and chip shop, Blackbull Road. Had a late walk on Leas, seeing Bastille Day fireworks going off in France.

Thurs, 15 July - To John's flat at 11.30 am and we walked to the Grand, where we had three pints of *London Pride* each, at Kepples (John had a meal). We then went to the Burlington hotel upstairs bar, where I left him. Removed some plaster.[13] Had a Warren swim and shower. Went back to John's flat in the evening to drink cider.

Fri, 16 July - 11.30 am to John's flat. We were going to walk to Sandgate, but John was lacking energy, so we just walked on the Leas and I helped him with his Sainsbury's shopping. Removed more plaster, had a Warren swim/shower. Saw Chris in the evening at Netia's house.

Sun, 18 July - Walk to the Burstin - no free *Independent* newspaper. Saw Netia, went with her and Tamsin in Netia's car to Flo's house near Botolph's Bridge. We had a sunny garden lunch with her and her young son, Remy, then we all went in Flo's car to the Rare Breeds Centre, Woodchurch. Perfect sunny day, beautiful countryside, visited St Rumwold's church, Bonnington, on the way back. Netia and I visited Brian and Jenny's[14] house and Jenny showed us around their lovely garden. Netia cooked a minced lamb meal back at her house. To John's flat with some home-brew.

Mon, 19 July - Had Radnor Park public toilet shit. To Cheriton library, buying a Megabus ticket. Went into town, met Charles Sturgis, sold him a book for £2. John also bought one for £2. Netia gave me £5. Saw her in the evening before going to John's flat to drink home brew. Had a Warren swim & shower earlier.

---

[13] From the outhouse ceiling.
[14] Brian and Jenny Oxley.

La Herradura, Thurs, 22 July - Slept OK in the Rock Room.[15] Had a walk to collect books from closing down Delphin book shop, was paid for one. Unpacked. I have suggested we just eat cold food at present - hence no cooking or washing up. John phoned - the *Daily Mail* has returned my book, which does probably prove that they all got delivered.[16] Feel upbeat again about the book's prospects.

Sat, 28 Aug - Phoned John, who has asked to advertise on my website.[17] Perhaps I'll forget the beach leafleting, (few Brit readers here anyway)[18]and I'll update my website and perhaps help John. Bought a Ryanair flight for 15 September (€49). Drank beer, heat wave on, was fractious with Roy.

Mon, 30 Aug - To village library computer. I need to update my website and possibly create one for John. Have spoken to Estepona teacher/writer, Peter Brookes, on the phone. He has borrowed a copy of the novel from the Glitterati book shop.[19]

Studley, Mon, 20 Sept - Made an 8.15 am departure[20] for walk to Redditch. Bought £1.15 stamps for books postage. Train to Birmingham, 1.55 pm Megabus to Victoria. Walk to Hotel InterContinental toilets, sunny, sultry evening. 7 pm National Express to Folkestone, John's flat 9.45 pm, for a welcome pint of cider.

Tues, 21 Sept - Slept and breakfasted at John's flat. Found Netia out, went into the town for a padlock. Was able to enter her outhouse to dump bag, but then I found Venetia in - am able to stay in her basement. To John's flat in the evening with some home-brew, followed by a full moon evening walk to Sandgate, with the sound of crickets on the steps up to the Leas. John is going to post books to Gardeners[21]as required.

---

[15] Cooler than diarist's bedroom.
[16] Diarist had posted twenty review copies of his novel's paperback edition, but afterwards wasn't sure he'd put the correct postage on them.
[17] www.vapourtrailsintheblue.com
[18] Diarist had been walking the beaches, handing out leaflets about *Vapour Trails in the Blue* to any book readers he saw.
[19] Glitterati Book Shop, Estepona.
[20] From allotment shed.
[21] Gardeners book wholesalers & distributors.

Thurs, 23 Sept - Made a start removing the wooden ceiling lathes from Netia's outhouse - very dusty work. To John's flat at 7 pm. He and I had a dinner invitation from retired charter surveyor, Peter Simmons and his girlfriend, Emma. We went to his flat (containing his collection of shaving mugs) and Peter took us all to Pinocchio's Italian restaurant, Canterbury.

Sat, 25 Sept - Went early to the Clifton hotel and met the Kristall TEFL course[22]director, Brian Almond, who agreed to let me do the course for a £180 discount price. Got cash from Barclaycard and began the course with six others. To John's flat in the evening with some home-brew (left over from last time).

Wed, 28 Sept - Got the bulk of the lathes down in the outhouse. To John's in the evening with some home-brew, very immature, not even quite brewed, in fact.

Sat, 2 Oct - To the library to note Waterstones branch telephone numbers, then to John's flat in the afternoon (with some home-brew). We began telephoning (free for John on Saturdays) the branches, ordering a copy[23]and giving a false name and address. Don't feel guilty – could benefit myself and Waterstones. Dusk Leas & Sandgate walk, more home-brew in basement.

Tues 5 Oct - Collated Netia's paper round leaflets and delivered half of them today, between her road and Victoria Grove. Drank home-brew at John's flat. Had a Leas/Sandgate walk as far as the Vasa Bar – formerly Miles Haven – before bed.

Thurs, 7 Oct - Finished Netia's papers. To a library computer, met Paul Harris[24]there, now editing local arts mag, *Folkestone Creative*. To John's with home-brew, phoned one or two Waterstones branches as myself, and they seemed happy to order copies. Had evening walk - wandered into the Leas Cliff

[22] A two day language teaching course the diarist had seen advertised in the *Folkestone Herald*.
[23] Of *Vapour Trails in the Blue*.
[24] Paul Harris, local history author, friend of Douglas Richmond.

Hall and found myself at a Herman's Hermits concert (with original drummer), listening to *Mrs Brown You've Got A Lovely Daughter.*

La Herradura, Wed, 3 Nov - Packaged a dozen more books to take to John's. To the internet shop for National Express tickets. Roy cooked some pasta, drank wine and quite a lot of beer, felt pretty joyless.

Stansted Airport, Sun, 7 Nov - Got a 6 am bus to Victoria coach station, where I was still making notes about the stories.[25] John's flat 1.45 pm, to the Quarterhouse Arts Centre at 4.30pm for a hurried judging farce with co judges, Gloria and Sarah, notes useless, none of my choices won anything, my speech too long, quips fell flat. Leas walk before Malaga airport gin at John's.

Mon, 8 Nov - Slept John's. Went into town, raw weather, shoes leaking. Bag of nuts and raisins lunch. Got more Waterstones telephone numbers from the library. At 6.15 pm I saw Steven Berkoff give a talk on his East End upbringing at the Quarterhouse, having been given a complimentary ticket. Drank gin before and afterwards with John.

La Herradura, Sat, 13 Nov - Phoned John. Did a Spanish version of my delivery invoice.[26] Walked to village supermarket, barbecued some sausages for hot dogs in the evening, drank brandy & coke and beer.

Tues, 30 Nov - Got a couple of more Waterstones orders - thirty books total now. There's no point in getting any more, as John needs a few in reserve for any reorders. Roy did a Chinese pork dish in the wok.

Sat, 4 Dec - Phoned John. There's nothing in the *Herald.* Have got a £100 fruit picking tax refund. Drank a pint, walked to the computer shop, then went up the river bed track to the hostal Verdiales, where I had a brandy. Continued drinking pints of

[25] Diarist had been asked to judge a children's writing competition in the Folkestone Book Festival.
[26] For sales to Spanish book shops.

beer back at the house, ranting about needing a change and going to live in Morocco, which will never happen, now the book has flopped. To bed 7 pm.

Mon, 6 Dec - A public holiday. John says Gardeners have sent a cheque for the first few books, meaning that they weren't on sale or return. If this is right then I've now sold over fifty, rather than just the nineteen in Spain. Got three more Waterstones orders, the last for the time being.

Sat, 11 Dec - Sent Mr Gage's book.[27] Phoned John, did financial admin. Had an evening walk to the Cyberphone internet shop - have incurred a £12 credit card late payment fee. I just didn't get the important break I needed with the book - the prominent review or help from some influential individual in the literary world.

Thurs, 16 Dec - Saw Pili Medina[28]at the school[29] during their 10.15 break. No more volunteers needed still. To a Herradura library computer, am still concerned with rectifying the bank account balance[30] and paying monthly credit cards online. Phoned John with a further unexpected Waterstones book order. A beer at the Sacrista bar?

Sun, 19 Dec - John says the *Herald* has done a paragraph on the book. Harsh UK weather. Did diary typing/editing.[31] Chicken cacciatore dinner, drank beer before and after.

---

[27] An order made on the novel's *www.vapourtrailsintheblue.com* website.
[28] Pili Medina, teacher, Sierra Almijara school, Nerja.
[29] Diarist was responding to an advertisement seeking volunteers to teach English on Adult Education courses at the school.
[30] After having an unauthorised overdraft.
[31] Of *Persistence! How I published a Great Novel from My Allotment Sherd - Diaries 1995 – 2010*.

Folkestone, Fri, 7 Jan - A shave in Sandgate toilets.[1] To a Sandgate library computer. To John's flat at noon and we drank home brew. To the *Folkestone Herald* office, to Waterstones (book still on shelf), visited Venetia (omelet snack), saw Chris. An evening Leas/Sandgate walk, drank more home brew with John.

Sat, 9 Jan - Stayed at John's. We were going to see Colin and Harold, but they are away. Phoned Margot and walked to her house for coffee. Lit her coal fire and cooked sardines on toast for two - friends again. Walked about Folkestone, finished home-brew with John.

La Herradura, Sun, 16 Jan - To Almuñécar boot fair with Roy. I walked back, did roof waterproofing. A roast chicken dinner, me complaining of oven/cooking oil fumes. John has had a benefit fraud inspector visiting him, the result of someone - probably V Crofts - telling them I have been staying there, and I have to sever all postal & accommodation address connections, and will now have no UK address.

Tues, 18 Jan - I phoned and wrote to the National Insurance Contributions Office, Newcastle, and got my voluntary contributions address changed from John's flat to the El Zoco de Nerja PO Box. Tunisian revolution sees president ousted - looks like a move towards democracy.

Wed, 19 Jan - Got two credit cards changed from John's flat to El Zoco. Cut and dyed hair. Drank beer, have gone back to drinking on Wed, Sat and Sun only. Am reading a boot fair purchase - the nightmarish *Rogue Trader*, by Nick Leeson. A daily walk to the cyber shop. The free library computers are down.

---

[1] After sleeping in hired car.

Sat, 22 Jan - I got John to send a book to *Folkestone Herald* book reviewer, Terry Sutton MBE, to whom I mailed some additional info. Roy's sister, Julia, has kindly agreed to allow her address to be used for Cefas.

Wed, 26 Jan - To the village to post an agreement form for a Halifax credit card, which I applied for at Christmas and have got - the last thing I will be able to do from John's address.

Sun, 6 Feb - Felt jaded. Wrote to the *Sunday Times* columnist, Rod Liddle (having got John to send a book to him). Drank a pint, walk to village letter box. Drank beer back at the house while hoovering the pool and sawing kindling wood. Slept, drank beer, Roy cooked a beef stew.

Wed, 9 Feb - John has a dozen or so books left and I dare say I could drum up some more Waterstones orders, but what's the point? Instead, I'm inclined to get him to send them to one or two individuals who might prove helpful. From 4 pm to 5.30 pm I sat in on another of Dan's lessons.[2] Am now due to give five lessons in his absence.

Sun, 20 Feb - John says a Terry Sutton review has appeared in the *Folkestone Herald*. John is sending books to a couple of more literary scouts (i.e. foreign publishing rights scouts). Did some lesson photocopying. Fine weather again. Roy cooked Robert Carrier's tournados au château recipe for dinner, with Jim's Pie Shop Irish steak.

Sat, 26 Feb - Phoned John, who is sending books to literary scout, Folly Morland, and to Caroline Montgomery, of literary agents, Rupert Crew Ltd. Drank beer in the evening, we cooked pizzas in the wood stove oven.

---

[2] Dan, volunteer English language teacher.

Sun, 27 Feb - Wrote a cover letters for the books John is sending. I also sent emails from the Best Alcazar hotel. Am making slow progress with the diary editing and now have 20,000 words, and am on course for 47,000+. Filet of pork dinner, with sautéed cabbage and jacket potatoes.

Sat, 5 March - Did language lesson preparation & photocopying. Wrote a cover letter to LAW literary agents. Rupert Crew have sent my book straight back to John. I'm only approaching one or two literary agents again to compliment the approaches I'm making to foreign rights scouts, Stayed up to watch a recent film version of *Brideshead Revisited.*

Thurs, 17 March - Had a nasty day long hangover, with headache compounded by an afternoon wank. Library computers are back up again and I'm trying to find or verify the addresses of any more literary scouts. John has sent books (those I re-covered)[3]to seven, plus one or two literary agents. Will any of them want to see me at the London Book Fair? Can't see it, somehow.

Sat, 19 March - Had a warm sunny walk to the Africa cyber shop. Almuñécar, wild flowers on the track behind the marina. Did online financial admin. Had some crab stick bisque on return to the house. Wrote two cover letters, after phoning John. Drank beer in the evening and was going to go for a stroll to the feria in the village, but went to bed at 10 pm. UN resolution results in NATO military action against Gaddafi.

La Herradura, Mon, 13 June - Walked to the Africa cyber shop, downloading a Corporation Tax Return form. John phoned - have had a reply from Studley Parish Council, saying they are still prepared to tolerate me living in Folkestone, but that the situation could change.[4] Am now thinking of *Persistence! How I Published a Great Novel from my Allotment Shed*, as a title for my diary book.[5]

---

[3] i.e. glued a new cover on.
[4] i.e. with respect for the need for allotment holders to be local residents.
[5] Published 2011, by Cefas Productions Ltd.

Fri, 17 June - Did monthly financial admin. Phoned the National Insurance Office, Newcastle, who have stopped debiting my voluntary contributions since I stopped using John's address (I now *live* at El Zoco de Nerja, 91).[6]

Birmingham Airport, Wed, 13 July - Slept in an airport shrubbery bed. Trains to Redditch, walk to Studley, arriving about 10.30am. Mowed the foot high allotment grass. To the supermarket and home brew shop. Unwound the hose and began brewing beer. Drank some birthday brandy and lemonade. Overcast weather turning sunny, my gloomy mood brightening. Kim and John phoned.

Birmingham Airport, Sat 16 July - Another shrubbery bed sleep, rain holding off.[7] Trains and walk to allotment, arriving 8.50 am. Went back to bed, to have breakfast, doze and a wank. Spent the rest of the day digging over the 2nd bed.[8] Phoned John and Venetia. I wish I could stop this diary, but I have so few friends and don't seem to make new ones. I can see it becoming an ever more dispiriting record, though, if I carry on.

Studley, Mon, 18 July - Made a 8.50 am departure and walked via The Slough and Rough Wood pathway to Redditch for a train. Visited Aston University Student Union book shop. Got Megabus to Victoria, had a Belgravia/Piccadilly walk in pleasant summer rain to Green Park toilets. Got 7pm National Express coach to Folkestone, arriving John's flat about 10 pm for drink and chat.

Folkestone, Fri, 22 July - Am feeling relaxed for the first time in ages. Went with Netia today in her car to Hythe, where we visited her daughter, Flo's, household in West Hythe, where Flo was with her grandchild, Alfie. We then visited Brian and Jenny Oxley, where Netia's daughter, Tamsin, was staying. I visited John in the evening, with a three litre bottle of Morrison's cider to share. Painter, Lucian Freud, dead.

---

[6] Nerja PO box.
[7] Diarist wasn't flying but stayed at the airport after returning late from a trip from Studley to London.
[8] Area under cultivation.

Tues, 26 July - Bottled some beer. Arrived at Margot's house at 10 am, to lever the flagstones of her fish pond terrace apart and fill the gaps with cement. I was there until 4 pm, drinking wine and having a pasta meal, then back in Folkestone I went to John's flat with some beer. Had a Leas/Sandgate walk afterwards.

Sat, 30 July - To a library computer for the hour a day allowed. Had an early evening Warren swim and spring outlet shower. Had breakfast and an evening meal from Netia. Saw Chris in the evening, before visiting John with some beer.

Mon, 1 Aug - To Margot's, where I cemented some bricks back into place in her front garden wall. Drank some wine, finished Margot's weekend steak & kidney casserole. A fun day, I walked back to Folkestone to visit John with some beer.

Fri, 5 Aug - I borrowed Netia's car and collected 1,700 Thomson Directories from Lockstore Ltd., Wotton Rd., Ashford. Delivered some cheese to Margot on the way back. Began delivering the directories, using Netia's paper round trolley. To John's with some beer, but he didn't drink any. Had a Leas/Sandgate walk.

Mon, 8 Aug - Took a day off from the deliveries. Walked to Margot's, where I painted one of her garden sheds with wood preservative. Drank wine and had meal and chat, and a buoyant walk back to Folkestone, where I went to John's with some beer.

Thurs, 11 Aug - Did Netia's paper round. To the Park Inn at 11.30 am, for a drink with Paul. To a library computer, doing the Thomson paper work. To John's in the evening with some beer (he saving his for another day). Had Leas/Lower Sandgate Road walk.

Leigh on Sea, Tues, 3 Jan - With Kim in his car to Wivenhoe, where we visited Carol and also Pam Dan. Back in Leigh I departed for Folkestone, arriving at John's flat at about 8.30 pm. Feel more relaxed now. Weather calm and mild.

Folkestone, Wed, 4 Jan - A 10.30 am drive with John, via Alkham and Sandwich, to Cliftonville, to visit Colin and Harold. They gave us smoked salmon baguettes and Christmas cake, etc. John drank Madeira wine, I drank coffee. Back in Folkestone I visited Netia, then returned to John's flat to drink home-brew with him.

Seabrook, Thurs, 5 Jan - Departed John's at 10 am, drove via Elham to Bishopsbourne and walked to Jocelyn Brookes's[1] water tower, on the Barham downs along Coldharbour Lane, finding it somewhat neglected now, but enough to impress any child still. To Margot's house for a relaxing afternoon, including a visit with her to her allotment at Peene. She went to bed early with my diary book.[2]

La Herradura, Sun, 19 Feb - Finished the 11 books as they are,[3] gluing the spines and sticking the covers on. Phoned John, who says he doesn't want to handle any further books. Roy cooked a Lubina for dinner, with asparagus and broccoli vegetables. Also an apple pie, with James Grieve apples.

Fri, 16 March - Am incorporating the scan[4] into the press release, which I'm writing in the form of a review of the diary book, which could be used verbatim. Am using some of the (unused) advice Margot gave me for the book cover. John phoned. He is talking about selling his flat and going to live with his mother in Salisbury.

Sat, 17 March - Worked on the press release. Phoned John, drank three pints of Steinberg - the cheapest supermarket beer - at lunchtime, then went for a village/seafront walk. The *feria* is here for the local San José holiday. Had three beers and tapas

---

[1] Jocelyn Brookes, Folkestone author of *The Orchid Trilogy*.
[2] *Persistence! How I Published a Great Novel from my Allotment Shed*, was just being published.
[3] Some copies were photocopied, rather than printed.
[4] Publicity photo of diarist.

at the Sacrista bar, continued drinking Steinberg back at the house. We had barbecued hamburgers (or beefburgers).

Sun, 25 March - With Roy to Almuñécar boot fair, where I bought a telephone for 2 euros, which works and replaces the defective house phone. Roy cooked Hunter's chicken/Chicken cacciatore dinner. John phoned, now not going to live with his mother. Andalusian elections today.

Sat, 14 April - Drafted a cover letter to send with the review copies. Phoned Carol and John. A boiled egg lunch, plus sweet things. Cold blustery weather, some rain. Some of the cats are ill.[5] A log fire in the evening. Barbecued hamburgers, drank beer, got indigestion. UN ceasefire observing mission in Syria.

Birmingham Airport, Sat, 28 April - Dozed on airport seating, leaning on books bag (33 taken). Trains to Redditch, checked newspaper addresses at the library, several of which had changed lately. Got stamps for the post cards enclosed with 19 of the diary books I posted. Got stamps for 12 VTITBs,[6] which I hope John will post. Walked via the lakeside path to the allotment. Mowed grass, rain threatening. To bed soon after 6 pm.

Studley, Mon, 30 April - Woke with a bad hangover in the night, slept again. Did another half hour digging. A 9.30 am walk via Priory Farm and the lakeside path to Redditch, where I posted two more books. Train and Megabus to Victoria, stamped the VTITB books for John in the library.[7] Got 7 pm National Express coach to Folkestone, arriving John's flat at 10 pm with some home-brew and brandy & lemonade.

La Herradura, Sat, 9 June - A morning walk to Zen II Net - updated website now uploaded OK. Am doing a glass fibre repair to a broken rubber breather, or cooling tube, that goes from a ventilation hole in the car's bumper to a tyre. Phoned John - an M&S credit card has arrived. No diary book post cards returned. No response to the diary book at all - things fizzling out!

[5] Belonging to landlady.
[6] Diarist's novel, *Vapour Trails in the Blue*.
[7] Near Victoria Coach Station.

Birmingham Airport, Fri, 13 July - Sat glumly on airport seating, unable to doze off. Early trains to Redditch, walked to allotment, arriving 8.30 am, to find grass waist high on the whole plot. Began cutting it with a hand saw, prior to mowing it. Bought and began brewing a beer kit. Ate sandw+iches, early to bed. Birthday phone messages from Kim and John.

Studley, Wed, 18 July - Felt recovered after a 12 hour sleep.[8] Bottled the immature beer, using no secondary fermentation sugar. Departed 9 am for a rain drizzle walk via The Slough to Redditch, where I went on a library computer and to the bank. Train to Birmingham, National Express coaches to Folkestone, arriving John's flat about 10.30 pm.

Folkestone, Thurs, 19 July - Did Sainsbury's shopping for John. I visited Venetia at noon. I can use her basement, but I have opted for her outhouse, as she has three language students in her busy house at present. Had a happy walk into the town before returning to John's to collect my bag. Had another town walk, went to the library, Lidl's and to Wilkinson's for a beer kit, which I began to brew.

Sat, 21 July - Made a passport application at the post office - could take four weeks. To Margot's, to prune her hedge and have a congenial day, with Jackie and Tony visiting. Began doing tax return on her computer,[9] but only got so far with it. Had drink, had a pleasant walk back to Folkestone, went to John's with a bottle of home-brew left from last year.

Wed, 25 July - Visited John. Walked to Margot's for a pleasant time, chatting over coffee and biscuits and doing one or two little jobs for her. Began digging out the stump of the palm tree.[10] Had a buoyant walk back to Folkestone, to John's with a three litre bottle of Morrison's cider. My HMRC download has overloaded Margot's computer.

[8]   Diarist had felt feverish.
[9]   For Cefas Productions Ltd.
[10]   Transplanted from Clifton Mansions and later cut down by Margot.

Sat, 28 July - To the library, to consult the *Writers' and Artists' Yearbook*, then use a computer to write to seven literary agents. I may as well send them some of the VTITBs I left with John, as none of the postcards I sent with the diary book review copies were returned. With Netia in her car to visit Brian and Jenny in St Mary's Road, West Hythe. To John's with some home brew.

Sun, 29 July - Sent off three VTITBs yesterday and prepared another four today to send. Visited Netia at 11 am and found John visiting her too. I walked with him into the town, helping him with his Sainsbury's shopping. Did wall plastering in the outhouse, went back to John's with some home brew.

Wed, 1 Aug A dawn expedition to Kingsnorth Gardens, to plant a Chusen palm tree cutting there.[11] Walk to Margot's, then to Hythe, to begin Thomson Directory deliveries in streets around the parish church - quaint area, up and down walking, hollyhocks everywhere. Did another batch along Seabrook Road. went weary to John's, arriving 9 pm with home brew. Team GB athletes doing well at London Olympics, haven't followed it, myself.

Sat, 4 Aug - Finished the Saltwood round, doing more deliveries in North Road and Seaton Avenue. Called on Julia[12]again, and found her in for a cup of tea and chat. To Margot's, Jacky and Tony visiting with grandson, Cameron, who did some gardening for Margot. To John's in the evening, arriving late with home-brew, but he wasn't drinking alcohol. US space probe, Curiosity, lands on Mars.

Wed, 8 Aug - Got a 7.30 am Canterbury bus for walk to St Dunstan's, finding that another internet shop/café there had just closed down, but a sign on the door directed me to Pure Magick, a novelty/gift shop nearby in the High Street, which had three computers upstairs. Had a two hour session, successfully submitting a tax return for Cefas. Had a buoyant

---

[11] From the palm tree stump in Margot's garden.
[12] Julia Horton, Roy's sister.

walk along the river to the coach park, ate sandwiches, swigged cider on return bus. Did Netia's paper round. To John's in the evening.

Sat, 11 Aug - An impromptu trip with Chris and Venetia to Etchinghill, coming back via Peene and visiting the crafts and vegetable shop restored barn,[13] near the Elham Valley Railway Museum. Did a cement repair to the outhouse rear wall. To a library computer. Netia did a barbecue, Flo there with son, Remy, also granddaughter, Charlotte, and her boyfriend and their infant son, Alfie. To John's afterwards with home brew, then returned with all the VTITBs.

Sun, 12 Aug - Saw Chris and Venetia before walking into the town, where I went to the bank till, Sainsbury's, a phone box to make a call to Roy, and the library, looking at literary agents' websites. Am wondering what to do with the VTITBs, which are no good just sitting there. Did more outhouse wall pointing repair work. Drank beer, to Sandgate on an errand for John, whom I visited.

Sat, 18 Aug - Netia had left to take a train to Brighton to see Tamsin, and on impulse I rushed after her and just caught her sitting on a stationery train and asked if I could borrow her car, and she gave me the key. Extracted nails from timber,[14] walked into the town and phoned Roy, found a giant sized unwanted TV in Earl's Avenue, which I got in Netia's car, as her TV is not working. To John's, new passport arrived there.

Wed, 22 Aug - To Cheriton library, noticing a bicycle repair shop - Cycle Power Products - near the Kentucky Fried Chicken shop. Took the bicycle there later, where owner, Fred Permeul, agreed to change the rear tyre, fit new brake blocks and fix defective gears for £30. To John's in the evening

[13] *George's Barn*, Elham Valley Railway Trust.
[14] Ceiling joists, found in skip.
[15] Diarist had been pruning some vegetation that was obscuring the view of the coast.

Sat 25 Aug - Woke early, rain still drizzling. Went and completed the sapling pruning job at the top of the Leas - satisfactory job.[15] Returned to my bed for a packet of custard cream biscuits and powdered milk & water breakfast and newspaper read. Had another doze, went to library, computers down. Did some pruning in Netia's garden, disposing of the cuttings on the railway embankment. Drank beer, took some to John's.

Wed, 29 Aug - Posted a diary book and VTITB to Claire Allfree.[16] Saw Netia at lunchtime with her grandson, Remy. Netia gave me fish finger meal. To John's with some home-brew - am drinking some every night this week.

Fri, 31 Aug - Finished pointing repairs to the rear wall, or the Ingles Lane side of the outhouse. To a library computer. Had a sunny afternoon walk to The Warren for a swim, shower and bare foot walk along the wet beach. Drank beer, had a final walk on the Leas, before going to John's with some (immature) home-brew.

La Herradura, Sat, 13 Oct - Had another early walk to Zen II Net, entering all the notes again with one or two minor changes.[17] Bought some kiosk *churros*, had with cocoa back at the house. With Roy to Mercadona supermarket, San Cristobal beach. We had a hamburger barbecue, drank three litres+ beer John phoned, talking about going to live in Salisbury again, with his mother going into a nursing home there.

Sun, 21 Oct - Am formatting the diary book for upload as a Amazon/Kindle e-book, which I feel OK about, unlike with VTITB. Phoned John, who is feeling anxious and in the dark about his mother going into a nursing home. Roy cooked smoked salmon & scrambled egg *brunches*, and a smoked haddock and mashed potato dinner. Drank Scotch & coke, Rueda white wine and beer.

---

[16] Claire Allfree, Books Review Editor, *Metro* newspaper.
[17] Diarist was entering some *extended notes* for Nielsen Book Data's *Enhanced Service*, to promote his books.

Studley, 26 Nov - Made an early departure for a walk to Redditch library, where I wrote and printed 12 cover letters. Train and Megabus to Victoria, having time to send a diary book and VTITB, with cover letter, to three newspapers from the nearby post office. National Express coach to Folkestone, arriving John's flat at about 10.15 pm, for brandy & chat.

Folkestone, 27 Nov - Packaged and sent to newspapers the remaining nine diary books and nine VTITBs I brought with me. To Netia's, she worried about selling her house. A 12.30 pm visit from Colin and Harold at John's flat. I then went to Saltwood for a cup of tea with Julia, then I phoned and visited Margot. Supportive chats from both.[18] Autumnal, rainy walk, felt better, more brandy with John.

La Herradura, Sun, 9 Dec - Wrote diary, phoned John and Chris Johnson.[19] Coffee with Geoff,[20] me talking about starting the *Trans-Med Review* magazine from Tangier. Fried egg & bacon back at the house, plus sweet fix.[21] Wrote a reply to a carer agency questionnaire.[22] Fried potatoes and cold smoked salmon evening meal, drank beer and wine. Watched Lean's *Lawrence of Arabia* on TV.

Sun, 30 Dec - Felt jaded with hangover. John phoned, saying he felt too weak to undress to go to bed or get down the stairs, and would have to go into a nursing home. I think it could just be his inadequate diet. Fed pets,[23]wrote diary, had a coffee with Geoff (he was drinking wine), a repeat of yesterday's lunch.[24](fried egg & bacon, toast/marmalade/croissants/honey, Roses chocolates) Did domestic/pet chores, made phone calls, reheated some of Christine's[25]Xmas dinner and drank some Torrox wine.

---

[18] The diarist's great friend and companion, Roy, had died on the 11th of November.
[19] Chris Johnson, Roy's brother.
[20] Geoff, hippyish ex RAF pilot friend of the diarist in La Herradura, supportive after Roy's death.
[21] Biscuits, cakes.
[22] Diarist was considering doing care work.
[23] Diarist's landlady, who lived downstairs and had many cats, was away.
[24] Fried egg & bacon, toast & marmalade, croissants & honey, *Roses* chocolates.
[25] Christine, partner of Chris Johnson.

La Herradura, Tues, 1 Jan - Did some admin and domestic chores. I have to do everything now, including any cooking, which Roy still did right up until that last Friday night before he got ill. Today I oven cooked a Jim's Pie Shop minced beef pie. John's doctor has visited him and changed his medication - crisis over.

Tues, 12 Jan - Did Sainsbury's shopping for John. To a library computer - am supposed to be doing an online study course. An afternoon walk, via Cherry Garden Avenue, to the snowy downs and a lane and footpath to the Cat and Custard Pot pub and back. I'm glad of a bed at John's, but otherwise I try not to inconvenience him, by going out for most of the day.

Wed, 13 Jan - I took John out in an Asda hired wheelchair. Cold sunny day. We were going to go to his hairdresser and bank, but instead we just went to Kepples bar at the Grand, where John had lunch and I had two coffees.

Thurs, 14 Jan - Did Sainsbury's shopping. A daily library computer hour. Had an afternoon promenade walk, passing the time before a 7 pm return to John's. This evening I cooked us both some sirloin steak, with mushrooms and leeks in white sauce, and oven-ready chips - all quite successful. I drank a bottle of Sainsbury's 7.5% alc. Perry cider, most enjoyably.

Fri, 15 Jan - I took John in a hired wheelchair to his hairdresser (Paul and Denis Crofts were there) and RBS bank and to Kepples for coffee. We then met David and Emma and David took us all to the Little Fish Shop, Sandgate, for a fish and chip lunch. Had an afternoon promenade and town centre walk and library visit. Got a Helping Hands phone call about two 14 day care work placements, beginning 27 March.

Sat, 16 Jan - Did Sainsbury's shopping for John. Phoned Margot, sounding unfriendly - doesn't want me to visit her. She really has become a terrible old dragon in her old age. Calm sea, an afternoon/evening walk to the end of The Warren concrete promenade, returning to John's at 7.30 pm. Bed 10 pm.

Folkestone, Tues, 22 Jan - A Wheat Biscuit and milk breakfast, shave Radnor Park toilets.[1] 10 am to John's flat. He has declined terribly - trembling and shuffling like an old man and his doctor thinks he could have Parkinson's disease. Did some shopping for him and one or two domestic jobs. I did some preparation at the library for the Helping Hands application.[2] Slept at John's, helping him into his bed.

Wed, 23 Jan - Visited Maureen, who used to work in the Chilham Sawmills[3]office, at her homely cottage, Shottenden Lane, Molash. She lives with her sister-in-law, Alice, and is still cheerful and friendly as ever. We had a reminiscent chat and she gave me one of Alice's frozen ready meals. Drove back via Pelham snowy lanes. Saw Netia, who is selling her house. Helped John with a warm flannel wash.

Thurs, 24 Jan - Departed John's at 10 am. Saw Charles Sturgis in town. To Margot's, she crabby at first but then OK. She doesn't look well. I did washing up and hoovering for her. I then had a tea and a chat with Julia in Saltwood, then another tea and chat with Mary Chapell in Headcorn, having found her name and address in Roy's wallet - childhood sweethearts. I then drove to Wivenhoe, arriving 10 pm to sleep in the car.

Studley, Sat, 2 Feb - Made a 10 am departure[4] for a walk to Redditch library, where I bought a coach ticket. Train to Birmingham, Megabus and National Express coaches to Folkestone, arriving John's flat at 10.15 pm. He is looking much better after a change in his medication. Have incurred another Coughton[5] speeding fine, £60, plus three penalty points.

---

[1] After sleeping in rented car.
[2] Diarist was applying to do care work for Helping Hands Homecare Services.
[3] Roy's family owned business.
[4] After sleeping in allotment shed.
[5] Village near Studley

Folkestone, Mon, 4 Feb - Another day spent mooching about. Did shopping for John. I feel relaxed being in Folkestone; love the sea air and am glad to have a bed at John's warm flat. Lunch is peanut butter or tinned sardines and bread, taken in Kingsnorth Gardens.

Tues, 5 Feb - Lucy Wilson, of Helping Hands, rang asking for a reference from Roy's sister, Julia, *then you will be ready to go*, she says.[6] Phoned Julia, not in, walked to Saltwood, still not in. Had a sandwich picnic and went the Hythe library, then found Julia in on my 3.30 pm return. We had tea and a chat and I gave her the reference form. An enjoyable return walk to John's.

Wed, 6 Feb - Went Sainsbury's shopping for John. Julia had delivered her character reference on my return. This I took to the library, to scan and email to Helping Hands. Had a Leas and Sandgate promenade walk before 7 pm return to John's. Bed 10 pm.

Fri, 8 Feb - I hired a wheelchair from Asda supermarket *Shopmobility* facility and pushed John to Keppels at the Grand hotel, arriving at 11.30 am. We had coffee in front of the wood fire, then I had more coffee and read a newspaper while John had lunch. Felt content. To the library in the afternoon, had a promenade walk, then visited town book shops and the library again, looking at care work text books.

Sun, 10 Feb - Called on Etelle at 8.30 am, and she gave me some breakfast and a *Sunday Times* read. To library - computers down. Changed mobile from Vodafone to cheaper Asda provider. To Margot's, for a cosy chat. Cut her toe nails, cooked meal. Freezing head wind on return promenade walk, sleet blowing horizontally. Had a bottle of wine and some curry, both given by Etelle, John declining a share.

---

[6] Diarist had completed a residential Helping Hands training course in January.

Sun, 17 Feb - To the library, buying a Malaga flight for 26 February. What awaits me there?[7] A pleasant sunny/misty afternoon walk to the Capel cliff edge café, back via Crete Way East and West. John's 7 pm. Ate tinned pork and lentil food, given by Etelle, and a bottle of Sainsbury's 7.5% Perry cider.

Mon, 18 Feb - Took John in an Asda wheelchair to Kepples at the Grand hotel, where he had lunch while I had a coffee. A pleasant sunny day, had my daily afternoon walk. I have started the online course of 18 care work study modules and tests to do for Helping Hands.

Tues, 19 Feb - A lovely, spring-like sunny day, crocuses about. Did Sainsbury's shopping for John. Daily library computer visit. The fourteen day holiday relief carer job, starting on 27 March, has been confirmed. An afternoon promenade walk to the Imperial hotel, Hythe, a perfect sunset (behind me) on return.

Wed, 20 Feb - With John to Kepples again, he for lunch, me for coffee. In the afternoon I met Chris on the Leas and he mentioned that Netia might be interested in selling the outhouse. I said I'd pay £20,000 for it. Drank some Sainsbury's Perry cider in the evening at John's.

Thurs, 21 Feb – Sainsbury's shopping and a Cheriton clinic visit for John. Weather very cold again. An afternoon walk through Shorncliffe Camp, visiting the Gurkha Regiment museum, where I was given a cup of tea. I went on down to Seabrook and back along the promenade to the Burstin hotel lounge bar before returning to John's. Visited Venetia, who served a rabbit-in-red-wine-sauce meal. She is prepared to sell the outhouse for £27,000.

Sat, 23 Feb - Made a 9 am departure from John's. Phoned Heidi,[8] who said that she is sick and that I must deal with her son in Germany. Got a National Express coach to Victoria, tube

---

[7] Diarist's landlady had given him notice to leave.
[8] Heidi Suri, diarist's landlady in La Herradura.

from Green Park to Ealing Broadway, then walked to Neil and Sandi's[9]house, Neil with stomach bug. Had a relaxing afternoon, playing with little Madelaine[10]and watching TV rugby. We had a Turkish take away evening meal.

La Herradura, Thurs, 7 March - Did I walk to the village Cyberphone internet shop? Phoned Netia re exchanging solicitor's names. There is a possibility of renting a garage from John Heal's friend and Crofts family relative, Richard Paine. Droitwich customer, Brian,[11] has died. Have another possible placement with a Mr Rees, in Cardiff. Have one electric light and a cold water tap in the bathroom.[12] Venezuelan president, Chavez, dead this week or last.

Sat, 16 March - Began packing Roy's records and my books.[13] John rang - the Allotment Committee/Studley Parish Council have given me notice to quite by the end of the month - upsetting news. Continued packing while drinking beer. Had a coffee and brandy at a village café, and then a drunken, tearful bout back at the house. Had a drunken evening walk to the village San José fair, and the campsite café, for beer and tapas.

Upper Witton, Birmingham, 6 April - The customer[14]and I had a little Grand National flutter at the nearby betting shop. We then met his two children and grandchild and friends at the Buffet Island *eat-all-you-can* Chinese restaurant, me included. Phoned John - my allotment eviction appeal has been rejected by the council, as I rather thought they might this time. I can't complain, have had the allotment twenty-one years, and while living in Spain as well.

---

[9] Neil and Sandi Simons, diarist's nephew and his wife.
[10] Madelaine Simons, Neil and Sandi's daughter.
[11] Brian, a prospective Helping Hands customer for the diarist.
[12] After an attempted forced eviction by the diarist's landlady, while he was away.
[13] Diarist was moving back to England.
[14] Diarist's current care work customer.

Thurs, 11 April - My last morning here. I've enjoyed my first Live-in carer placement. Washed and tumble dried the bed linen for the return of the customer's permanent carer, who arrived at 2 pm. He took me to Chester Road station, then I got the 4.33 pm London Midland train from New Street to Euston for tube and National Express coach to Folkestone, arriving John's 10.15 pm. Drank some Malaga airport whisky with water on the way. Margaret Thatcher died this week.

Fri, 12 April - To Netia's (out). To the library, then I returned to John's with a Shopmobility wheelchair and went with him to his hairdresser, bank and to Kepples bar, where he had lunch while I read a newspaper. After returning the chair I went to Netia's and she gave me some late lunch, and later an evening meal, while watching *Les Misérables* musical on video.

Sat 13 April - Richard Paine showed me his garage near Godwin Road, which I have rented for six months (£300). To Fred's bicycle shop, Cheriton, and Morrison's supermarket, and to a library computer. Had an afternoon harbour and Sandgate promenade walk in light rain and wind. Netia out, drank cider, including a pint at the View bar[15] on the Leas. Flowering red current fragrant on Leas sunken pathway. Cooked steak with chips and peas at John's and we watched US Masters golf.

Sun, 14 April - I woke after a melancholy dream about Roy. Read a newspaper and ate muesli in bed. To Netia's (out). To a library computer, but then needed a harbour toilet pee. To Morrison's for John. Sunny afternoon, had chips and a dish of seafood meal on the East Cliff sands, then a promenade walk to Sandgate, where I had a cider at the Sandgate hotel and, on impulse, a £3 *opening anniversary celebration* roast beef lunch at the Sixty-Six restaurant near the Royal Norfolk hotel. Drank cider throughout the afternoon. Met Chris on the Leas.

---

[15] Formerly the Salisbury hotel.
[16] From the allotment.
[17] Diarist had left his keys at the care work customer's house and had had to break into his allotment sheds.

Studley, Tues, 16 April - At 7 am I bicycled[16]via Aston Cantlow to Carwise Services at their Weston Road Industrial Estate depot, Stratford, to hire the Ford *C-Max* again. Got diesel. To the customer's house (out).[17] To Warwick race course, to attend a speed awareness course, thus saving the three license points. To the customer's house again, got my keys, returned to the allotment to load as much stuff from the sheds as I could, without sorting it out, including stuff from the caravan and Dad's house. A motorway drive from Warwick to Folkestone, arriving John's 1 am.

Folkestone, Wed, 17 April - Unloaded the stuff into Richard's garage, then he and I went to Netia's, who cooked some food for us while we chatted about the garage rental deal. Margaret Thatcher's funeral was on TV. A motorway drive via Heathrow to the Henley-in-Arden exit and to the allotment. Loaded car, had an 8.45 pm arrival back at John's.

Thurs, 18 April - At 7.30 am I began depositing the load into the garage (having a curt exchange with an elderly resident there, who thought I was blocking his neighbouring garage). Felt dismal on the motorway drive to Henley, brighter having a farewell cup of tea in the shed of allotment old timer, Rolland. Returned my main gate key to the council office. Returned to John's with the last load of stuff, much of it rubbish, arriving about 7 pm. I'm glad the decision to leave the allotment has been made for me, I'd have stayed there forever otherwise! Thank you, Studley!

Axe, France, Thurs 9 May - Made an early start to catch the ferry,[18] but then had a puncture on the motorway from Limoges. I just got up a slip way to a service area and managed to change the tyre - a good effort - with the help of a discovered Mercedes instruction manual and jack. Continued

---

[18] Diarist was moving his possessions from La Herradura to Folkestone in a hired van.

via Blois and Rouen, listening to catchy French pop music - shed a tear hearing a Sardou song about a seventy seven year old woman, formerly with blond hair. Reached Calais 6.30 pm. I'd missed my *Rodin* ferry but was put on the 7.30 pm *Berlioz*, where I sat facing the sunny forward bar windows watching Dover approach. Arrived John's before dusk. To Sainsbury's for some cider.

Folkestone, Sat, 11 May - A relaxing day. To Fred's Cycle Shop, Cheriton. Did Sainsbury's shopping for John. To a library computer - have been offered another week's care work. To Netia's in the evening and she gave me some Shepherd's Pie. I was going to drive her to Hythe, but her grand daughter, Charlotte, took her, so I stayed watching TV and drinking perry. Blossom on trees and Kingsnorth Gardens pretty with tulips and hyacinths and rose coloured maple tree leaves.

Sun, 12 May - Wrote diary, ate muesli and biscuits and drank milk in bed. To the library, accepting the week's care work, beginning on Thursday. Saw a Noel Redding[19]exhibition there. A peanut butter sandwich lunch at John's. Had a Leas/ Sandgate walk (including woodland path to the Clarendon pub). Visited 'Netia, spending the evening there watching TV and sharing a meal.

Mon, 13 May - Phoned Helping Hands - the week's work offer has fallen through. To Worthington's solicitors - the outhouse purchase is still on. To Fred's Cycle Repair Shop, Cheriton, then to Asda car park Shopmobility, for wheelchair hire (£2). With John to Kepples, he for lunch, me to sit by the fire with a coffee and newspaper. Richard Paine was there. To Netia's in the evening, was given a meal, Chris was there.

---

[19] Noel Redding, base guitarist with the Jimi Hendrix Experience, who lived locally.

Tues, 14 May - Did Sainsbury's shopping for John. To Cheriton library and Folkestone library - Ryanair's website is not loading properly. Netia gave me some lunch and we went in her car to pick grandson, Remy, up from school. We returned to Netia's for another meal - meatballs for Remy, Duck à l'orange for Netia and myself (using oranges I brought from Spain).

Wed, 15 May - To John's Cheriton surgery and Fred's cycle shop. For £30 he has now put some front wheels and foot rests on the old wheelchair I found on the Leas - did I mention it? three or four months ago. Went with it to Cheriton library, buying a one way Monarch flight for £79. Daily wank, am feeling fit. Another Duck à l'orange meal at Netia's.

Fri, 17 May - John changed his mind about another wheelchair outing, so I went to the library instead, buying a Ryanair return flight from Spain, on 26 May (47€). Netia gave me some lunch, then I took the wheelchair and some stuff to the garage before getting the 2.50 pm National Express coach to London. Walked to Gloucester Place bus stop S, for a mini Easybus to Luton airport (one hour late). Ate a snack beforehand at Marylebone station.

Stansted Airport, Mon, 27 May - Slept on the airport floor and some seating. Got the 6.30 am National Express coach to Victoria for tube to Ealing Broadway, where I had a biscuit and milk breakfast and newspaper read on the sunny common, before walking to Denmark Road, for a relaxing morning with Neil, Sandi and Madeleine. We all walked to a pub garden for lunch. I then returned to Victoria for a 4.30 pm coach, arriving at John's about 7 pm. Had a Leas walk before dusk.

Folkestone, Tues, 28 May - To the garage store. A sweet leaves-and-flowers-of May scent, Alexanders on the Leas. To Sainsbury's and the RBS bank for John. Netia gave me some lunch and we watched TV, with a visit from daughter, Flo, and

[20] Folkestone cinema.

grandson, Remy. An evening Leas walk, retrieving wheelchair from garage.

Wed, 29 May - To the library, booking coach travel. Did more shopping for John, then took him in the wheelchair to the Grand hotel, where he had lunch at Kepples, while I had a coffee. To Netia's, where she gave me some lunch and we watched TV. To the Silver Screen cinema[20] in the evening, seeing a current remake of *The Great Gatsby* - good acting and production, script with lapses but staying faithful to the spirit of the book.

Upper Witton, Birmingham, Sat, 1 June - Kept to daily routine for the customer, with an afternoon wheelchair trip to the nearby Circle shops, buying some new potatoes at a butcher's shop. In the morning I went to the nearby betting shop for John, putting a £2 each way bet on *Ruler of the World*, in the Derby, and the same bet for myself. The horse won, and we made £20 each.

Thurs, 6 June - Took the customer to his ex wife's house,[21] then prepared for the return of his permanent carer. I left at 2.30 pm, for a sunny walk to Chester Road station. The London Midland train to Euston was delayed by a broken down freight train at Rugby - missed my Victoria coach, got a train from Charing Cross (£31) and sat in an empty carriage with a half bottle of vodka and fizzy orange, the *Evening Standard* newspaper and the June dusk outside - bliss! Was slurring-voiced drunk at John's.

Folkestone, Fri, 7 June - Ate muesli and milk and read newspaper in bed. To the garage for the wheelchair. Made a brief visit to Netia, then I took John to his bank and Kepples, where he had lunch while I had a coffee. To the library and a walk to the harbour in the afternoon, the evening spent at Netia's, with a meal and TV. Feel buoyant.

---

[21] The diarist was driving the customer's vehicle.

Sat, 8 June - Ate muesli, biscuits and chocolate, drank milk and read newspaper in bed. To the library, finding that the outhouse Land Registry document had been emailed from the solicitor's. Saw Netia, briefly. A coffee with John at Kepples, then we were taken by Peter and Emma to the Little Fish Restaurant, Sandgate, for a fish and chip lunch. John and I watched a Red Arrows display on the Leas afterwards. I went to Netia's in the evening, fora meal and TV.

Sun, 9 June - Made and fitted some bent plastic pipe arm rests to the wheelchair. To a library computer. Took Netia in her car to Brian and Jenny's house, West Hythe. To Sainsbury's for John, then with him in the wheelchair up the Leas, Chris there. Meal and TV at Netia's in the evening. Drank two 1½ litre bottles of Sainsbury's Lambrini Perry.

Malaga Airport, Sun, 23 June - Slept OK on airport seating. 7.20 am Ryanair to Birmingham, had more sleep on plane and on the 11.20 am Megabus to London. Read a newspaper in Ebury Park and strolled in nearby Pimlico, viewing antique furnishings in shop windows. Got the 4 pm National Express to Folkestone, John's 7 pm. Retrieved wheelchair, saw Chris on Leas. Visited Netia, who gave me a meal.

Folkestone, Mon, 24 June - To the library and Worthington's Solicitors. We are now waiting for the *search* to be done. With John to Kepples, where he had lunch and I had coffee and a newspaper read. Returned the chair to the garage before getting the 5.07 pm Charing Cross train and 7.30 pm Megabus to Birmingham International, arriving 10 pm to sleep/doze on seating.

Bidford on Avon, Sat, 6 July - Cooked two fried breakfasts, then the customer's[22]son came at 9.15 am to take him out for a couple of hours. I phoned John and Venetia, then visited the library, to check emails - search has been returned. My solicitor

---

[22] Diarist's present care work customer.
[23] Felix Dennis, magazine publishing entrepreneur.

is now querying a covenant preventing change of use of the outhouse to a habitable dwelling. With customer twice to the Bull's Head pub and once to the British Legion Club. I did a barbecued hamburger, mostly eaten this time. I don't usually read self help books, but I am enjoying *How To Get Rich*, by Felix Dennis.[23] It's too late now for me to get rich, although I had a shot at it with the novel and Cefas. Now it's just a case of my survival. A military coup in Egypt this week.

Alcester, Mon, 29 July - Helping Hands say I won't be going back to the customer before the return of his permanent carer on Thursday.[24] A sunny walk from Alcester[25]to his sons' precision engineering factory in Bidford, one of them fetched my bag from the customer's house. A bus to Stratford, coach to London, train to Folkestone, arriving John's about midnight.

Folkestone, Tues, 30 July - Got the wheelchair from the garage, did Sainsbury's shopping for John. Saw Netia, who is hoping to complete the outhouse sale this week, money needed for her daughter's house purchase deposit. Hot weather, took John in the wheelchair on the Leas. To Netia's in the evening, had a meal there with her and her young French language student, Morgan.

Wed, 31 July - Overnight rain storm. Phoned my solicitor, Mr Coley, and at 2.30 pm I went to sign everything needed to complete the purchase. With John to Kepples beforehand, where he had lunch while I had three pints of Whitstable brewery bitter, which felt like a celebration, although I still haven't quite made the purchase yet. Continued drinking beer, to Netia's in the evening.

Thurs, 1 Aug - Did Sainsbury's shopping for John. To a library computer. Very hot weather again, had a sea swim at the bottom of the Zig Zag Path, and also watered the palm tree cutting there and the one in Kingsnorth gardens. Drank home-

[24] Diarist's customer had been hospitalised with possible dehydration.
[25] Diarist had been staying in Helping Hands' hostel accommodation in Alcester.

brew, found in the outhouse from last year. Did Netia's *Kent Messenger 'Extra'* paper round, had a meal with her in the evening.

Fri, 2 Aug - Purchase completion still awaited - some mortgage details to be updated by Netia with the Land Registry. An afternoon walk to The Warren for a spring water shower and I ate a chips and sausage meal there. In the morning I went to a music shop in the Old High Street and bought some second-hand tuning keys, with which to repair Netia's acoustic guitar. Collected a hired van for John at the nearby Northgate Vehicle Hire, near Folkestone West station.

Sat, 3 Aug - To Netia's (out) and a library computer. Drank home-brew in the outhouse, then at 12.30 pm John and I met Richard Paine at Kepples, where I paid him another three months garage rent. Continued drinking beer, walked to the downs,[26] to look for orchids (after Jocelyn Brooke). A pint at the new Firkin Bar, Cheriton Place. John and I then had fish and chips with Peter and Emma in Sandgate, on me (£50).

Sun, 4 Aug - Had mournful dreams about loneliness. With John in his hired van to Salisbury, via the motorway and Nether Wallop, to meet his sister, Melissa, at their mother's house, which is up for sale. John collected a few things and we had some lunch there, then they went to see Mrs Heal at the nearby Harnham Croft nursing home. I had a walk into the city centre, viewed the cathedral copy of the Magna Carter. 9 pm return to John's flat to unload. I was last in Salisbury forty years ago with Roy.

Mon, 5 Aug - My customer has died, incredibly. I phoned the Alexander hospital[27] and the ward nurse said he'd been *very poorly for two days with bleeding in the head.* Did Sainsbury's shopping for John. To a library computer. Saw Netia in the evening, had a meal, Chris there.

---

[26] Hills behind Folkestone.
[27] Redditch hospital.

Wed, 7 Aug - I returned stuff to the garage using the wheelchair (now sold to John for £50). To a library computer. Departed John's 12.20 pm, for trains to London and Birmingham International, for my 8 pm Ryanair flight to Malaga. Phoned the late customer's son from the airport, who told me he'd had a fall in hospital, which doesn't surprise me, as he'd kept trying to get out of bed while I was there.[28]

La Herradura, Sat, 10 Aug - Took more stuff to C/Mezquita.[29] Phoned John and Netia from there. Returned car to H Suri house - she has still been targeting everything I ever did in the garden. Drank four+ pints, went to the El Meurte beach bar, and back there again at 11 pm, after a sleep and with a hangover. Had three gin and tonics, there was a Spanish *thrash rock* band playing, I slept a while on the beach, then made my way gingerly back to the house, gin and tonic in hand. I would have stayed the night on the beach, but for a fresh breeze.

Folkestone, Tues, 27 Aug - Got the bed board upstairs, and a mattress that was already in the outhouse fits Roy's king-sized bed.[30] Feel really pleased with it. Have also assembled the white lacquered table that was my computer table in Spain. With John today to Kepples, he for lunch in the restaurant, me for coffee and newspaper read in the bar. To his bank afterwards and more promenading on the sunny Leas. US/UK/ France consider retaliation, after the use of chemical weapons in Syria, an act denied by Assad government.

Folkestone, Thurs, 29 Aug - I arranged more furniture, Did 11 am Sainsbury's shopping for John, preceded by a slight contretemps with Netia, who wanted help to move some heavy doors from downstairs in the outhouse, so a prospective buyer for her kiln there could see it better, but I couldn't see the point, and Chris helped her instead. I put everything back how it was later. Continued reading *One Day*[31] in the evening.

---

[28] The diarist and customer's two sons had visited him in hospital.
[29] Diarist was in the process of moving some possessions to a new rented flat in La Herradura.
[30] Diarist had just returned from Spain with another van load of possessions.
[31] Novel by David Nicholls.

Fri, 30 Aug - At 11 am I wheeled John to the White House Clinic, Cheriton, and while he saw his doctor I went to Wickes DIY store. We then went via a sunny Leas to the Clifton hotel's Leaside Lounge, John for tea, me for coffee and read of a *Country Life* magazine. Felt proprietorial. To a library computer later, buying a flight ticket, and to Sainsbury's.

Mon, 2 Sept - To a library computer, then I took John to the bank, chemist, supermarket and the Clifton hotel lounge, where he had a scampi & chip lunch, while I had a coffee and a read of a *Country Life*. A long sunny spell of weather is continuing. Drank some home-brew. Gave another diary book to Charles Sturgis, the first having been posted to the wrong address. David Frost[32]dead (having, frankly, looked half dead for years on TV).

Tues, 3 Sept - To a library computer, paying credit cards and buying coach travel. Did Sainsbury's shopping for John. Am getting a daily barrowload of stuff from the garage. Had an afternoon swim with Netia near the Mermaid cafe, afterwards she stood me a hamburger at McDonald's. Drank home brew with John.

Wed, 4 Sept - To Wilkinson's and the library, making preparations for a two week care job. Began the transportation of my paintings from the garage to John's flat, for interim storage there. Cut hair. Watered and cut around palm tree cuttings in Kingsnorth Gardens and Lower Sandgate Road, both sickly. Tinned sardine/peanut butter diet, drank home-brew in the evening.

Sat, 21 Sept - Drank milk, ate custard cream biscuits and read the newspaper in bed. To John's at 10.30 am, went to the chemist for him and to Wilkinson's for a home brew kit, which I later started to brew. Made two wheelbarrow trips to the garage, to get all the tools I could find. Saw Netia in the

---

[32] David Frost, TV presenter.
[33] Dave Harney, UK depot manager for Spanish Way To Go van hire company. The diarist was in a dispute with them about extra charges.

evening and Chris, had fish and parsley sauce meal. To John's with home-brew. Feel good. Dave Harney[33]is refusing to talk to me on the phone.

Tues, 24 Sept - Began replacing one of the existing pair of stable doors from the outhouse giving onto Ingles Lane/ footpath with a resized door fame and door that were among the unwanted stuff Netia was storing here. Did Sainsbury's shopping for John. Began brewing some beer. Am doing nothing creative or artistic, but I don't feel concerned about it somehow.

Wed, 25 Sept - At noon I took John shopping in the town, then via the Leas to the Grand, he for a Kepples restaurant lunch, me to sit in the bar drinking Whitstable Brewery bitter and reading the *Daily Mail.* Continued drinking afterwards while working on the door frame. A dusk walk to the garage, to take some more paintings to John's, but I had a tiff with him and ended up taking all those he was already storing to Ingles Mews[34]in a drunken huff.

Thurs, 26 Sept - Did further Sainsbury's shopping for John. Daily free computer hour at the library, trying to complete some paper accounts for Cefas, but am being diverted from this by an email exchange with Way to Go, me complaining about the dashboard damage they said I did. Door frame now in position. *One Day* was a great read, had brilliant dialogue and characterisation. Probably better, if tamer, than VTITB.

Fri, 27 Sept - Began sawing the old door to size. Library computer hour. Radnor Park public toilets are there for a shit, if Netia's basement door is locked. A dusk walk up Castle Hill Avenue and via the town and Leas, to get more pictures from the garage. Bouverie Road West eateries are quite busy, quite a number of the customers Londoners, I would guess. Syringed John's ear this week, unsuccessfully.

---

[34] Diarist's initial name for his outhouse home.

Sat, 28 Sept - Got the resized door screwed on the door frame (using hinges from another door Chris told me about, in a skip in Christchurch Road) and it looks fine, though it had a glass window that, despite a metal grill behind it, could invite a break in attempt. A mortice lock from Wilkinson's went straight into the slot and key hole from a previous one. I feel very pleased to have access now via Ingles Lane.[35] Drank home-brew, saw Netia, to John's with more home brew.

Folkestone, Thurs, 31 Oct - Had a sound sleep.[36] Blustery autumnal weather, gloomy indoors, Netia out. John rang, which cheered me up. Did some admin paper work by the morning daylight. Sawed a bit off the new door, to make the lock work easily. Dusk at 4.30 pm, got two paintings from the garage and went to the library, open 'til 8 pm on Thursday. Had a pint of home brew. Oh, I recall that after dawn today I went and sawed the top off a view obscuring sapling at the top of the Leas, but I got the wrong tree.

Sat, 2 Nov - A porridge and custard cream biscuit breakfast. Radnor Park toilets shit. Saw Chris on return, then Netia, back from a holiday in Harrowgate. I got two paintings from the garage, then Netia gave me an egg on toast (additional) breakfast. Began brewing some cider. To John's with home brewed beer in the evening, which I began drinking beforehand, by my new open front door, lit by an Ingles Lane pathway street light.

Mon, 4 Nov - Wet gloomy morning. Saw Netia, she having a flu cold - went and got medicine for her, then took John in his wheelchair to his hairdresser, bank, chemist, supermarket and the Clifton hotel, where he had lunch and I a pot of coffee. Sunny day, as from 11 am. Helping Hands phoned and I accepted a job for tomorrow. Saw Chris and Netia again in the evening, drank home-brew to keep the flu at bay.[37]

---

[35] A footpath, rather than a lane.
[36] After returning from Spain.
[37] Diarist didn't usually drink alcohol on Mondays.
[38] From care work job.
[39] The diarist's latest skip find.

Fri, 22 Nov - Unpacked,[38] did some paper admin work. John phoned. I saw Netia and did her paper round, then she gave me some lunch. Showery weather. In the afternoon I began sawing the door from the skip[39]to size, to replace the existing flimsy door to the upstairs room. Saw Netia again in the evening.

Sat, 23 Nov - Ate muesli and half a packet of custard cream biscuits for breakfast. Found some shelf storage space for books and records, have brought a barrow load a day from the garage. To a library computer. Began drinking weak home-brew cider, bottled hastily before last departure. Sawed door, got another barrow load of books and records. To John's with cider for me, home brewed beer for him.

Wed, 27 Nov - Stored some books and tidied up a bit, then at 11.30 am I took John in the wheelchair to the bank, chemist, supermarket and the Clifton hotel lounge, where he had scampi and chip lunch and I a pot of coffee. Sawed a bit more off the door. Daily library computer hour. Drank some weak immature cider.

Sat, 30 Nov - Feeling bright. Lay in bed reading the Oliver Reed biography[40]and eating muesli and custard cream biscuits. Phoned Neil. Walked to the B&Q DIY store, buying a letterbox (£29.99). To the library, buying a coach ticket. Drank cider, made departure preparations,[41] 5 pm went to garage plus a Sandgate Esplanade walk. To John's with cider, he drank orange juice due to his medication.

Folkestone, Tues, 17 Dec - Did a little film script work.[42] At noon I wheeled John to his bank, chemist, supermarket and the Clifton hotel, where he had lunch. While we were there Helping Hands rang. I've been sacked! Devastating, upsetting news! It's because I got the customer's medication wrong on

---

[38] From care work job.
[39] The diarist's latest skip find.
[40] *Evil Spirits: A Life of Oliver Reed*, by Cliff Goodwin
[41] For Spain.
[42] Diarist had begun writing a screenplay.

the last job.[43] I have to admit I made the mistake, but I never though the consequences would be so drastic.

Fri, 20 Dec - Oh, I feel down, diary! Will I be able to get another job? I won't get a reference from Helping Hands. To a library computer, investigating other companies. I would have earned £1200+ with that Christmas job.[44] This evening Peter Simmons and Emma took John and me to their flat for a meal - grilled fish and veg, apple crumble and ice cream sweet.

Sat, 21 Dec - A Radnor Park toilets shit. Changed a light bulb for John and washed my hair there. This week I put the letter box up on Ingles Lane gate, but I don't know what my number is. Wet stormy weather. A 5 pm walk to Margot's, but there was just her bedroom light on. Returned to drink cider and brandy, took some home-brew to John's   .

Mon, 23 Dec - Wet windy weather. Did noon Sainsbury's shopping for John, went on a library computer, then delivered the shopping at 2 pm. Worked on door, got a barrow load of stuff from the garage. To bed at 7 pm, but got a phone call from Steven and an incoherent Margot, resulting in me walking in a headwind rain gale to Horn Street to stay the night.

---

[43] In Glossop, Lancs.
[44] Diarist had accepted a care work job over Christmas and the New Year.

Seabrook, Thurs, 2 Jan - Margot[1] is recovering, but is back in bed.[2] I attended to her, and went on her computer. At 1 pm I walked to John's flat, taking him to his bank. The address of Mews Cottage[3]has been confirmed by the council. At the garage I found the Plaza Ermita pastel,[4] which Carol wanted to buy, and Tony too, damaged by rain – the garage leaks like a sieve. All the foreground figures are affected, some ruined. Sawed the top off the cottage garden door, which now fits. 8.30 pm return to Margot's. Anyway, I'm grateful to Helping Hands for helping me through the first year after Roy's death.

La Herradura, Sun, 2 March - Had an incapacitating hangover and just lay on my bed after some porridge. Phoned Margot and Kim, John phoned later. A 2 pm seafront walk, having coffee at the Saca Corchos café. 4 pm scrambled egg and bacon, wrote this diary. Had a Jim's Pie Shop steak pie with mashed potatoes and cheese sauce, drank a glass of Montilla. Was drunk last night. Have aged in the last year - do I look old? Ukrainian crisis continuing.[5] Ian Fleming said they could be the cruellest of all people, which has always coloured my view.

Seabrook, Sat 15 March - Got up about 9.30 am for some porridge and a weekly shower. Wrote some further thoughts on Margo.[6] Cooked a fried brunch. Walked to Folkestone, buying a lager home brew kit at Wilkinson's. At Mews Cottage I have started digging around the patio drains and I took a bucket of rubble to a skip. To John's, finishing the Malaga airport gin with him and starting the lager kit brew-up there. A full moon stroll back to Margot's.[7]

---

[1] Margot Johnson (unrelated to Roy Johnson), secretarial services provider, travel courier.
[2] The diarist had been staying with Margo since the 23rd of December.
[3] The diarist's present name for the outhouse.
[4] One of the diarist's works done in Nerja.
[5] Border strife with Russia.
[6] Margot Johnson had died on the 8th of March.
[7] Diarist was *house-sitting* in Margot's house.

Sun, 16 March - Felt sluggish. Wrote diary, went on computer. Steven and Michelle and their son, Thomas, visited. I then had a fried breakfast before walking to Mews Cottage. Beautiful warm, summery day. Cleared some foliage in the patio, took rubble to skip, collected the brew bucket of lager from John's. Cooked some frozen chicken back at Margo's, with basmati rice. My life's more about survival than creativity now.

Wed, 19 March - This week I ordered a Lamb electric motor/ air pump on eBay (£138, new) and this evening it was delivered by Parcel Force to John's flat, as I really can't receive parcels at Ingles Lane. My bus pass has also arrived, after the second application I made, usable on local buses all over England. Bought a £50 Monarch flight to Malaga on 14 April.

Sat, 22 March - Porridge, shave and my weekly shower here. Practised making the funeral address, did some financial admin, then had an 11 am walk to the cottage and to John's flat. Peter and Emma then arrived in Peter's Mercedes to take us to the Little Fish Restaurant, Sandgate, for a fish and chip lunch. Dumped some earth on the railway bank and rubble in the skip. Went back to John's with some home brewed lager, had tipsy pleasant walk to Margot's.

Mon, 24 March - A morning walk to Folkestone, visiting charity shops and buying black shoes, trousers and tie (£9.50), To John's, borrowing a black jacket. Lunch at pipe, if it still functions.

Fri, 28 March - With John at noon to Northgate Van Hire near Folkestone West station, where he booked a hire car in my name, a Ford *Focus*. We then went via the Leas to his RBS bank, a stationery shop and Sainsbury's then back up the Leas, John for lunch in Kepples restaurant, me for coffee and a newspaper read in the bar. Did work in the patio before my evening return to Horn Street.

Sat, 29 March - Got up early to write and email a letter to Anne Greatex, of the Good Care Group. Bus to Sandgate (using bus pass for the first time), walk to Northgate Van Hire, then with John in a new Ford Focus to the Black Horse, Monks Horton, where John had lunch while I read a newspaper outside in beautiful warm sunshine. The pub's long-standing owner, restaurateur Nicola, formerly of the Lismor hotel's L'Escargot/Nicola's restaurant in Folkestone, is now back there running it himself with his family. We then went via Brook/ Hastingleigh lanes to Canterbury, where John bought underwear at Marks & Spencer. Began another brew back at his flat. Slept at Mews Cottage. Am feeling better.

Sun, 30 March - I drove John in his hire car to Salisbury, via the motorway and Nether Wallop to his sister, Melissa's, house, where we had lunch. While they visited their mother in her nursing- home, I had a walk to the Cathedral. The Chapter House, with Magna Carter, had just closed, I bought a reproduction & info booklet from the gift shop. Tea and scones at Melissa's before we returned, via Stockbridge, Chichester and Hastings, arriving John's 10.30 pm, then I drove to Horn Street.

Mon, 31 March - Returned John's hire car, walked to his flat then with him to his bank, my bank, Smith's post office counter, then back up the Leas to Kepples, John for lunch, me for coffee and a chat with an elderly gay resident there, Nick, who sports an eye patch and who lived in Paris for twenty years, and was the boyfriend of John Profumo's[8]brother. A late lunch at the cottage, did patio work before an evening walk to Horn Street.

Thurs, 3 April - Anne Greatex, of Consultas Care, has declined my job application, after I sent her the letter about Helping Hands. Disappointing. Did VTITB editing.[9] I do some daily digging around the patio drains, dumping the soil on the

---

[8] John Profumo, Tory minister who resigned over the Christine Keeler scandal.
[9] For Kindle edition of novel.

railway embankment and the rubble in a Castle Hill Avenue skip. Got the full brew bucket back from John's in the wheelbarrow.

Sat, 5 April - Daily porridge/shit/wash & shave, went on Margot's computer, cooked scramble egg on toast, with smoked salmon and some cake from the funeral wake. A promenade walk to Folkestone library, getting Kindle Direct Publishing info printed (Margot's ink cartridge empty). Am chipping out a drain inspection hole in some concrete pathway in the patio. Dispersed a pile of soil on the embankment. To John's with home-brew, drank more back at Margot's. Wrote diary.

Fri, 11 April - Began an application form for the Good Companions *Care at Home* Agency, Carlisle. Walked and bussed to Folkestone, went on a library computer. Lunch at the cottage then at 2.30 pm I took John in his wheelchair into the town via (and back along) Earls Avenue and the Leas. Had a pint of home brew. I had been going to get more dumped piping and glazed window frames, but didn't. Bus return to Seabrook, drank more home-brew, cooked fish cakes.

Sat, 12 April - I went early on Margot's computer, trying to upload scans in a zip file. Ate porridge, mowed lawn, completed the Good Companions application form. Walked and bussed to Folkestone, posted the form, uploaded the scans OK from the library, but another problem arose with the text. Am almost there though. Lunch at the cottage, drank home brew, had a blossomy pipe-search walk to Folkestone West station. To John's with home-brew, then a mild moon lit walk to Margot's. Cooked some steak.

Thurs, 29 May - Did a film score hour,[10] then at 11.30 pm I took John via the Leas, the RBS bank and Sainsbury's to Kepples, where he had lunch while I sat at the bar talking to (the Rt. Hon.) Nick, again, who lives at the Grand. He spent three months in Tangier in 1963, going to the Parade bar and

---

[10] Diarist meant film script hour.

he talked of David Herbert[11]and David Edge.[12] To the Nightingale Homecare office again,[13] Shearway Business Park, for a passport photocopy for them.

West Ealing, Thurs, 31 May - A boiled egg breakfast with Neil[14]and his family, then lazed around over tea and newspapers. I departed after a shower for Victoria, bought a 4 pm coach ticket at the library then walked to Tate Britain for a pee, saw Phyllis Barlow large *flotsam and jetsam* sculptures there. Sauntered back, then ran, but missed the coach. A Mall walk for Charing Cross train (£21). To John's 7 pm with some home brew.

Folkestone, Sun, 1 June - Had mournful dreams about loneliness. Ate porridge flakes with milk and biscuits in bed. Wrote diary, did a film script hour after a Radnor Park toilet shit and cottage shave. To a library computer then at 2 pm I took John via the Leas to Sainsbury's, we met Peter Wagstaff there and at the village fete being held on the Leas. John stood me a pot of coffee - he having tea - at the Clifton hotel lounge. Tinned sardine meal, 8.30 pm to bed to read - bought reading glasses earlier at Poundland, need quite strong ones now at +3.00. Chris says it's due to ultra violet light damage.

Wed, 4 June - Am using the little Camping Gaz stove to make tea and coffee, getting water from John's and some from the public toilet hand basin. Cottage life is not unlike the allotment shed, but I've no complaints - I have a bed, roof over my head, no neighbours, no rent or mortgage, and no domestic bills, either, yet. A mid week home brew evening drink. Kim phoned from New York.[15]

---

[11] Hon. David Alexander Reginald Herbert, writer & socialite.
[12] David Edge, eccentric gay Tangier resident.
[13] Diarist had been interviewed for care work there the day before.
[14] Neil Simons, diarist's nephew.
[15] Kim was acting in an Alan Ayckbourn play in New York.

Sat, 7 June - Ate custard cream biscuits and read a newspaper in bed. Daily 8.30pm Radnor Park toilets shit. Did a film script hour, then to John's at noon and we went to the Shepway Airshow on the Leas - sunny with tents and crowds all along the Leas. John had a sandwich lunch and tea at the Clifton hotel lounge, me a pot of coffee and *Daily Mail* read. To his flat again in the evening with some home brew, then I had another stroll on the Leas.

Thurs, 12 June - After eating porridge flakes and reading newspaper cuttings in bed, I have a Radnor Park toilets shit, then return with some bottled water with which to shave and have a sponge body wash - all a lengthy process. At 11.30 am I took John to his bank, a greetings card shop, Sainsbury's then up the Leas to Kepples, he for lunch, me for coffee and a newspaper read in the bar. We went on the Leas again afterwards (with no dog shit these days)[16] Today I completed my registration with the Manor Road doctors' surgery/clinic - blood pressure and diabetes tests OK . Rio World Cup about to start.

Sat, 14 June - At 5.30 am I went to the top of the Leas again to prune some saplings. I then ate custard cream biscuits and had a newspaper read in bed, before my toilet & wash routine. Netia gave me some more tea and some egg and bacon. Did a film script hour, then went and got a double mattress, in good condition, dumped in Earls Avenue. To a library computer, chipped cement off some old bricks. To John's with home brew at 10 pm, went to bed on new mattress.

La Herradura, Thurs, 26 June - Got the 7.10 am Malaga bus and the train to the airport, like yesterday.[17] Did a bit of film script work while awaiting my 12.50 pm flight, which left at 2

---

[16] Diarist was recalling his 1999 Leas clean-up campaign.
[17] Diarist had missed his flight, after trying to take an electric drill through the security check, and then going to hide it, for future retrieval, outside the airport.

pm. Trains from Gatwick, arriving Mews Cottage at 7 pm. To John's flat at 8 pm, to iron a shirt and some trousers. Am feeling calm, after a stressful, costly episode yesterday.

Folkestone, Sat, 28 June - Ate muesli, had shave, made 8.20 am Radnor Park toilets visit. At 10 am I continued breakfast with Netia (boiled egg) and French language student tutor, Thierry, whom she is accommodating. Bought a beer kit at Wilcos. Used my library computer hour on VTITB's *Free Kindle Download* promotion, notifying other sites about it's 10 to 14 July running schedule. To John's with home brew and I started another brew there.

Wed, 2 July - A 9 am library computer hour, then at 11.30 am I went to John's and we went via the Leas for lunch, on him, at Paul's restaurant, to celebrate his (John's) 60th birthday. We both had the roast of the day - turkey. We went back on the Leas afterwards, in warm sunny weather, then in the evening I returned to John's with some home brewed lager.

Sat, 5 July - A custard cream biscuit breakfast in bed. At 9.15 am I went to a library computer, purchasing a coach ticket. Netia then gave me some fried egg and bacon. Afterwards I delivered some of her *Kent Messenger 'Extras.'* Went back on a library computer, further advertising the 10 - 14 July free VTITB promotion. Bottled the last brew. Went to John's in the evening with some of the previous home brew and started the next brew there.

Wed, 9 July - To a library computer, my hour extended to two, on request. To my bank where, concerned by the thought of losing everything in a fire, I took out some house insurance (£201). At 2 pm I took John to his bank, then back up the Leas to the Burlington hotel, he for a pot of tea, me for a pot of coffee, on him.

Sat, 12 July - I went at 6 am to water and prune around the palm tree cutting again (at the bottom of the Zig Zag Path), but some more kids were in the cave just near there. Netia gave me an egg and bacon breakfast. To a library computer - there's only nine more downloads - free VTITB promotion a flop. Would paid advertising have made much difference? Delivered Netia's *Kent Messenger* 'Extras,' went back on a library computer. Had an afternoon sleep, to John's with some home brew. Wet dull weather this week, not cold.

Thurs, 17 July - Hot weather. Began cutting a small trap door in the floor boards by my bed, to give internal access via a ladder from downstairs, the outside stairs (which I would like to enclose) being too public. 3 pm to John's, taking him in his wheelchair to his bank and Sainsbury's and up and down the Leas. We had some home brew afterwards and I began another brew at his flat. Malaysian passenger jet shot down by Russian separatists in Eastern Ukraine.

Sat, 19 July - Overnight thunder and lightning. Ate chocolate and biscuits in bed. Shave, began film script hour, interrupted by the need for a Radnor Park toilet shit. Had a hot chocolate and newspaper read in the nearby café. Resumed film script hour, boiled egg lunch. An afternoon library computer visit, did Lidl shopping, got some water piping out of storage. Tinned hot dog sausage meal, to John's with home brew.

Thurs, 24 July - Took CRB certificate[18](arrived yesterday) to the Nightingale Homecare office. Return to cottage, applied for a Land Registry deed and plan (£14). To John's at 4 pm, taking him shopping in the town and on the Leas. Had cabbage and egg meal, steamed together in a little water and eaten with pepper and a squirt of ketchup.

---

[18] Criminal Records Bureau check.

Sat, 26 July - 8.15 am shit and daily water bottle refill at Radnor Park toilets. Did a film script hour or less. A sunny walk to Smith's post office counter, my bank, Lidl and a library computer. Lunch, doze, screwed sawn bits of floor board to some hardboard. To John's with home brew, started a stout kit there. A 10 pm Leas walk, very mild, bars all looking busy.

Thurs, 31 July - Did a film script hour before taking John to his bank and shopping, then we went back up the Leas to the Grand, John for lunch, me to chat in the bar with Nick, who talked of a partnership he had had with Lady Sarah Churchill, running an haute couture shop in Athens. Bottled the home brewed stout. Saw Venetia and Chris later, Netia giving me a meal. Gave a diary book to Chris.

Sat, 2 Aug - Had a custard cream biscuit breakfast, got water from the public toilet, Did financial admin. Steamed eggs and cabbage at noon, then walked to the bank, Wilcos (for beer kit), Tontine Street Opt Out of Doors camping shop (for Camping Gaz cannisters) and the Burstin hotel (for a shit). Washed my behind back at the cottage, read/dozed then worked on the new skip door, while drinking home-brew. Took some to John's and began another brew there, bringing it back in the wheelbarrow.

Thurs, 7 Aug - To the Nightingale Homecare office, finding manager, Shelly, still not there. At 2.30 pm I took John shopping in the town, then we went back up the Leas to the Burlington hotel, where he stood us pots of tea and coffee, which we had out of doors on an artificial grass patio in the sun. Drank some home brew in the evening.

Sat, 9 Aug - An 8.15 am visit to Radnor Park toilets. The annual Donkey Derby and boot fair is on in the park. Bottled the beer, phoned P&O ferries, Dover. Shopped for some new summer clothes (£35). Had steamed egg and cabbage lunch. Cleaned the old bicycle (Nick's), tyres and gears OK. Put another bolt on the door. Drank home brewed stout, went to John's with some home brew, after a tinned hot dog sausage meal.

Tues, 19 Aug - Hangover. Resumed cottage activities,[19] beginning with muesli, a wash and shave and a Radnor Park public toilet visit. To a library computer, making my remaining credit card payments for August. Did a film script hour or less. To John's with home brew in the evening, started another bitter kit there, bringing it back in the wheelbarrow.

Sat, 23 Aug - Made a sluggish, newspaper-reading-in-bed start, then made phone calls, resulting in my going by train to Ramsgate, and taxi to Margate, to cover for Nightingale manager, Ian, who was with a twenty seven year old female service user, along with another male carer, Josh, aged twenty one, in her home. I was there from noon to 4 pm. I then got a bus back to Ramsgate's sunny harbour area and train to Canterbury, for bus to Folkestone. Netia gave me a meal. To John's with home brew. An American journalist was beheaded by a British jihadist in Isis Islamic terror state on the Iraq-Syria border.

Wed, 27 Aug - I have no cash and I forgot to bring all of the La Caixa bank details[20] to transfer some. Walked to the Nightingale office, being asked to care for a transvestite overnight on Friday evening, in Margate.[21] At 11.30 am I went with John to his bank, Sainsbury's, and the Burlington hotel, where he had a bar lunch and I a pot of coffee and *Daily Mail* read. To the library later to type a permission-request-for-pipe letter.[22] Went to a talk at the Grand one evening this week, given by Michael Stainer[23] on Art in Folkestone. Etelle was there with a friend, and we walked back together afterwards in the rain.

---

[19] After doing care work in Thanet. [20] From Spain.
[21] Diarist was to do a night shift with *Rebecca* (not his actual female name), an adult male service user with a psychotic infantile complex, who lay on his back like a baby all night, one hand sticking and unsticking bits of parcel tape to the lino floor.
[22] To lay a water pipe on neighbouring private land.
[23] Michael Stainer, hotelier & manager of the Grand hotel, Folkestone.

Ramsgate, Mon, 6 Oct - I left the service user's house at 9.30 am for buses to Ramsgate (calling at Nightingale's office), Dover and Folkestone. How valuable my bus pass is being! Took John to his bank, getting there just before its 4.45 pm closure. To bed at 7 pm.

Fri, 10 Oct - Service user is recovered.[24] He is noisy and pinching and grabbing again. With him to the Westwood Shopping Centre, Ramsgate, and we had another walk in Hartsdown Park, Margate. He then had a McDonald's *Drive Thru* lunch - chicken nuggets and chips. I arrived back in Folkestone 4.08 pm, took John to his bank, Sainsbury's, his hairdresser's and up the Leas.

Sat, 11 Oct - My day off, had habitual pre dawn wash and shave, tidied up room. At 10 am Netia gave me an egg and bacon breakfast. To Wilkinson's for a beer kit and to a library computer. Egg & cabbage lunch, did a film script hour, then I moved one hundred bricks found in a skip on Thursday evening. Drank beer, took some to John's and began another brew there. Earlier, I bought an electric brewing heater at a new home brew shop in Sandgate Road.

Ramsgate, Mon, 20 Oct - Made a 9.30am departure from Marrose Ave.[25] for a buoyant, sunny bicycle ride to Folkestone. Found a few post-harvest Coxes apples in orchards, had a picnic at Coldred, called on Janet MacFarlane[26]again. Folkestone 4.15 pm. Made a Will-making appointment at Worthington's Solicitors. To John's with some home brew,

Folkestone, Thurs, 23 Oct - At 10 am I made a Will at Worthington's, leaving Jack[27] the house and Kim the contents. Took John to his bank, Sainsbury's, and the Burlington hotel, where he had a steak lunch and stood me a pot of coffee. Nightingale rang to ask me to work at the weekend, I said yes. A boozy, late-closing-day library computer visit. Got sausage

---

[24] Diarist's temporary care work client in Deal had had a fit two days previously.
[25] Home of diarist's regular care work client.
[26] Janet MacFarlane, proprietress of MacFarlane's Nurseries, had been a friend of Roy's.

and chip meal from the chip shop at the bottom of the Road of Remembrance.

Sat, 25 Oct - Trains via Ashford and Margate to Birchington, arriving at the Canterbury Road home of three Down's Syndrome *service users* at 9.30 am. They are two female and one male, the male being away this weekend. One of the females also went out for the day, leaving me and carer, Stuart, to take the other to a Margate seafront amusement arcade. Both the females have sweet, simple natures. 3 pm bus return via Canterbury. To John's with home brew.

Ramsgate, Mon, 3 Nov - I left Marrose Avenue at 10.30 am and just caught the 11.17 am Dover bus from Ramsgate, arriving at Folkestone at 1 pm. To Lidl supermarket, to John's flat. His American half sister's husband has been killed in Kansas, in a light aircraft accident. Had an afternoon read and sleep, then I went to John's again with some home brew, having drunk some at the cottage beforehand. Jack Bruce[28]died a week ago, 71   .

Folkestone Wed, 5 Nov - Had a rainy walk to the Nightingale office, excusing myself from a meeting next week. At noon I took John to his bank and Sainsbury's, then back up the Leas to the Grand, where he had lunch, while I had coffee and a chat in the bar with the Rt. Hon. Nick Armstrong, who talked of featuring in Nigel Dempster's *Daily Mail* gossip column. To a library computer later, drank beer and had a bonfire night promenade walk from the Rotunda beach to Sandgate. Am now registered to vote here. Am now fully back in the system in the UK, after twenty five years of little *official* participation or registration anywhere.

---

[27] Jack Michell, the diarist's son.
[28] Jack Bruce, vocalist, base player & song writer in Cream.

Fri, 7 Nov - Made departure preparations, after realising my flight was tomorrow, not Sunday. Felt relaxed about it and had no urge to drink. A lunchtime walk, giving bus pass application forms to Nick at the Grand and John at his flat. Saw Chris and Netia in the evening before getting the 9.09 pm train, changing at Tonbridge and Redhill for Gatwick.

La Herradura, Sat, 29 Nov - Was up 4 am, got 7 am Malaga bus and a Monarch flight to Gatwick, then trains to Folkestone, arriving 4 pm. To Lidl supermarket, Wilcos and the library - there've been 45 downloads.[29] Drank home-brew, went to John's with some and started another brew there, bringing it back in the wheelbarrow.

Folkestone, Sun, 30 Nov - Had to get up in the night and drink more beer. Slept again until 10 am. Made preparations for tomorrow,[30] then at 12.30 pm Netia gave me some chilli con carne. To the library - forty nine downloads. Had a shit at Burstin hotel toilets, then at 3 pm I took John shopping in the town and did a small maintenance job on his wheelchair. Afterwards I drank home brew at the cottage.

Ramsgate, Mon, 15 Dec - I left Morrose Avenue at 9.20 am, after the carer handover. Called at the Ramsgate office, then got the 10.17 am Dover bus, sitting at the front on the top deck and having some nips of whisky and water. Arrived Folkestone at noon, did Lidl shopping, took John to his bank, Sainsbury's and the Burlington hotel, for pots of tea and coffee. Drank home brew at cottage. Doing this care work keeps me off the booze for a lot of the time.

Folkestone, Tues, 16 Dec - Am hoping to make some Christmas visits this week. Got up after dawn, for a prolonged wash/shave/Radnor Park toilet visit. Did a film script three quarters of an hour, paid credit cards on a library computer, had a tinned sardine lunch. Knocked a brick out of the patio garden

---

[29] Diarist was holding an Amazon five day free Kindle download promotion for his diary book,
[30] Ramsgate care work job.

wall - I intend making a pedestrian gateway. To John's with home brew.

Ramsgate, Thurs, 25 Dec - The service user was with a bad back, and I was with a sore throat and headache, and we spent the day lying on the sofas watching TV. John, Kim and Nick phoned, I phoned Jack. At 6 pm the service user cooked a turkey breast-with-stuffing-and-bacon ready-to-cook meal that I'd got from Marks and Spencer, plus some roast potatoes.

Mon, 29 Dec - I left Morrose Avenue at 9.30 am. Made an office visit, got 10.17 am Dover bus, arrived Folkestone at midday, finishing yesterday's cooking wine on the way. Did Lidl shopping, then for a couple of hours before dusk I began, or resumed, digging footings for the patio pedestrian gate pillars. I have a heavy cold. Frosty evening, to John's, starting another brew there.

Sat, 3 Jan - Had a Lidl custard cream biscuit-and-mug of tea breakfast in bed. A 10.30 am wheelbarrow walk to Wickes, Park Farm Road, for more sand and cement. Ate two boiled eggs back at the cottage. Knocked the bottom rows of bricks out in the patio doorway and cemented them into pillars either side. The old cement pointing is very crumbly. To a library computer. To John's with home brew to share.

Thurs, 8 Jan - Had breakfast with Netia again. Worked on the door pillars, skimming finger tips with the cement pointing. Bottled the last brew and began drinking it immediately (or after a library visit). Took some to John's to share. Twelve cartoonists and policemen at Parisian *Charlie Hebdo* satirical magazine murdered by jihadist fanatics - dastardly act done in the name of the prophet and hate-ridden Koran.

Tues, 3 Feb - Emptied the room downstairs of everything, stored chock-a-block, floor to (sagging) ceiling.[1] This took all day, with everything put along Ingles Lane pathway to get wet in drizzling rain - can't be helped. To John's last night with home brew, starting another kit there. Cold weather, frost on Sunday night.

Fri, 6 Feb - I've got to get rid of everything that's now on the pathway; it can't come back into this tiny cottage, and I'm in no position to sell any of it or even take it to the municipal dump. Many books and art magazines have been spoiled by damp, and this morning I found that all my personal exhibition catalogues have been spoiled or ruined. My oil paintings seem OK. I thought it was Saturday and I went to John's with some home brew, which we had anyway and I stayed the night.

Ramsgate, Sun 1 March - The company thought I was doing an extra two days, but I said I couldn't and left after an 11 am carer handover . I was going to Charing Point to Point race meeting, but on the train to Canterbury John rang to say it was last weekend. Got a bus to Folkestone, drank and bottled some

---

[1] Diarist had woken the previous day to find the whole floor of the upstairs room had given way in one corner.

beer. Had a sunny Leas walk. After dark it was raining and I wheelbarrowed some stuff to Cheriton charity shop doorways. To John's with home brew.

Folkestone, Thurs, 5 March - Netia gave me breakfast - salad with oriental dressing, bacon omelet, toast and homemade marmalade - bless her. At noon I took John shopping and to Keppels, where he had a restaurant lunch and I coffee and a newspaper read in the bar. Crocuses are lovely in Castle Hill Avenue, more planted than in former years. Delivered some of Netia's *Kent Messenger 'Extras'* before dusk.

Sat, 7 March - Had a sound sleep, got up after dawn for wash & Radnor Park toilet visit, either having a shit or emptying the shit bottle there and getting tepid hand basin water to wash an item of clothing daily. Netia gave me another breakfast then I finished the patio gate brick laying. Drank home brew, took some to John's to drink with him.

Thurs, 2 April - Today or yesterday I went to the Tontine Street Outdoors shop for Camping Gaz cannisters. To John's at 10.30 am, beginning a lager brew there then taking him shopping in the town and to Kepples, he for a restaurant lunch, me for coffee and a newspaper read in the bar with it's log fire going there. A 4 pm walk to Folkestone Fixings, Park Farm Road, looking at jig saws, then I bought one - another Bosch - for £69.99 at Wickes.

Sat, 4 April - Walked twice to Folkestone Fixings for a bulb and then a photocell switch, which I fitted. The street light now works OK (as discovered in the evening, when they came on) and the light does not stay on all the time, as it did before, defectively. Had an egg and bacon brunch, began drinking gin and orange, got a train to Charing, arriving at the Point to Point, for the ultimate race. Put a tenner on *There You Go, Son*, which was the only finisher, won £6.60. A pint in the beer tent. To John's with gin and orange.

Sun, 5 April - Easter Day and it's also the daffodil/primrose/ flowering red currant season. Woke about 9 am, dozed again until 11 am - why not, in my own home here? Wrote diary, cut hair, got tepid clothes-washing water from the public toilet. At 1.45 pm I went with John on the Leas, staying two hours in warm sunshine, me reading old newspapers. We then had a couple of drinks at Kepples. Back at the cottage I had a Goblin steak and kidney pie, with cabbage and a pint of home brew.

Mon, 6 April - Easter Monday. Wrote up diary, had fried egg, bacon and bread. From 2 pm to 4 pm I took John on the Leas again, then we went to the bar at Kepples. Did a little gate post work before dusk. Had another Goblin pie and cabbage meal. The Goblin pies are now in a plastic pot, but seem the same. Chris Ashman, of European Sound Studios,[2] died recently, 65.

Ramsgate, Mon, 13 April - Left Hope Lane at 10.30 am after the carer handover.[3] To the Red Cross office near the Hornby factory (wheelchair borrowed by the Morrose Avenue client hasn't been returned). Spring sunshine, Alexanders on Margate Road. Got train, cottage 1 pm. Began drinking home brew lager, did Lidl shopping, went on library computer. To John's in the evening, drunkenly starting another lager brew.

Folkestone, Sat, 18 April - I have never been *clubbable* but it would be somewhere to go.[4] The membership is pretty sedate, certainly at lunchtime, with many elderly local residents. I'd enjoy the King's Road walk there. This morning I posted an American Express card, found on Albert Bridge, to their London office. Washed hair with hot water from the railway station loo. To John's with home brew in the evening.

Sun, 19 April - Drank tea, ate custard cream biscuits, read one of John's gay magazines in bed. Wrote diary, had an egg and bacon fry-up, like yesterday. Finished the gate posts. To John's at 4.30 pm, cutting his hair and taking him on the Leas. He is

---

[2] Folkestone recording studio where the diarist had recorded some of his music in his twenties.
[3] Diarist was working with a new client in Ramsgate.
[4] Diarist had been to the Chelsea Arts Club the previous day.

an invalid now, hardly able to walk at all. He had a meal at Kepples and we afterwards sat in the bar with Nick and his dentist partner, John. Nick bought a VTITB, which I went and got.

Sun, 26 April - A letter yesterday from the Chelsea Arts Club, inviting me to further ingratiate myself with the existing membership. Felt sluggish today. To the library (closed) and by bus to Cheriton library, emailing Nightingale Homecare. I think Ray[5]is suspicious of me - he has a defensive attitude. A noon fry-up, then I had a doze, then I began work on making the patio wall door. To John's with home brew.

Mon, 27 April - To a Cheriton library computer? At noon I took John to his bank and Sainsbury's, then to Wilcos for myself, then back up the Leas to Kepples, he for a restaurant lunch, me for bar coffee and a newspaper read. Did afternoon patio gate work; am making it out of skip joists. Tinned Lidl chicken curry and baked bean meal.

Wed, 29 April - Voted Liberal Democrat by postal vote in the forthcoming General Election, in the hope that the present coalition government will continue. Can't bring myself to vote Tory, despite being a minor property owner. Voting seems like the last step in my UK rehabilitation, after my unofficial life in Spain. To John's with home brew in the evening.

Thurs, 30 April - Am working on Cefas (or my personal income & expenditure) accounts, covering three months worth of receipts per day. From 2 pm to 4 pm I took John to Sainsbury's and on the Leas. I sorted this month's receipts at the library, which stays open until 8 pm on Thursdays. I also paid some credit card instalments.

Sat, 2 May - With John to Northgate Van Hire where he hired a Hyundai *Blue Drive* saloon car, somewhat tank-like. We then went in convoy with Peter Simmons to the Black Horse at

---

[5] Ray, permanent carer of the diarist's present Ramsgate client.

Monks Horton for lunch, Peter being John's guest and me paying for myself. I had Duck a l'orange main course. We all had soft drinks. John and I went to Marks and Spencer and the Parrot Inn in Canterbury afterwards. Drank home brew with him at his flat, more back at the cottage.

Sun, 3 May - With a hangover I drove at 7 am in John's car to Peene allotments, to dispose of some old gardening tools over the gate. Returned to bed until 10 am. Had a quick fry-up then John and I went to the Inkerman pub, Rye harbour, for lunch - me cod and chips, John scampi and chips. Drank lemonade there and at the Standard Inn in Rye afterwards. We returned via Littlestone. Overcast day, still spring-like. A sister to Prince George born to Kate and William.[6]

Mon, 4 May - May Day bank holiday. To Salisbury with John for lunch at his sister, Melissa's, house, then they visited their mother at her nursing home. I saw her too. Tea and cake at Melissa's, then John and I returned along the A27. We went to the White Dog at Ewhurst Green, where three acoustic guitarists were taking turns playing 60s numbers. Arrived Folkestone after midnight.

Tues, 5 May - I took two wheelbarrow loads of early typed drafts of the novel to the municipal dump. Returned the car then walked into the town via the Leas and the Undercliff - sunny breezy morning, Alexanders fragrant. Bought a charity shop blazer (£6.99), also a colourful shirt. Made departure preparations. Visited John at 7 pm, before getting the 8.14 pm Tonbridge train and trains to Gatwick.

Gatwick Airport, Wed 27 May - Had a North Terminal seating kip. Had a wash & shave before 8.30 am Redhill train then via Tonbridge to Folkestone, arriving cottage at 11.30 am. Have a slight snivelly cold and upset stomach. Bought bread at the next door Co-op shop. To John's in the evening with home brewed lager. Nightingale have said they are downsizing in

---

[6] The Duke and Duchess of Cambridge.

Thanet, and have advised me to contact the Folkestone office for work.

Folkestone, Fri, 29 May - Resumed the course work for the Care Certificate, begun in Nightingale's training course week. At 12.15 pm I took John to his bank then shopping in the town and to Kepples. Chris and his sister, Mary, and Margaret were in the restaurant. I had coffee and a newspaper read in the bar, then a pleasant and sweet May rain-smelling walk to the cottage, for an umbrella for John. Worked on the door. Lidl tinned herring-in-pepper sauce meal.

Sat, 30 May - To the library at 9 am, buying a June return flight for £127. To Netia's, where I was given some breakfast. I put her car battery on charge. Between noon and 3.30 pm I did another Care Certificate course work module. Worked on patio door. Drank home brewed lager and took some to John's.

Wed, 3 June - Am doing Care Certificate course work, one module a day - have fifteen to do. To the library, printing a list of the care work I'd done in Ramsgate for the Folkestone Nightingale office. Some daily afternoon patio door work. My article was accepted by Bill Dinsmoor.[7] To John's in the evening, had dusk walk up Leas.

Sun, 7 June - John and I had been going to go by bus to Canterbury, to Peter Simmons's 75th birthday luncheon, but John said his sister, Melissa, was visiting him, due to some family crisis, so I went alone. About twenty five people were there at Pinocchio's restaurant. We shared mixed entrées then I had sea bass for my main course. Visited John in the evening. He wasn't talking sense - was he having a psychotic episode?

---

[7] Bill Dinsmoor, Editor, Streetwise Magazine, Nerja. The diarist had sent him an article about a trip he'd made to the Cannes Film Festival in May

Mon, 8 June - Did a Care Certificate module then had a noon walk to the Nightingale office, seeing rota manager, Emma. At 2.30 pm I visited John, who said some new medication he'd begun taking was giving him hallucinations, including the imagined Melissa visit yesterday. Started a lager kit there. Lidl tinned chicken curry evening meal.

Wed, 10 June - Did Care Certificate work in the morning and patio door making work in the afternoon. In the evening, I went to John's with some home brew, but he did not have any. He is really very unwell, mentally and physically. I fear the outlook isn't good for him. Sawed a bit of uneven hardboard carpet underlay out from his bathroom floor.

Fri, 12 June - I took John shopping. He has gone back to his old medication but is still being peculiar, ordering twelve bouquets of flowers for people he knows. We then went by bus to Canterbury, where he had lunch and I coffee at the computer café (no computers there now) off the High Street. Sunny day and we sat outside. Back in Folkestone we went up the Leas, then at 7 pm I went to Fenner Close, Golden Valley, helping to get the ex RAF regular current client to bed. I got there   late.

Sat, 13 June - Ate custard cream biscuits and drank water in bed. To Sainsbury's for powdered milk. Had a wash and shave, made public toilet visit. Did photocopying at the library. Had a fried egg, bacon and bread with baked beans then a jam sandwich brunch. Kim, Peter Simmons, Netia and Melissa all telephoned today about John. Did patio door work. At 6 pm I walked to Fenner Close, for three quarters of an hour spent helping to get the service user to bed.

Mon, 15 June - I took John to the Red Cross, by Folkestone West station, and they lent him a four wheeled Zimmer frame with seat, for use in his flat. He then kept an appointment to see his doctor at the White House clinic, Cheriton.[8] Did some monthly financial admin.

Wed, 17 June - Did monthly financial admin, including checking credit card balances, at the library - under £5000 owed now. In the afternoon I located some hinges for the patio door. The door is heavy but seems OK on the hinges I found. To John's, neither of us having any alcohol.

Sat, 20 June - Had lunch with Netia and teenage French English student, Madi, whom Netia is accommodating and teaching. Made three visits to Fenner Close; a fourth, at 7 pm, was cancelled. Am using Nick's old bicycle, have bought new tyres for it. I am doubled with a colleague on breakfast and bedtime visits, solo for in-between visits. Drank home brew, visited John, who drank water.

Mon, 22 June - Had one call today at 8.30am at Fenner Close. I help wash and dress the service user and get him downstairs for his medication and breakfast. Took John to his bank and Kepples then at 4.30 pm to the White House clinic, finding he'd postponed his doctor's appointment, but fortunately a doctor saw him anyway.

Thurs, 25 June - No care calls today. At 11 am I went to the Film Club,[9] seeing World War II Franco-German love story, *Suite Française*. Sunny weather outside, had a dish of whelks at the harbour before a cottage lunch. Took John to the chemist and on the Leas for an hour. The patio door has turned out well. My next project is getting a mains water supply connected.

Sat, 27 June - Made six care work calls during the day. Beautiful weather, went back to the cottage in-between times. Did a gammon steak, egg, bread and baked bean fry-up about noon. Began drinking home brew at 8.30 pm, back from the

---

[8] Diarist recalls that on the way to the clinic John had said that he did not want to go, but then found himself still continuing to be pushed there anyway.
[9] The Classic Film Club screened its films on Thursday mornings at Folkestone's Silver Screen cinema.

last call. To John's. His doctor has increased the dose of his old medication. Islamic State jihadist gunmen kill thirty five beach holiday makers in Tunisia, mostly British.

Wed, 1 July - Record temperatures. Submitted Cefas Abbreviated Accounts at the library then I went with John to a garden party in Sandgate Road near the Metropole, given by his gay friend, Barry. Seven people were there, including a former *Gay News* writer called Nick. I got drunk and fell asleep in the garden in some shade.

Thurs, 2 July - Got an 8 am phone call from John's upstairs neighbour, saying John had fallen on the stairs and had been stuck there all night after returning from the party in a taxi. We got him into his flat and I tended to him throughout the day. He doesn't seem to have hurt himself but is very sluggish in bed. I drank endless mugs of tea all day, John was also very thirsty at first. Phoned Jack on his birthday.

Fri, 3 July - Am doing no more Nightingale work, but am now tending to John. He is slightly more active, but can hardly walk at all. Phoned his sister, who thinks he should be in a home, which he will have to do now, if he doesn't start having some home support.

Sat 4 July - Every day I wake feeling sad at not doing any creative work, then I feel OK on getting up. To John's, after phoning his sister to suggest he needs the services of Nightingale Homecare. Meanwhile I have asked Venetia to call on him daily. Drank home brew in the evening, had a sunny Leas walk at 7 pm, then called on John for the last time at 9 pm.

Leigh on Sea, Mon, 6 July - A quiet morning. Kim and I had a ham salad lunch with some of his home grown new potatoes. Got a 2 pm London train, left a message on Kim's answer phone about his treatment of Alison[10] - unwise, no doubt. Folkestone 7.30 pm, did quick flight bag packing, drank home

---

[10] Alison, partner of diarist's brother, Kim.

brew then visited John before getting the 9.14 pm Tonbridge train and trains to Gatwick, sleeping on North Terminal seating. Greeks vote *No* to EU bailout terms - good news for us, frankly.

La Herradura, Sat, 11 July - Returned to the Frigiliana shop, taking six hours to finish the job[11] - an unpaid day's work, in effect. A 5 pm Herradura return, to have a doze and drink three or four litres of beer. Had a midnight shamble to El Meurte beach bar but it was closed, I could see, looking down from the pathway. Despondent, I had a gin & tonic at Antonio's Los Arcos bar and also visited the Bacuba disco bar near to me. John is now being visited by National Health Service carers.

Sat, 18 July - Phoned John. Angie, of Nightingale Homecare, is going to see him. Did a film script hour. Bought a £117 return September flight at the Cyberphone shop. Saw Geoff at a café. At 4.15 pm I drove to Mojacar, taking about two and a half hours on the motorway. Had a pint at the Patio 2000 bar - good Reggae band there. I then walked up and down the sea front, having another pint at Patio 2000 whenever I passed by again. At 3 or 4 am I slept in the car. The Greeks are still in the euro, against all predictions.

Gatwick Airport, Wed, 29 July - Felt fine on waking at 8 am.[12] Airport toilet wash & shave, trains to Folkestone, cottage 11 am. Saw Chris and Netia, Netia is OK after being hospitalised with heart or angina pains. A 1 pm walk to the Nightingale office, returning via Park Farm industrial estate. An attractive woman was smoking by the pond near the hospital - why couldn't I have said something to her? Did some wood preserver painting. To John's, went to bed around dusk.

Folkestone, Thurs, 30 July - Phoned Christine Johnson - Chris Johnson died two months ago from heart problems. He'd had a hip operation before Christmas. I saw a doctor at the Manor

---

[11] Diarist had begun cleaning four sofas at the shop the previous day.
[12] After having an alcoholic journey from Spain.

Road clinic about updating my inoculations. Had a dental check up at the NHS dentist in Sandgate Road (£18). John is in dire straights, is no longer able to use the stairs. I visited him at 8 pm and began a beer kit brew there. Did Lidl shopping earlier and went on a library computer.

Fri, 31 July - I got a 10 am Dover bus (passing a nasty car & motorbike accident outside the Plough pub) and then a Sandwich bus, to collect a pair of shoes ordered by John there. Back in Dover I had a walk to the Eastern Docks - ferries unaffected by some trouble caused by migrants in Calais trying to get to England through the tunnel. Cottage 3 pm, had a sleep, did patio steps wood preserver painting. Had a Lidl tinned herring meal. UK weather cool and sunny - bliss!

Wed, 5 Aug - Did a film script hour. Had a noon lunch then walked to Graham's Plumbing Merchants, Park Farm Industrial Estate, via the hospital fish pond. The attractive woman smoker was there, I said hello and she smiled back, but clearly didn't welcome distraction from her cig and mobile phone. *Have a nice afternoon*, she repeated. She works in hospital admin. Had a Fenner Close evening call. Saw John, who asked me to contact the local vicar for him.

Thurs, 6 Aug - To Manor Road vicarage, under renovation for a new vicar. I had two breakfast time calls - Fenner Close and Churchill House. Did a film script hour, walked to Tontine Street for Camping Gaz cannisters, had a dish of whelks at the harbour. Did internet research on John's condition, which could be Parkinsonism, brought on by his schizophrenia medication having suppressed his dopamine levels. He did change to a better medicine for this reason a couple of years ago.

Fri, 7 Aug - Had one morning Churchill House call and one evening Fenner Close call. In between I did a film script hour, had a sleep and did some wood preserver painting. Yesterday I phoned the church/parish Benefice Office secretary and a vicar is visiting John today. The Plough road accident motorcyclist was not badly injured.

Sat, 8 Aug - A bicycle ride to Summer Court[13] for the 7 am to 2 pm shift. Had lovely promenade rides there and back, temperate and cloudless; it's a privilege to to have the health to enjoy this and be going and helping people in poor health, and be paid for it too. Swigged some beer on the way back, continued drinking at the cottage while bottling the last brew. To John's, with some earphones for his radio. The priest came and gave him communion.

Wed, 12 Aug - An 8 am Fenner Close call, working with colleague, Grant, and getting the service user washed and dressed and down stairs in the stair lift and medicated (or with his self administered medicines prompted). An afternoon walk to a plumber at the top of the Dover Road, then I had a Warren swim and shower. Delivered some of Netia's papers. To John's, beginning another brew there. Today I had an idea for publishing another volume of my diaries, based on my motorbike.[14]

Thurs, 13 Aug - Did a double shift at Summer Court, 7 am to 11.30 am and 2 pm to 9 pm. Lay on the bed in the staff flat during the break. There was a thunder storm during the day. I got only slightly wet going on the bicycle and it was dry and mild coming back. It would give Cefas something to do, publishing more diaries. No one's interested in them, but it seems a bit of a waste just writing them and stuffing them into an old suitcase.

Wed, 19 Aug - Did the Summer Court 2 pm to 9 pm shift. Swigged some beer on the bicycle ride back and went to John's, drinking some more and doing some laundry for him.

---

[13] Sheltered residential apartments in Hythe, managed by Nightingale Homecare.
[14] From 2000 to 2005 the diarist had a small Honda H100S motorbike.

Fri, 21 Aug - To Summer Court 7 am to 2 pm. At 4 pm I went to John's, who had said he felt he might be able to get down his stairs with my help, but then he said he couldn't. Bottled the last brew back at the cottage, went early to bed.

Wed, 26 Aug - At 7.30 am I went back to the Hire Station, Park Farm Road. The petrol engined breaker/tarmac drill is not going properly, so I returned with an electric engined breaker and a petrol generator in the wheelbarrow. With these I punched two foot wide lines along the private driveway near to the wall, without anyone's permission.[15] Netia was agitated about it, also the Co-op shop girls - I told one to get lost. Rainy day, hard work, made a good effort. Drank beer, went to John's.

Mon, 31 Aug - A bank holiday. Steady rain. Wrote diary, did some financial admin. To John's at 3 pm, doing some laundry for him. He manages two or three trips to the kitchen per day, but otherwise lies on his bed listening to the radio with headphones. Ingles Lane neighbour, Mike, was burgled recently.

Wed, 23 Sept - Began laying the barrier pipe in the twenty feet of trench I'd dug, back filling behind it. Worked dawn to dusk, body protesting, neighbours protesting, feeling anxious, but carrying on. Drank beer afterwards then at 8.30 pm I went to John's, drinking more beer and doing his laundry and starting another brew.

Thurs, 24 Sept - On John's suggestion I rang Peter Simmons, chartered surveyor and property landlord, who said the owner might issue a High Court Injunction against me, costing me thousands. I believe him and in the afternoon I took the pipe out of the trench - I've lost my nerve. Danny Reece[16] has informed someone called Charles Hagger.[17] Is he to do with the owners?

---

[15] Diarist was intent on laying a pipe, to connect his property to the water mains.
[16] Danny Reece, headmaster of the PRU school neighbouring the diarist's cottage.
[17] Charles Hagger, owner of the PRU school building, leased to Shepway District Council.

Fri, 25 Sept - John has a bad leak coming from his bathroom ceiling and today I took my ladder to examine the outside down pipes. To the library, typing a letter for John to send to the flat tenant upstairs and his landlord. Finished refilling the trench. Had a conversation with Danny Reece, who went to Alcester Grammar school and whose mother lives in Alcester.

Sat, 26 Sept - Saw Netia, back from a trip to Vienna with Tamsin. Typed John's letter again at the library then I went to Wood Avenue branch library to print it, as the main library printer wasn't working. Took the letter to John's, had cottage sandwich lunch, drank beer, had a sunset Leas walk - told off three 12 year olds playing football by the Leas Cliff Hall, intimidating pathway pedestrians.

Wed, 30 Sept - Wheelbarrowed to Wickes, Park Farm Road, for sand and cement. Cemented a bit of the refilled trench. Qualified plumber, Darren Sutton, visited and I paid him £40 for advice. Ingles Lane footpath now looks like the best alternative for the pipe. Had an email from Charles Hagger, owner of the PRU[18] school next door, threatening legal action. John phoned, wanting to go the the Black Horse, Monks Horton, this evening. Delivered some of Netia's papers, drank beer.

Fri, 2 Oct - Lovely *Indian Summer* weather. John can manage his stairs again and today I took him to the Clifton hotel, he for lunch, me for a pot of coffee and newspaper read. Am feeling brighter, being back at Summer Court. All Nightingale Staff are being retained by Meritum,[19] another family owned business which started at about the same time as Nightingale. Got more sand and cement. Tinned kippers-in-rape seed oil meal.

---

[18] Pupil Referral Unit (PRU), for pupils excluded from a state school.
[19] The care company now managing Summer Court.

Tues, 13 Oct - Got a bag of sand and a last bag of *cold lay* tarmac from Wickes. Began brewing some beer with water from Netia. I don't think I'll be seeing much of John for a while - he is in his *honeymoon period* with his lady carers coming in three times a day to cook his meals. I had already lost him as a home brew drinking partner. Russian bombing intervention in Syria, to prop up President Assad.

Sat, 17 Oct - Worked 7 am to 9 pm at Summer Court, having a nap in the staff bedroom from 11.30 am to 2 pm, plus a biscuit lunch. Phoned John from there, but little conversation. Quite happy, I think he is, safe in the bosom of the National Health Service, with his carers and feeling relieved to be still in his flat. I said I would take him out again, but he shows no interest in doing so.

Thurs, 5 Nov - By making use of the wheelchair and the cinema stair lift, I took John to the 11 am Film Club. I saw Beach Boys/Brian Wilson[20]film, *Love and Mercy*, John saw the other film. Afterwards he had a bar lunch in the lounge of the Clifton hotel, while I had a pot of coffee. We then went to visit a lady he knew in Grimston Gardens (out), then we took a bus to Hythe, me to go to the shoe repair shop (closed). Rainy bus return, rain continuing for Bonfire Night. Had boozed-up Leas and Lower Sandgate Road promenade walk, where there was a steady, temperate on-shore breeze. A few fireworks were going off in the drizzle.

Thurs, 3 Dec - To the 11 am Film Club, seeing Anglo-French/ Normandy *Gemma Bovary*. Had cottage sandwich lunch then at 2 pm I went to John's to go to the bank for him, but I didn't. Began another brew there. John can only inch his way around his flat, but not painfully, and he seems perfectly content there, with his lady carers looking after him. He doesn't have much conversation these days, and it's a bit dispiriting going to see him. Britain joins Western coalition bombing ISIS in Syria this week.

---

[20] Brian Wilson, Beach Boys songwriter & vocalist.

Tues, 8 Dec - This morning I was phoned by Kent Social Services about John, who wasn't able to move from his bed to let his carer in last night. He is now in the William Harvey hospital. I phoned his neighbour, Beth. Made a token film script effort. At 3 pm I bicycled for a 4 pm to 8 pm shift at Summer Court.

Wed, 9 Dec - Got the 9.40 am bus to the William Harvey hospital, going via Saltwood and Brabourne/Smeeth. Sunny calm day. John was in J2 Ward, under assessment. He is OK, but weak and bewildered and bedbound. I then went to Canterbury for him, to try and locate one of his carers, Lara, now working as a beautician there. Drank beer on the bus, going via Wye and Chilham - about forty new housed have just been built on the Chilham Saw Mills[21]site. Continued drinking beer, to bed 8 pm.

Thurs, 10 Dec - Saw James Bond, *Spectre*, at the 11 am Film Club - expensively made twaddle, indifferent script. Ate peanut butter sandwiches on a 2 pm bus to the William Harvey hospital, delivering a mobile charger to John and other items. 5pm return bus; to Lidl supermarket and a library computer. Tinned herring meal, to bed 9 pm.

Fri, 11 Dec - I go to the public toilet between 8 pm and 8.30 pm, to shit or empty the shit bottle and get some tepid water, to wash an item of clothes or my hair, and also to drink. Made a feeble film script effort, walked to RBS bank for John. Muesli/ tinned sardine lunch, then at 2.30 pm I bicycled to Summer Court, for a 3.30pm to 8.30pm shift. Pleasant nocturnal return, blown by prevailing westerly wind.

Sun, 12 Dec - Delivered Netia's papers at 7 am today and yesterday (also last week) At 10.30 am I visited Peter Simmons about John. A care home could be his only option. At noon Netia gave me some pea soup. I then went to the library to book a Calais day trip for us on Monday, on a *Folkestone*

---

[21] The Johnson family business, for which the local council would not grant planning permission for houses at the time it closed down.

Express £3 offer. Did 4 pm to 8.30 pm Summer Court shift, drank four pints on 9.30 pm cottage return.

Tues, 15 Dec - Slept seven hours. Felt fine[22] peddling to Summer Court for the 7 am to 10.15 am breakfast shift. Weather calm and mild. Bottled some home brew on return, then I took John's wheelchair on a bus to the William Harvey and took him to the hospital café for a coffee. He said he felt worried. *What will happen to me?* he asked, and I said he'd be looked after, whatever happened. He's going to be bed or armchair bound from now on. He said I could begin another brew at his flat, which I did.

Sat, 19 Dec - Delivered half of Netia's newspapers at dawn. Completed the Network Rail application form at the library, and sent it with maps and photos.[23] Festive looking town centre, feel removed from it - don't reckon much to Christmas these days. Had a bacon and egg fry-up then took some clean clothes to John, who is now in the Broad Meadow Rest Centre, Park Farm Road. Phoned Jack earlier. Drank home brew.

Sun, 29 Dec - John could be soon to die. I went to see him this afternoon, and that is my opinion. He sits head slumped into chest, dull eyed, faint tremulous voice. He seems to be fading away. It's the schizophrenic medication, I reckon, but nothing's being done about it. Earlier I went with Netia in her car to visit Brian and Jenny Oxley, at West Hythe. Drank some home brew in the evening with Netia, Chris there.

Tues, 22 Dec - To John's flat in the morning, renewing the bulb above his outside door and trying to get his TV working next to his bed, having moved it from the lounge. I went to see him in the afternoon and he seemed somewhat better, quite perky. Maybe he will be able to return to his flat. Am in touch with his sister about it, and afterwards I went to Wickes and bought two key safes for his door (£47).

---

[22] After a Calais day trip the previous day.
[23] Diarist was applying for permission to lay a water pipe on railway land.

Fri, 25 Dec - At 10 am I did some Registry filing, then I visited John at the Broad Meadow Rest Centre. He wasn't as bright as last time, although he smiled at me wearing my Christmas hat[24](and looked hilarious with it on). I then bicycled to Summer Court for the 2 pm to 8.30 pm shift, the hat worn once again. Had another calm, moonlit ride back, drank four or five pints of home brew.

Sat, 26 Dec - Boxing Day. At noon I visited John, Richard Paine there too. After a cottage egg and bacon fry-up I did some Registry filing, then at dusk I went to John's flat and began drilling the holes to fit the key safes. Drank four pints of home brew, ate sardines and peanut butter with bread.

Sun, 27 Dec - A 6 am bicycle ride for the 7 am to 2 pm Summer Court shift, my last as things stand, perhaps until February. Do they still need me? A couple of the girls who left have come back and they are now overstaffed. Took John's wheelchair to the rest centre and we went into the town and up and down the Leas. Drank home-brew, ate chocolate, having also been eating chocolate in the Summer Court staff room - gifts from residents there.

Chiswick, Thurs, 31 Dec - Nick, Lexi[25] and Biff[26]gave me a lift to the tube on their way to Wiltshire. Walked from Sloane Square to Victoria via Pimlico village. Ate chocolate, got the 1.30 pm 007 Dover coach, getting off at Canterbury for a free 16 bus to Folkestone. Bought a drill bit at Wilkos and got one of John's key safes fitted, using Dad's old hand drill. Drank tea, had sardine & peanut butter meal.

---

[24] A woollen pom pom hat, decorated with twinkling fairy lights.
[25] Lexi, Nick's fiancée.
[26] Biff, Nick's Labrador.

Fri, 1 Jan - Feel OK on the whole; a bit mournful about failed/abandoned creative career. At sixty four, I know I look a bit silly to others, being alone all the time. I **am** a silly person. Phoned Carol and Hugh Tulloch. This morning I fitted John's other key safe, then went to see him at Broadmeadow Rest/Care Centre.[1] Saw Paul Crofts on the way. Did cottage Registry filing, sardine meal, bed before 8 pm. There's little I can do after dark, except drink home brew and/or listen to the radio.

Sat, 2 Jan - Did morning Registry filing and a bit of film script work. To a library computer at 4 pm, paying credit cards and buying a 28 Jan Malaga to Gatwick flight (£17). To John's flat, putting keys in the key safes. Drank home brew, set traps for mouse/rat - got to be done, after finding the place where it's been pissing/shitting/nesting.[2]

Sun 3 Jan - Spilt a bottle of piss on the floor boards. At 8.15 am I visited Etelle who ran a bath for me, gave me breakfast and a *Sunday Times* read, and bade me farewell with chocolate, etc. Did some Registry filing by the gloomy cottage day light, then visited John at 4 pm. He said he felt depressed. I said we're trying to get him back to his flat. Phoned Melissa later. Drank home brew and ate tinned hot dog sausages and onion.

Mon, 4 Jan - Wrote up diary, did Registry filing. Having tried to get John's TV - which has an indoor aerial - working beside his bed, today I moved it back to the lounge, the only place it will work. Visited him about 4 pm, before his 5 pm evening meal. Tinned chicken curry for me.

Tues, 5 Jan - Finished filing cuttings and pamphlets in the Registry, a continuing habit of mine. To a library computer. This afternoon I moved one of John's single beds from his

---

[1] Broadmeadow Registered Care Centre, Park Farm Rd., Folkestone.
[2] Diarist had been hearing rodents in the night.

spare room into the lounge, so he has the option of using it to watch television. Am sleeping around ten hours a night, with some vivid dreams.

Wed, 6 Jan - In the afternoon I hoovered the carpets in John's flat. We are having heavy rain again and the leak in his bathroom is as bad as ever, after cleaning the gutters failed to fix it. Visited John afterwards. He wasn't able to walk to the dining room and had to go in his wheelchair. Says he feels sad and depressed. Phoned Jack. Drank beer in the evening.

Fri, 8 Jan - In the morning I took John in his wheelchair to the door of his flat, where we met his neighbour, Beth, then we went up the Leas. He has not been able to get out of bed, unaided, for the last three days, or walk to the dining room with the Zimmer frame. Afterwards I had a conversation with Lisa, the Occupational Therapist, who thinks John probably now needs residential care, which is hard to disagree with.

Sat, 9 Jan - A 10 am walk to Kent Auction Galleries, Heathfield Industrial Estate, re stamps and three pictures that John has in the Collectables auction today. I visited John, then returned to the auction and was the under-bidder for the pictures, which sold for £48. One had belonged to Roy, sold to John after we left the flat for £10. The stamps fetched £100. Took John in the wheelchair to the Asda supermarket café. He fell out on the way back, banging his head, not very badly.[3]

Sun, 10 Jan - Yesterday morning John said: *time's running out for me* and *I've lost my sparkle.* I'm in a quandary about whether to delay my return to Spain and help John return to his flat by sleeping the nights there. If I don't he's likely to go into residential care next. I saw him in the morning and in the afternoon. Netia gave me an oriental dish evening meal, watched TV, drank home brew, Chris there.

---

[3] The wheelchair, which had no seat belt, had suddenly got stuck in a pot hole and John's fall was a salutary lesson for the diarist as a carer.

Mon, 11 Jan - I proceeded with my departure preparations, gloominess worsened by the radio news that David Bowie, not the sort of person who dies, did so at sixty nine. Had to rush, going to John's flat, his bank and briefly to see him before getting the 11.14 am Tonbridge train, thence to Gatwick. Felt calmer, got the 3.25 pm Monarch flight to Malaga, had a pleasant pavement table coffee near the bus station before getting an 8.30 pm Herradura bus, arriving C/Mezquita about 10 pm.

La Herradura, Tues, 12 Jan - It didn't feel right leaving John, but I decided to do so and then go back earlier than 28 January, if necessary. I feel disheartened about things - sorry for John, and for Davis Bowie, and sorry for myself. Sunny weather, went to the seafront mini-market shop, then had another promenade walk at sunset, seeing Geoff in a café and having a beer with him. Cooked a spaghetti-in-pasta-sauce meal.

Sun, 17 Jan - Slept off hangover. Have a cold, now with a cough which gets worse when lying down to sleep, dammit. At 9.30 am I phoned Melissa - John is to be in the Broad Meadow Centre another two weeks. It is still possible he will return to his flat. They are reviewing his medication. Ate porridge, wrote diary, did a film script hour. Had a lunchtime promenade walk, with a coffee in the Chorillo café. Cooked a fry-up brunch, with another orange, yogurt, marmalade and croissant sweet. Cleaned the apartment windows. At 5 pm I began drinking beer and brandy. To bed about 8 pm.

Thurs, 21 Jan - This morning I did a little film script work, then used my tablet on the library's WIFI signal. Tinned sardine lunch, have little appetite. Phoned John, who sounded stronger. Felt dire in the afternoon - horribly empty and unfulfilled; nothing much done with my life, nothing but old age to look forward to, etc. Finished curry. At 7 pm Dave[4] rang to say the car is mended.

---

[4] Dave, proprietor of the *Team La Noria*, garage, Nerja.

Gatwick Airport, Fri, 29 Jan - Slept on some seating before passport control, much to the immigration officers' surprise, when I went there at 6 am, with no other passengers about. Got early trains to Folkestone, arriving at the cottage at 9 am for a mug of tea, then I went by bus to Hythe and saw manager, Darren, at Summer Court. I am not on the next fortnight's rota, and he said he will call me when I am needed. This is worrying, as I suspect I am not really needed there. I then visited John, who is better mentally but worse physically, after a medication adjustment. Had a cottage lunch, then I visited Meriton's Shearway Business Park office to say I would do some hourly work for them.

Folkestone, Sat, 30 Jan - Had a twelve hour sleep. The public toilets were closed at 8 am, so I had a shit at the Burstin hotel. Did some token film script work before visiting John at 11.30 am. He won't be returning to his flat and could be going to Spade House Nursing Home.[5] Had a 1.30 pm fry up and ate some Xmas gift toffee and Smarties, managing to break a tooth on the Smarties. Delivered a copy of the Cannes Film Festival article[6]to Etelle. Had a Leas walk, Netia gave me a meal in the evening, Chris visiting too. To bed listening to David Bowie talk about his career on Radio 4.

Sun, 31 Jan - Washed socks with tepid Radnor Park toilet water. Wrote diary, did a film script hour. Cooked an egg, bacon and bread fry up, with baked beans. To John's flat, meeting his neighbour, Beth, and her two young daughters, and seeing them again at the Broad Meadow Care Centre when visiting John. Drank six or seven pints of home-brew, steamed a Fray Bentos pie with cabbage. Rat not caught in trap, there's no further sign of it.

---

[5] The former home of H.G. Wells. The diarist had once had a painting studio in a garden shed there, which had been used by Wells to write in.
[6] Written by diarist and published by *Streetwise* magazine, Nerja.

Mon, 1 Feb - I don't recall the day exactly. Doubtless I did some film script work. Receipts say I bought some sale price boxer shorts from Peacocks (£5) and a Gatwick to Malaga return flight in March for £75, booked on a library computer. A daily visit to John at the Broad Meadow Care Centre. Beth and her two young daughters were there again today.

Wed, 3 Feb - Had a 9.05 am appointment at Dental Care, Sandgate Road, where a young female Asian dentist in a headscarf put a built up white filling in my broken tooth. Felt a bit fragile afterwards and rueful about the cost (£116). As I'm not earning anything I'm trying to eke out my last wage packet. I don't feel optimistic. I don't feel able to accomplish anything, big or small, any more. John is waiting to go into Spade House Nursing Home.

Sat, 6 Feb - Washed a cardigan, made a minimal film script effort. Had a fry up brunch and some Xmas toffee. Read the cuttings in my Registry *Fraud* file. At 2.30 pm I walked to Spade House,[7] finding John in the lounge in his wheelchair. It seems very relaxed and homely there. After he returned to his room I continued watching an old episode of *Colombo*, with a radiant Faye Dunaway playing a guest leading role. At 6 pm I returned to the cottage to drink beer.

Sun, 7 Feb - At 6.15 am I got a call from Summer Court night carer, Emma, asking me to do the 7 am to 2 pm shift, but it was another false alarm, as I discovered when I got another call while bicycling down Sandgate Hill. Felt cheesed off, returned to the cottage for my usual Sunday. Bought a beer kit at Wilcos and began brewing it at John's flat. Steamed some Sainsbury's *Basics* tinned stewed steak with some potatoes and cauliflower. Drank home brew but was not cheered up - felt bad, in fact.

---

[7] Renamed Wells House Nursing Home.

Tues, 9 Feb - To Fenner Close at 8.30 am. The client there, with Parkinson's disease, now stays upstairs, and in fact he was asleep throughout my call and I just chatted with colleague, Grant, and Celine, a Polish nurse who lodges with him. Returned to the cottage at 10 am, to do a film script hour, then to Lidl's and a library computer. Am now in touch with Network Rail Assets about laying the water pipe in Ingles Lane.[8] Visited John from 5 pm to 6 pm.

Wed, 10 Feb - To Fenner Close at 8.30 am, The client is much weaker than the last time I saw him, and in fact he is in an identical situation to John, although he has been able to stay in his home, with his Polish lodger being there at night to help. Netia gave me some mushroom and walnut soup and pancakes made with chickpea flower. Screwed some planking at the bottom of the cottage stable door, to make it rat proof. Drank home brew (as per Wed, Sat & Sun drinking pattern). UN brokered truce in Syrian war this week.

Fri, 12 Feb - To Fenner Close from 8.30 am to 9.30 am. At 11.30 am I visited Meritum's office. Things don't look good for me - I'm not being *rostered* for any hourly calls, I'm just covering absent staff. I think they're giving me minimal work, hoping I'll go away. Glum return to cottage for lunch. Delivered the rest of Netia's papers, worked on rat-proof door. Saw John at 6 pm. He is now bedbound, being hoisted onto commode or wheelchair. Lidl tinned herring meal.

Wed, 17 Feb - Collected the CDs from Hythe Camera Shop, with the three tape cassettes of Roy's Coastline Radio show dubbed on them. Phoned and walked to Julia's house, giving her a set of the CDs, as she'd previously requested. We had a chat over tea and coffee. Bus return to cottage, did an afternoon film script hour, drank beer, visited John with clothes

---

[8] On the railway side of the dividing fence.

and items from his flat. Am taking some of his clothes to charity shops.

Thurs, 18 Feb - A boiled egg breakfast with Netia, then I saw *Brooklyn* at the Film Club, set in '50s Ireland and New York - had a good first half. Cottage lunch, felt despondent most of the day. There's no work from Meritum. To the library late closing evening, filling in and sending a care work application to a London company. On the way I left a bag of John's clothes outside the Rhodes Minnis Cat Sanctuary charity shop.

Fri, 19 Feb - A 10 am walk to the Meritum office. Am still on their active staff list, and roster lady, Cath, gave me one or two calls on Sunday (and later one or two by phone, on Monday). I don't think they are deliberately ignoring me, just badly organised. Felt brighter on return walk, went to Lidl's, did an afternoon film script stint, then began another brew at John's. Ate sardines and peanut butter lunchtime and evening.

Sat, 20 Feb - Made a brief film script effort, then walked to Kent Auction Galleries, who were actioning some more of John's possessions, including that watercolour of Roy's which wasn't in the last sale. It didn't sell at all, although John made over £900 from other lots. To a library computer, researching Ingles Lane footpath ownership. Visited John - am helping with his financial arrangements. Drank beer before, during and after the visit. David Cameron has renegotiated our membership of the EU - small gains made.

Tues, 23 Feb - A morning film script hour. To a library computer, printing a form and info on getting a Land Registry search done on who owns Ingles Lane footpath. Cottage lunch and newspaper read lying on my bed. At 5 pm I visited John with more items from his flat. Staff came to put him on the commode, and I went downstairs to the lounge, then left, as John wanted to sleep. Cold weather, below 5° in cottage.

Wed, 24 Feb - Found Radnor Park toilets closed, got some warm water from the railway station toilets to wash my hair. Did a film script hour. Took two bin bags of John's clothes to charity shops, then went on a library computer, buying coach tickets. Drank home brew in the evening. The Wed, Sat & Sun drinking pattern is quite arbitrary - I drink on those days and don't drink on the other days, whether I feel like drinking or not.

Thurs, 25 Feb - Had bacon, egg and beans with Netia, then I went to the Classic Film Club, seeing Spielberg/Tom Hanks Bridge of Spies. Visited John at 4 pm, taking some financial stuff from his flat. A female solicitor from Rootes and Alliott also visited, to discuss John giving Power of Attorney to his sister, which the solicitor didn't think worth doing. I stayed with John until 8 pm. His head is now slumped down in his chest and seems locked there, and he can now only move his arms.

Fri, 26 Feb - At dawn I delivered half of 'Netia's newspapers. At 10 am I visited the Meritum office. They have no calls for me. I returned to the cottage then visited Kent Auction Galleries, withdrawing Roy's watercolour from future sales, as agreed with John. To Lidl's and a library computer in the afternoon, buying a rail ticket. Cut some Ivy growing up the cottage from next door. At dusk I delivered the rest of Netia's papers. Tinned herring meal, tea to drink.

Mon, 29 Feb - I spent most of the day digging and pulling the Ivy root out of the near corner of next door's patio.[9] Wintry day with a sleet shower. In the evening I visited John. I suggested I sort through all his papers at his flat.

---

[9] The next door property was vacant at the time.

Tues, 1 March - I think Netia gave me some breakfast and also some Thai fish soup she had made. I then spent the rest of the day, until after 7 pm, sorting through John's papers at his flat, putting at least 95% of it in bin bags - old bills, leaflets, junk mail, etc. I microwaved a frozen meal that was in his fridge.

Wed, 2 March - Made repairs to an old wooden fence panel that was dividing my patio from next door's patio. Did some more sorting at John's in the afternoon. I imagined someone doing the same thing for me at the cottage one day, throwing everything out. Microwaved another frozen meal there. There is a lot of news about the Syrian refugees arriving in Greece from Turkey, and also Britain's EU *in or out* referendum to be held in June. I feel minded to vote out.

Thurs, 3 March - Had an egg and bacon and mushroom soup brunch with Netia, then I suggested visiting Brian and Jenny, on the way taking John's bin bags of paper to the municipal refuse dump, to which Netia was agreeable, so we did this in her car. Tea and home made marmalade biscuits at Brian and Jenny's St. Mary's Road house, which I do like visiting. In the evening I took a cardboard box of family photos, letters, school reports, etc., to Wells House for John. Did more fence panel repairs and wood preserver painting earlier.

Sat, 6 March - At 7.30 am I did half of Netia's paper round, then had a 10 am town walk, posting the Land Registry form and returning via Castle Hill Avenue and John's flat. Made a brief film script effort, ate beans and hard steamed eggs, dozed, then sorted some of John's financial stuff. At 4 pm I began drinking beer while screwing the fence panel in place, then I walked to Wells House with the last of John's paper work from his flat. Mentally he seems OK again. Drank more beer there and on cottage return.

Folkestone, Fri, 25 March - Raining here. I arrived at the cottage at 1.30 am.[10] At 9 am I felt OK, went to the public toilet at 10 am, then I did a little film script work. To Sainsbury's for bread and back via the Leas, on a cloudless, sunny Good Friday. After lunch I cut back some brambles growing on the railway embankment, then at 5.30 pm I visited John. He seems stable now, bed bound, but OK mentally. Sunshine all day and it was still pleasant on the 8pm return walk, the smell of spring in the air.

Sat, 26 March - To the public toilet soon after it's 8 am opening - the time I usually aim for. Did a film script half hour, slept another hour then went into the town for John and to his flat, meeting Beth there, who told me that she and her partner, Martin, and the children are going to rent John's flat from Melissa. Later I began brewing some lager there - my last? Cut more brambles. Took four pillows to John from his flat. Drank home brew all evening.

Sun, 27 March - Slept off hangover. Wrote diary, made a miserable film script effort. Ate chocolate biscuits (John's), phoned Melissa, went to John's flat, retrieving a chair and a small table then I took the chair with me when I visited John at 5.30 pm. Drank beer there and back at the cottage, ate sardines, listened to a French pop radio station. I'm happy to be of help to John - I wouldn't be seeing anybody otherwise!

Tues, 29 March - At 10 am I went to a library computer, paying credit cards and buying a return Malaga flight in May, for £63. I have no income here, and hardly any in Spain, and I'll have to draw on the remainder of Roy's money soon.[11] I'll get £70 a week state pension in July. I visited John at 2.30 pm, taking the small folding table from his flat. He dictated one or two personal and financial letters. John's the only social contact with anyone I have.

---

[10] From La Herradura.
[11] i.e. diarist's inheritance from Roy.

Wed, 30 March - Made my daily film script effort, an hour or less. A morning visit to John's flat, retrieving a small wooden stool. Beth's partner, Martin, was there doing renovation work - new window frames, plaster/ceiling repairs, new toilet, bath & shower, etc. I don't need to earn much, but I can't even manage to earn that amount to support myself. How could I ever have supported a family? What a dud I've been.

Thurs, 31 March - To John's flat again, retrieving some school photos at the bottom of a cupboard and some books he wanted. Met Beth and her two young daughters, Lila and Ophelia, on the way there in Kingsnorth Gardens, and saw Martin again at the flat, which is now in a state of upheaval. At 5 pm I had a pleasant walk to Horn Street and asked Steve if he could take some files off an (obsolete) floppy disc and email them to me. He gave me Margot's (unused) wheelchair, with which I returned.

Fri, 1 April - To the library, printing the last few film script typed pages emailed by Steve. At 10 am I returned the four wheeled walking aid, borrowed by John from the Red Cross, then continued to the Meritum office. They had nothing for me - I'm obviously finished there, although no one's officially told me. At 2.30 pm I visited John, taking the wooden stool, then at 5 pm I continued to Horn Street and collected the floppy disc from Steve.

Sat, 2 April - From 7 am to 10 am I followed my daily breakfast/wash & shave/public toilet routine, including the washing of an item of clothing. I did a film script hour then at lunchtime I went to John's, to retrieve his briefcase and remove the door key safes. Ate baked beans and raw broccoli for lunch, began trying to type the printed film script pages on the tablet - very fiddly. At 4.30 pm I began drinking beer while re-stacking all the skip bricks, to see how much of a wall they would make. Aunty June[12] died, 84.

---

[12] Aunty June, diarist's mother's sister.

Tues, 5 April - Daily film script stint. Phoned the Ramsgate Red Cross with a view to giving them Margot's wheelchair, to replace the one borrowed for the Morrose Avenue service user, but their office has closed there. To Sainsbury's and Smith's, for myself and John. At 3 pm I visited him with some of his books, mostly self instruction paperbacks on how to get rich. Am making preparations to build a brick wall between my patio and the neighbouring patio.

Fri, 8 April - After returning from the public toilets I began brewing a lager kit, using water brought from the toilets (and stored in a large plastic container). What else can I do? Anyway, there's nothing wrong with the water. My daily film script stint is now spent on the second typed draft, using the tablet, which I can charge up here, like my mobile phone, thanks to the electricity line from Netia's house, although I can't repay her by doing her paper round any longer.[13] Visited John at 3 pm with more of his books.

Sat 9 April - Cold, wet weather. After a toilet visit I went to Coral's book makers, putting a Grand National bet on for John and a £1 each way bet for myself. Did a tablet stint then I went to the library, trying to complete, scan and send another care work application form, but I couldn't concentrate - I just printed the form. Baked bean lunch, slept, began digging the patio wall footings trench. Drank lager, listened to a French radio show on the Velvet Underground's music. My horse, *The Last Samurai*, came second in the 'National. Neil phoned earlier; he may be making a visit.

Wed, 13 April - Spent a soulful morning looking for something about Nanny's[14] Will in my box of old letters. Did some minimal script typing then at 2.45 pm I visited John and

---

[13] The newspaper was no longer being printed.
[14] The diarist's maternal grandmother. The children of a service user had complained that the diarist had left their father's bedroom in an untidy state.

made out one or two cheques for him, to be posted or paid in at his bank. Did trench digging before dusk, drank tea and ate some discount price Sainsbury's *hot cross buns*.

Wivenhoe, Thurs, 14 April - Went to the bank for John. At 11am I had an appointment with Meritum director, Charlotte Jones, about the customer complaint,[15] but she wasn't there and it's been rescheduled. Got the 12.14 Charing Cross train, a train from Liverpool Street to Colchester, then one to Wivenhoe, arriving at Hugh Brogan's Park Street house at 4.30pm.[16] To the Co-op shop, then I oven-cooked a cod-in-breadcrumbs-and-seed-topped ready meal for Hugh T. and myself. I drank tea, Hugh a bottle of Sancerre.

Folkestone, Tues, 19, April - To the library, then I posted a job application to SweetTree Home Care Services. At 3pm I visited John, writing a cheque or two for him. He has started some modest share investing, better than horse betting and something to interest him. Did trench digging afterwards, in and behind the roots of a Laburnum-type shrub in the corner of the patio, which I'd like to save, largely to aid summer privacy in the patio.

Fri, 22 April - While I was at the library Sweettree Homecare Services rang to invite me to an interview on Thursday. Felt cheered, though they said I'd be doing dementia work, which I've got to expect to do, to be sure of earning money. Visited John at 3pm, writing cheques and letters to post for him. He has a pleasant room and a good standard of care at Wells House Nursing Home, certainly the best he could expect on the National Health. Pop star, Prince, died yesterday, 57. Pro EU president Obama visited the UK this week.

---

[15] The children of a *service user* had complained that the diarist had left their father's bedroom in an untidy state.
[16] Diarist had been asked by his friends, Hugh Tulloch and Hugh Brogan, to provide a few days Live-in care support for them, after Hugh Tulloch had broken his arm.[17] Disclosure and Barring Service check.

Tues, 26 April - I see today, from Wilco and Wickes receipts, that this morning I bought and began brewing a beer kit and in the evening DBS[17] and reference checks, and a four day training course, so London here I come, working anywhere in the M25 circle. Made a lunchtime wheelbarrow trip to Wickes. At 4.15 pm I saw a doctor at the Manor clinic about a Hepatitis B jab and was told my employer should arrange it. I then visited John. Had Lidl tinned herring evening meal.

Wed, 4 May - At 3 am I woke and drank two pints of lager in bed. In the morning I went to John's bank, Sainsbury's and to my bank, then I cemented a two brick high row of broken bricks in the back of the trench. I balanced the existing make-shift fence panel on this and can now complete the whole wall without disturbing it or troubling neighbour, Guy, when he returns.[18] Made a 3 pm visit to John, had a lovely May undercliff road walk back, with a sunlit France in the distance. Drank lager, packed flight bag, got 8.14 pm Tonbridge train, thence to Gatwick, to sleep on North Terminal seating.

La Herradura, Sun, 15 May - Wrote diary. Worked on the EU letter.[19] A 1 pm walk to the seafront shop and village, on the first warm beach weather day, by the look of it. Melissa phoned - John is in hospital with a chest/bladder infection, also Noravirus has been making a resurgence - it doesn't sound good to me. Did more EU letter work, drank beer and at 7 pm I had another promenade walk and a drink with Geoff in a café. Tinned fabada meal, drank brandy & coke, took some selfie photos with mobile phone. I spent £4,600 last year, plus 3,000 euros rent. This includes about £2,000 for food and £1,200 credit card debt repayment. A week ago Leicester won the Premiership league title. Sadiq Khan succeeded Boris Johnson as London mayor.

---

[17] Disclosure and Barring Service check.
[18] After a custodial sentence.
[19] Diarist was writing to the *Daily Mail* about why Britain should leave the EU.

Folkestone, Mon, 30 May - A public spring holiday - overcast windy weather. Had a noon walk with wheelbarrow to Wickes for sand and cement. At 3 pm I visited John, who has recovered after his chest infection hospitalisation (not Noro virus). I helped him with his correspondence. Having been funded for his care home, his other benefits have been stopped, so he has no cash income at all any longer.

Wed, 1 June - To the library, paying credit cards. Began brewing another beer kit. I am also resuming an hour a day's film script typing on the tablet, the result of not liking to think that I am finished creatively. Visited John at 2.30 pm and wrote a couple of letters that he dictated. Drank five pints of home-brew lager and bitter. It was another very windy day.

Thurs, 2 June - To the library, paying domain name annual registration fees to GoDaddy.[20] (Withdrew £100 from Gibraltar NatWest to pay into Folkestone NatWest, to cover this, although I ended up paying with a Pay Pal registered credit card). Forgot to take reading glasses, bought another pair from Poundland. Visited John today, not yesterday. To Wickes this morning for sand and cement, did afternoon/evening brick laying, like yesterday.

Wed, 8 June - Did a daily minimal film script stint, typing on the tablet. At 11 am I visited John, and after the staff got him in his wheelchair I pushed him very slowly along Radnor Cliff Road, to the seat at the bottom of the Metropole steps. It was a lovely sunny warm day. John's head is locked over his left shoulder, and his neck begins to ache sitting in the wheelchair. Afterwards, I drank some beer. To Wickes at 7 pm, for sand and cement.

Sat, 11 June - At 10 am Netia gave me breakfast, then we went in her car to visit John at Wells House Nursing Home, then to her sister, Flicky's St Mary's Road cottage, then to Brian and Jenny's house near her. Their garden really is delightful, with

---

[20] For diarist's www.vapourtrailsintheblue.com website

many unusual shrubs and trees planted over thirty five years. Mild, summery weather. On the way back we went to the café on Hythe esplanade where Netia's daughter, Flo, works at the weekend. Did some bricklaying, drank beer, had dusk walk up the Leas grass.

Sun, 12 June - Daily 8 am to 10 am breakfast/wash/toilet routine. Wrote diary, did film script typing. Bought some vests for John from Primark and visited him at 3 pm. He says he feels well, but his voice is weak. Drank beer there and while doing a fortifying repair to some wooden fence panelling on the patio wall - two young kids have been climbing across the patio to enter the back door of a neighbouring house. Dusk Leas grass walk. It seems a good year for Elderflower this year.

Stamford Brook, Sun, 19 June - I left Aylmer Rd[21]at 8 am, for a quiet sunny walk to the tube for Victoria. Wrote diary and had a discreet plastic bottle pee while sitting on an Ebury gardens seat, before getting the 11 am Folkestone coach. Swigged some brandy at Ashford, then home-brew at the cottage and during a 2.30 pm visit to John (after a buoyant walk up the Leas grass). Drank more beer while cleaning some bricks of old cement, ate sardines and a bar of dark chocolate, to bed at 8 pm, listening to a transistor radio (an old one of Dad's, which I do believe was originally on sale in his Lodge Park[22]hardware shop) On Thursday Labour MP, Josephine Cox, was shot dead by a racist nut case in her Yorkshire constituency - a terrible event, which could influence the EU referendum outcome.

Thurs, 23 June - EU Referendum Day. Slept off hangover. I have a ballot paper, but I intend abstaining after all my time in Spain, which let me earn a bit of money unofficially (plus enjoy the coffee and tapas). I still hope we leave though. At 2.30 pm I visited John, also not voting. John's head is now in a

---

[21] Diarist had been staying with his nephew.
[22] Lodge Park housing estate, Redditch.

permanent sideways position, but the staff have told me not to tuck any more pillows under it to raise it a little. Did brick laying, afterwards, and went at 8 pm to Wickes, for sand and cement.

Sun, 26 June - Felt anxiety on waking.[23] Wrote diary then did tablet typing from 10 am to 11 am. To the bank cash dispenser and a library computer. I was going to visit Dukes Bar[24]at 1 pm, on the way to John's,[25] but it was closed, so I returned to the cottage for a tinned sardine lunch, then visited John at 2.30 pm, finding Colin and Harold also visiting. They both looked well and it was good to see them. Did some brick laying and drank beer back at the cottage. Had a dusk Leas walk, Dukes Bar still closed.

Wed, 29 June - At 2.40 pm I saw John. He seems to be getting worse again. His arms are now being affected. I noticed, and his left hand is useless for holding anything, even a letter to read. He was distant and subdued, but comfortable, he says. Drank some home brew and did brick laying back at the cottage, then at 8 pm had a pint at Dukes Bar, Jessica[26]serving.

Tues, 12 July - To Sainsbury's at 9 am for powdered milk and porridge. Had a wheelbarrow trip to Wickes for sand and cement. At 2.45 pm I visited John. He's still stable, mentally. He gets frustrated, he says. The staff are changing his bed position regularly, and he can now only move his right arm feebly and just about hold a beaker. Did brick laying afterwards, until dusk. I have been thinking of halting this record of my doings, being 65 tomorrow. Will I?

Thurs, 14 July - Slept off hangover then had an ineffectual morning. From 2.40 pm to 4.30 pm I visited John. Did brick laying afterwards. Had a wank yesterday, as I continue to do in my old age; had one today. Theresa May became PM this week.

---

[23] Diarist had been concerned about the EU referendum result and his care work prospects.
[24] At Windsor hotel, Folkestone.
[25] i.e. Wells House Nursing Home.
[23] Diarist had been concerned about the EU referendum result and his care work prospects.
[24] At Windsor hotel, Folkestone.
[26] Jessica, Dukes Bar's current barmaid.

A sniper shoots several policemen in the USA, after a black suspect is killed by policemen during a road check.

Folkestone, Fri, 16 Sept - Rain has ended the fine weather spell. I found myself trying to raw plug a makeshift toiletries shelf over the sink, but they wouldn't *take*, so I just bashed nails through the shelf bracket holes to fix them. Saw John at 2.30 pm. His voice has got noticeably fainter.[27] Worked on the brick wall, packing cement behind it to try and correct a two inch wavering from the vertical at the top.

Sat, 17 Sept - Netia gave me an egg-on-toast and jam-on-toast breakfast, and I stayed until noon. To a library computer, verifying tomorrow's flight. Visited John again, as did Peter Simmons and his present lady friend, Catherine. Did wall cementing before dusk. I've been building the wall by eye judgement only and what I've done is not quite vertical. Drank home-brew, had two pints at the Windsor hotel's Duke's Bar.

La Herradura, Fri, 23 Sept - Feel really well, mentally and physically, this week, but this morning Melissa rang to say John is hospitalised with a chest infection, and that the next twelve hours are critical. This sounds like the end - he can't go on, surely. It's no surprise, and I don't feel that affected by it, although I had thought of him this week, just lying there while I'm here in the sun. I cleaned several carpets for Swedish couple, the Marners, off the track up to the Punta[28]from the village. Cooked a battered fishy evening meal, had an ice cream and tinned peaches sweet.

Sun, 25 Sept - John can go on. Melissa says he pulled through his chest infection. Apparently he woke up and was asked if he wanted to be resuscitated the next time it happened and he said *yes*. Dusted my bedroom and pruned the driveway shrubs. Drank Rosa's whisky [29]with coke. Saw Geoff in the village,

---

[27] Diarist had been doing a Live-in care work job in London.
[28] Punta de la Mona, La Herradura.
[29] A present from regular carpet cleaning clients, Alfonse and Rosa Mettel.

after having a brandy and coffee at the café Conchillo. Got the 5.30 pm bus to Nerja, met Carol[30] and we had gourmet tapas in Plaza Cavana then went to Linda's Bar. Got the 9.45 pm return bus.

Gatwick Airport, Fri, 7 Oct - Slept North Terminal seating until 7 am.[31] Airport shave & shit, had hard boiled eggs, defrosted peas and fresh milk for breakfast. Wrote up diary. Trains to Folkestone, arriving at the cottage at 11.30 am. Visited Netia and went with her to a clothes buying shop in Bouverie Road. She then gave me a chicken Kiev lunch. At 3 pm I visited John, finding him in better shape than expected after the hospitalisation crisis. Brewed some beer at dusk, was in bed listening to *The Archers* at 7 pm.

Folkestone, 10 Oct - Slept off a crashing night time headache. Phoned Sweet Tree co-ordinator, Michael - my carer profile and that of another carer has been sent to a prospective client. Wrote up diary,[32] had a noon walk to a library computer. Cottage muesli/tinned sardine lunch, saw John at 3 pm. Did patio wall brick laying work. Tinned chicken curry evening meal, eaten cold from tin.

Tues, 11 Oct - A noon walk into town, buying vests for John at Primark, where I also bought a £16 pair of shoes for myself. All my shoes are worn out, many of them Roy's, although I have decent footwear for the care work. Delivered John's shopping at 3 pm and did some letter writing and paper work for him. Made a 6 pm wheelbarrow trip to Wickes, for sand and cement.

Wed, 12 Oct - Have resumed a daily token film script stint on the tablet. Colin and Harold rang, and after they visited John I met them at the Leas Cliff Hall café. Peter Wagstaff and John's

---

[30] Carol Golding, Wivenhoe resident, frequent Nerja visitor.
[31] Diarist had just returned from La Herradura.
[32] From the previous day's rough draft.

shopper friend, Tony Fox, were there too. Colin and Harold came to see the cottage - good to see them sitting on my sofa! Colin was adamant that I couldn't live here, not without toilet, water and electric light, and that I should go on the council housing list. Drank beer afterwards, did a Wickes wheelbarrow trip. I felt great back at the cottage.

Sat, 15 Oct - Netia's gone to Barcelona for the weekend with Tamsin. Did noon brick laying then cooked a fried brunch. Went to see John, doing shopping for him on the way. He seems to bear his condition with equanimity. He can only move one arm feebly, but he still signs documents, if illegibly, and takes an on-going interest in his affairs. Got boozed up back at the cottage, listened to Absolute Radio Saturday rock music programme. I have been reading Nabokov's *The Enchanter*, a strange precursor to *Lolita*. It has his inimitable style, but is a pretty minor work, I think. Bob Dylan wins Nobel Prize for Literature.

Wed, 19 Oct - Phoned Sweet Tree and booked one of their in house training courses, *Personal, Stoma and Catheter Care*, for next Monday afternoon - got to show willing. Visited John from 3 pm to 5 pm, writing a letter or two for him. I then drank beer before, during and after a dusk wheelbarrow trip to Wickes, for sand and cement (£6.44).

Sat, 22 Oct - Woke in the night feeling too good to sleep - had two 4 am pints of home-brew in bed, then slept 'til 8am's film script half hour, then I had a bacon and egg breakfast with Netia. Did brick laying, saw John 3 pm to 5 pm, during which I walked back to Sainsbury's for some Fruit Pastilles for him. I was swigging home brew and continued boozing while brick laying until dusk. I had a couple of drinks at Duke's Bar - only hotelier, Mick, and a couple of elderly customers were there. Phoned Kim today.

Wed, 26 Oct - At 8 am Etelle gave me some breakfast again - fried potato & sausage *patatas bravas*, and a newspaper read, then I did some gardening for her. Did cottage brick laying for an hour, then visited John from 3 pm to 5 pm. He has a cold. Did more brick laying at dusk, while drinking home brew. Sweet Tree have asked me to do a couple of single day's Live-in work with another client. I feel really good, generally - don't know why this should be.

Sat, 29 Oct - Rewrote some notes taken during the shadowing.[33] Boiled egg lunch. To Sainsbury's for John, then I went to visit him 3 pm to 5 pm. He was OK, dozing and listening to Classic FM radio on a mono earphone I got for him lately. I sat doing sewing - shortening some some care work trousers. There was another garden bonfire next door at the cottage, so I just drank beer and listened to Absolute Radio.[34] I also had two cans of beer at Duke's Bar at the Windsor hotel and a Leas grass walk.

Wed, 2 Nov - No rain lately,[35] went twice to the public toilet for water, needed for washing myself and laundry. I get two or three litres per visit. The tablet battery was flat, so I did some filing instead of typing. Visited John 3 pm to 4.30 pm. It is dark now at 5 pm. Drank home brew, used the step ladder to sit on top of the new patio wall. Ate peanut butter sandwiches and listened to Absolute Radio.

Sun, 6 Nov - Went twice to the public toilet. Wrote diary, did film script hour. Ate two fried egg sandwiches. Did fence wood-preserver painting. Visited John at 4 pm and found that he can't now use his arm to reach his mouth. I fed him Twiglets, Fruit Pastilles and his cheese on toast tea when it came. Drank home brew at the cottage. Heated some tinned stewed steak with a sliced carrot. This week a High Court ruling complicates the government's Brexit implementation plans.

---

[33] Diarist had *shadowed* another carer working with a client in Tooting the previous day.
[34] Rather than do any brick laying.
[35] Diarist collected rain water to use.

Tues, 8 Nov - Donald Trump just beat Hillary Clinton to the US Presidency - as amazing as Obama's win. It could be disastrous - huge borrowing to boost the economy, appeasing Russia, being protectionist, maybe resulting in some catastrophic war. Saw John this afternoon. He was very sluggish, apparently he couldn't talk yesterday. His doctor was there - they are going to further adjust his medication.

Sat, 12 Nov - Am sleeping about ten hours a night, certainly on non-drinking days - nothing else to do in the dark. I get up with the 7 am dawn, after listening to Radio 4 news, but they have started having cricket on the longwave then, on old, non-digital radios. Did a film script stint and some paperwork/admin. Began drinking at 2 pm, visited John, who seemed a bit better. Fed him his cheese on toast 5 pm tea. Had a can of beer (all they've got) in Duke's Bar on the way back, ate tinned sausages, heated with a chopped onion. Continued boozing on the 8.09 pm Tonbridge train and trains to Gatwick.

Gatwick Airport, Thurs, 17 Nov - Had a seating sleep until about 7 am.[36] Toilet wash & shave, trains to Folkestone, arriving cottage about 11.30 am (after mistakenly going on a Tonbridge to Tunbridge Wells train). To Lidl's and a library computer. Met Netia outside her house. Have little appetite and a minor cough & sniffle. Made care work job preparations. To a library computer again, paying credit cards, then on to see John at 5 pm. His sister rang me on my return to the cottage. Did more care work job preparation by torch light, before bed at 8pm. Am still reading Emma,[37] a *Miss Bossy Boots* kind of girl.

Marylebone, Thurs, 8 Dec - Sweet Tree carer, Carmen, relieved me at midday.[38] I went to the nearby Barley Mow pub for a couple of pints, having seen in a local magazine an article about a short film that the pub management and staff had made there. Bought some vodka and orange juice in a Strand

---

[36] Diarist had just returned from La Herradura.
[37] By Jane Austin.
[38] The diarist had a Live-in care work job in Marylebone.

Tesco shop, to drink on the train. Visited John at 7 pm, having a beer at Duke's Bar before and afterwards. Former barmaid, Jessica, was a customer there. John is now immobile, apart from one hand, or its fingers, and lying all curled up on pain killers, complaining they don't reposition him enough.

Folkestone, Fri, 9 Dec - I went to see John again at 9.30 am, writing Xmas cards for him. After a midday return to the cottage I got the 2.09 pm Charing Cross train and Northern Line tube to Whetstone/Totteridge. At 5 pm I arrived at the client's Greenview flat, relieving permanent carer, Sebastian. The client had just recovered from a bout of diarrhoea. Cooked salmon cutlets with broccoli and potatoes, which we shared. On Tuesday, while with the client in Manchester Street, Marylebone, I was sitting on the sofa reading *Emma*, the client and his wife in their respective armchairs, when Manchester Street was mentioned in the novel - quite a coincidence, as the client's wife agreed.

Wed, 14 Dec - Had a slothful porridge/toilet/shave routine. Netia gave me some additional egg/jam/toast breakfast. Went to the RBS bank, for John, and Sainsbury's. I visited him at 4 pm, opening Christmas cards and other correspondence for him. Drank some beer back at the cottage. On Sunday Russian/Assad forces were about to take Aleppo, with the civilians there in dire straights.

Fri, 16 Dec - Went to the RBS bank for John and did other shopping for him. Made credit card payments on a library computer - £2,300 now owing. Cottage lunch then I cleaned a few bricks of cement. Visited John at 3 pm. Spent an hour attending a *relatives of the residents* meeting, then fed John puréed food at 5 pm. Melissa rang me and she spoke to John. I left about 7.30 pm. Drank home-brew and began packing for the care work job.[39] Some Aleppo civilians were allowed to go to rebel held territory. Are the rebels Muslim fundamentalists?

---

[39] For the diarist's Marylebone client, a former doctor.

Stamford Brook, Mon, 9 Jan - A tube strike was on, had a 11.30 am walk with Nick to the Duchess of Cambridge pub bus stop, me for a 94 bus to Marble Arch, then a rain drizzle walk to Marylebone Road for a crowded bus towards Kings Cross, walking the last bit past the impressive St Pancras hotel. Got High Speed train to Folkestone (£20.25), cottage 3.30 pm. Visited John at 5 pm and wrote some letters for him, return walk in squally rain, bed 7 pm. Last Monday Carol told me that Hugh Tullock had died - saddening news.

Folkestone, Tues, 10 Jan - Slept a bit fitfully. After porridge flake/wash/public toilet routine, I went shopping in the town for John. Netia gave me some lunch. Chipped cement off old bricks before dusk, then took John his shopping. He dictated another letter, saying in it that he couldn't move at all now, but hoped a change in schizophrenic medication would restore him to health. Fed him his 5 pm scrambled egg and ice cream meal - he can only eat soft food. Back at the cottage I ate some tortilla crisps he'd given me. Phoned Carol today.

Sat, 14 Jan - After a twelve hour sound sleep, I felt fit. Went shopping for John and to his bank cash dispenser. Did some tidying back at the cottage, none done lately. Ate Christmas cake given by John, cleaned more bricks, have enough now for the final two rows of the patio wall. A sunset walk to Wells House taking John's shopping. Drank home-brew back at the cottage and had two cans of John Smiths beer at Duke's Bar. Got a sausage & chips meal on the way back. It is cold - just above freezing. Had a reality check moment - me, about to spend a frugal, lonely old age in my poor cottage.

Sun, 15 Jan - Tidied a bit then took my diary and financial admin to the warmth of the library Reference Room.[1] To the RBS cash machine for John. Netia gave me some roast chicken dinner, or lunch, which restored me. Wheelbarrowed to Wickes for sand and cement. Positioned a row of bricks before dusk, drank home brew and heated a tin of stewing steak, while listening to Absolute Radio on the digital portable radio.[2]

[1] Folkestone Library Heritage Research Room.
[2] A recent purchase.

Tues, 16 Jan - Had an 8.45 am dental check-up appointment, teeth OK (£20). Had some 10am breakfast with Netia, then I worked on the final row of patio wall brick laying, having to go to Wickes at 2 pm for more sand. The wall is now complete, although I'd really like to have it two stories high, to accommodate an upstairs toilet, as well as downstairs toilet/ shower. To the RBS bank for John, saw him at 6pm. Melissa phoned me later.

Tues, 31 Jan - Had a sluggish breakfast time routine, although the cough is suddenly better. Netia gave me some mid morning breakfast/lunch. Went on a library computer, paying credit cards, and being cheered by seeing further Sweet Tree wages in my bank account. Visited John at 4 pm, wrote a letter or two for him and fed him his 5 pm tea/supper. I was back at Netia's at 7.16 pm and she gave me soup and a sausage and sautéed potato meal, Chris was there briefly.

Wed, 1 Feb - Another inconsequential day, did no film script work, didn't even find time to write up this diary from its rough first draft. Netia gave me some 11 am breakfast, then I spent an hour packing for the care work job, then I returned to her for some freshly home baked spinach tart. Went shopping for John and to his bank, saw him from 4 pm to 6.30 pm. Drank four pints of home brew back at the cottage.

Fri, 24 Feb - Followed my usual breakfast time routine to 10 am. Paid credit cards on a library computer. Cottage lunch and doze. Visited John at 5 pm, taking his stamp catalogues.[3] Fed him his puréed evening meal and did some correspondence and paper work for him. He has had the police visit him, apparently, about a homosexual assault he suffered in 1988. Saw Etelle on the way there.

Sat, 25 Feb - Had a custard cream biscuit breakfast. Did shopping for John and got cash from his bank's dispenser. After a cottage lunch I went on a library computer then to see John. Fed him his 5 pm meal, turned the pages of stamp

---

[3] Diarist had bought some stamp collecting catalogues for John at Stanley Gibbons stamp dealership in the Strand.

collecting magazines for him to read. Drank home brew back at the cottage, plus two tins of John Smiths bitter at Duke's Bar, the only other customers, as usual, being an elderly quartet of the hoteliers, Mick and Marjorie and their two friends.[4] Bought some sausage and chips on the way back.

Mon, 27 Feb - Felt jaded and gloomy. Tomorrow's Venice trip seems like a chore, I'm ashamed to say. I only booked it because I swore to Hugh Tulloch I'd go last year, and never did. He and Hugh Brogan went numerous times. Overcast damp weather. Visited John at 5pm. I wasn't going to mention the trip to him, but I did when saying I'd see him on Friday. Bought a better mobile phone today, a second hand Samsung A3, for £129, to get the *People Planner* app needed for care work.

Venice, Fri, 3 March - Found my ticket invalid for the 8.10 am airport ferry, had to get another company's 8.40 am ferry (15€). Had a quick walk to the Lido beach, then on the ferry I chatted with two Scottish women who'd been here during the carnival. On my 10.15 am Easyjet flight to Luton a Venetian woman beside me told me about a holiday home to rent near Venice. Got a Green Line bus to Victoria then a 3.02 pm train from there to Folkestone, arriving at 5 pm. Had a pint of home brew then went and saw John, not looking well at all again. I showed him my Venice selfie photos and wrote one or two letters and cards for him. Drank more brew back at the cottage, my consciousness was still swaying from the ferry boat! - Venice was a beautiful dream.

Sat, 4 March - Had a duck egg breakfast with Netia, showed her the selfies. Unpacked and tidied, went shopping for John - what a shame to sully the impression of Venice in my head with mundane reality. Sorted some receipts before going to see John at 5.15 pm. He looked as bad as could be, to me, and said he would die if he didn't go to hospital, but the staff didn't think it necessary. I fed him some ice cream and he did perk up after that. Made a 7.15 pm return to Netia's, who gave me a

---

[4] Mick's sister and her husband.

battered chicken meal, Chris there, I enthused about Venice. My arm is still painful.[5] Ingles Meadow Garden Centre has closed for redevelopment - boo!

Sun, 5 March - At 8.30 am I began writing up my Venice diary. Visited John at 10 am, finding him looking somewhat better. I don't think a doctor or hospital could do anything for him. I stayed a couple of hours then went to Netia's for lunch - veg soup and her Thai fish stew. She showed me a *Daily Express* £1 Calais day trip offer and I booked one at the library for Tuesday for myself, Netia unable to come. Walked back via Castle Hill Avenue, crocuses out. Was going to go back to Netia's again, but drank too much brew and went to bed about 8 pm.

Mon, 6 March - Went shopping for John in the morning. After lunch I re-read Cyril Connolly[6] on Venice, who took a jaundiced view of its rapacious gondoliers and pigeon shit - at least they must have done something about the pigeons since the 'sixties. At 4 pm I had a slice of spinach tart with Venetia, then I visited John from 5 pm to 7 pm. He is stable again and I'm helping him renew his *international pen pal club* and stamp swapping activities.

Wed, 8 March - To the library for flight check-in and boarding pass printing. At 12.30 pm Netia gave me some Thai fish stew, then toast with some Brie I'd brought from Calais. Visited John from 5 pm to 7 pm. Got the 8.30 pm Tonbridge train, Gatwick at 10 pm.

La Herradura, Tues, 14 March - Was up at 4 am to make ready for the 7.30 am Granada bus. Wrote diary at Granada bus station (after buying 10 euro reading glasses at a kiosk there). Bus to the airport for the 12. 05 pm Easyjet to Gatwick, where the weather was better than rainy Granada. Folkestone 5 pm, visited John at Wells House Nursing Home. Had 7.30 pm return walk, the air sweet and fragrant with springtime. Went early to

[5] Diarist had begun having a shoulder pain two weeks earlier.
[6] Cyril Connolly, author and literary critic.

bed. Claire[7]didn't look homeless. Her builder husband left her in October, she said, after cleaning their joint bank account out of £30,000.

Folkestone, Wed, 15 March - Had a sound sleep, am feeling better. Saw Netia at her door - she has a cold. To the RBS bank for John and a library computer. Cottage lunch then I began cutting brambles on the railway embankment. At 5 pm I saw John for a couple of hours. He asked me how he looked and I replied as positively as possible. He is being looked after well there. Drank beer at the cottage, to bed at 9 pm - had to pee several times in the night.

Fri, 24 March - A routine day. Am not able to change the Orange email account[8]wholesale over to Gmail, due to some glitch. To save some past emails I am copying and pasting them individually, a tedious task. At 5 pm I visited John. Slowly, slowly, his decline continues. His voice is a barely audible whisper now, and he is losing weight. However, he is still alert and interested in things. He dictated a couple of letters. A 7.30 pm return to the cottage for Lidl tinned herrings and tea to drink.

Sat, 25 March - The client is now likely to return home on Monday or Tuesday.[9] At 10 am I went and had breakfast with Netia and Tamsin, Chris scarpering on my arrival. I know I tread on his toes a bit, visiting Netia, but we are really OK, he and I. Tamsin looks well. Did shopping for John and went to the library. At 5 pm I visited him and fed him his scrambled egg and jelly sweet meal, plus some chocolate afterwards. To Duke's Bar on the way back, hoteliers, Mick, and his wife, sitting in the bar with their two or three Saturday drink friends as usual, plus one or two other customers. Drank home-brew before and after.   .

---

[7] Claire, an Englishwoman the diarist had met in La Herradura, hitching a lift with her two lap dogs and a laundry bag of possessions.
[8] Orange was discontinuing its *Free Serve* email service
[9] The diarist's Marylebone client had been hospitalised with a chest infection.

Sun, 26 March - Made a sluggish start, with a custard cream biscuit tea-dunked breakfast. Did a film script hour and wrote diary. Chicken soup lunch, had a sunny walk into town and to a library computer. Visited John from 5 pm to 7 pm. On the way back the painted Leas Cliff Hall lights were on, my handiwork proving effective.[10] With luck they will leave them as they are. The walk back from John's is most pleasant along the Lower Sandgate Road and up to the Leas. Drank beer, had a tinned stewed steak with mushy peas Sunday dinner.

Marylebone, Thurs, 5 April - Misgne[11] visited before Carmen[12] relieved me at noon. It was a glorious sunny day outside. I went on a Marylebone library computer, then I had a picnic lunch in Paddington Street Gardens, many others doing the same. To the Stanley Gibbons stamp dealership in the Strand, for John, and Tesco Extra, for a small bottle of vodka and some orange juice. These I began swigging on the 3 pm from Charing Cross. Felt buoyant, sitting in the sun with trackside primroses - a host of them at Pluckley. Visited John at 5 pm, a bit tipsily. Afterwards I had halves of lager at the Salisbury and Carlton hotels, both have been revamped. Drank beer and ate a chip shop meal at the cottage; was very enjoyably pissed. A week ago Theresa May triggered Article 50 and Britain's EU exit. She's been handling things well, but I still think *no deal* is the most likely outcome of the Brexit talks to come.

Fri, 7 April - Slept off hangover, made a sluggish start to the day. After a film script stint I went to Wilcos for a lager kit, then went on a library computer. Began brewing the kit after lunch and visited John at 5 pm. Etelle had visited with some food, and as John wasn't hungry I ate his evening meal. Had a lovely Lower Sandgate Road/Leas evening return walk, Alexander and flowering red current fragrant, Leas grass recently mown. There are a few bluebells outside the cottage on the embankment land.

---

[10] Diarist had modified some electric lighting, to make it less glaring when looking at the sea view from the Leas Cliff Hall at night.
[11] Misgne, carer from the Health Vision agency.
[12] Carmen, SweetTree Homecare Services carer.

Sat, 8 April - Did a film script hour then went shopping for John and to a library computer. I still can't transfer Orange email to Gmail in one go, so am dealing with the emails and email addresses individually. Measured the length of Ingle Lane footpath - a hundred and sixty feet to my door. Visited John, taking and checking some Scratchcards for him (like I did yesterday) To Duke's Bar, where I played pool with someone, arm hurting like hell. Drank beer at the cottage, listened to radio music.

Sun, 9 April - Slept off a hangover, got up 8 am and began a film script stint before 10 am, but then went to have breakfast with Netia - a fry-up, plus toast and marmalade. Wrote diary back at the cottage and had a brief doze, before arriving at Wells House at 3 pm, for John's afternoon tea party. Colin and Harold and John's ex-shopper friend, Tony Fox, were the other guests. It was bizarrely pleasant, chatting over tea and John's chocolate cake, with him lying a complete invalid in front of us. Drank beer at the cottage, ate tinned stewed steak and mushy peas.

Mon, 10 April - At 8 am I made an appointment at the Manor Clinic and saw a doctor at 10.10 am, who prescribed some anti-inflammatory cream for my shoulder pain. After dithering, I got trains to Ashford and Bromley South, for a bus to Oakley Road and a walk to City Irrigation Ltd, buying another twenty five metres of barrier pipe and a connector (£242). To Wells House, visiting John until 7.30 pm. Tinned curry meal.

Tues, 11 April - Was up at 6.15 am, to do a bit on the film script before my 8.15 am toilet visit - am trying to keep it going. Carmen phoned me to say the client has stopped responding at all, is now comatose. Surely I won't be going back, am feeling resigned to it. Began digging a water pipe trench on the railway side of the fence - have got to take steps towards getting the water mains on. I'm seeing John every day and doing things for him - time consuming, but he can't have long, either. Wheelbarrowed to Wickes for sand.

Thurs, 13 April - Resumed my current routine, with an 8 am start to it. A daily computer hour, still dealing with the Orange to Gmail change - an absolute bane. A daily trench digging hour or so, with my weakened left arm. What have I done to it? Is it rheumatism, here to stay? A daily John visit, usually feeding him his 5.30 pm meal, which is often just the sweet. I can hardly catch what he says, even holding my ear to his face, I have to do lip reading now. In Margate, on Wednesday, I knocked on *Rebecca's* door and a carer said she/he was still there.

Fri, 14 April - I've hit some concrete just a few inches down in the trench. Today or yesterday I was going to have breakfast with Netia, then it was changed to lunch, but I started listening to a Radio 4 phone-in programme on care work and I went to Netia's with my mobile phone held to my ear, leaving her a bit miffed. John looked terrible on my visit - grave faced, as if stricken with his predicament. He ate some chocolate, partly regurgitated. He really only has one bed position. The nurses express regret that he can't be made more comfortable.

Sat, 15 April - The client has died. Sweet Tree texted me and I got another from his son. Poor Odette,[13] she was clinging on to hope. I'm out of work, but feel OK about it - they'll find me something. After the getting up routine I went to a library computer, opening a Tesco savings account for myself and paying a credit card instalment for John. I have got his bank account accessible online. Saw Netia in her garden. The trench looks impossible to do; my arm feels a little better. Drank beer, went to Duke's Bar, where hotelier, Mick, talked about a London – Edinburgh *blowpipe* transport idea - an idea that I've previously mooted there.

Sun, 16 April - Easter Day. I felt a bit vacant. Ate chocolate biscuits, had a 9 am toilet visit, did a film script hour. Had some 12.45 pm lunch with Netia and felt grateful for it. Have ducked an invite from Kim to go to Leigh. They are hospitable, but I'm never really relaxed there, Kim so touchy. Also, after that

[13] Odette - not the client's real name.

episode when Roy died,[14] I swore I'd never let it happen again. Saw John at 5 pm, not looking great. Fed him the sweet of his meal and read to him. Cottage beer, tinned stewed steak with mushy peas and carrot meal.

Tues, 18 April - Resumed my current routine. At the library I suddenly succeeded in changing the Orange/Free Serve email accounts to Gmail, a relief. I am now digging a trench a few feet out from the fence on the railway land. They do allow utility pipes on their land, but you are supposed to have official permission and pay a fee. Will I get away with it? Saw John from 5 pm to 7 pm. Theresa May has called a snap election over Brexit. I wish she hadn't - I'll have to vote for her now.

Wed, 19 April - At the library I bought a return ticket to Malaga, 16 to 24 May, for £53. Rang Sweet Tree to enquire about doing other Live-in work. A daily film script stint, just pecking at it. A daily visit to John. Today after my 7 pm return I did trench digging for an hour before dusk. Drank about five pints of home brew.

Thurs, 20 April - At 11 am Netia and I saw *La,La,Land* at the Silver Screen cinema's Film Club, at my invitation, then she stood me coffee at the Asda supermarket café and lunch at her home. Saw John from 5 pm to 6.45 pm, then walked back to the Leas Cliff Hall and used a voucher that Netia had to get £10 off a £28 ticket to see an Ellen Kent production of *La Bohème*, with soprano, Ecaterina Danu as Mimi.

Fri, 21 April - At 9.30 am I telephoned Odette Did a film script stint then went to Lidl's and the library, still saving old emails on memory sticks. Bought bicycle brake blocks at the Bicycle shop opposite the library. Visited John at 5 pm. His doctor and a dietician have seen him, after he'd been looking quite deathly the last two days, but today he was looking better and showing interest in things again. Fed him a little food and read to him. He is now having some protein milk supplement.

---

[14] When the diarist's brother had visited him in La Herradura.

Sun, 23 April - Followed my getting up routine to 10 am. Made a miserable film script effort, wrote diary. Had a noon library computer hour then cottage lunch, then did trench digging - very slow going. I just have to get the water on somehow if I'm going to stay here indefinitely, but the job seems impossibly daunting and problematic. For instance, I could take all summer on the trench and then be stopped by the railway company at the last minute. Saw John, subdued and withdrawn again. He knows he hasn't got much to live for. Drank beer, had a stewed steak meal.

Tues, 25 April - The client's funeral was today. I am refraining from phoning Sweet Tree about finding another client. I have some money in hand, and I need to get some work done on the water pipe project. To Lidl supermarket and then Wilcos for a lager kit, which I started brewing. Daily film script and library computer hours. Today I did some trench digging after dawn, and some more before dusk, after seeing John.

Wed, 26 April - Sweet Tree phoned me today about another client and emailed his Care Plan. Visited John from 5 pm to 7 pm. I'm walking there via Kingsnorth Gardens, Jointon Road, Earls Avenue and the Leas grass, and returning along the Lower Sandgate Road and up pathways to the Leas and Castle Hill Avenue. I love the Alexander and flowering red current fragrance. Am enjoying another lovely springtime, while poor John is completely cut off from it.

Thurs, 27 April - Phoned Netia at 10 am and had some breakfast with her, Tamsin visiting. At 11 am I saw American film, *Manchester by the Sea*, at the Film Club. My script is surely too long for a film, it will have to be much chopped down. Saw Netia again afterwards. Did afternoon trench digging before visiting John. This week he has suddenly lost his interest in things. Today he said he was going blind. The old lilac tree in my patio is still alive and blooming again.

Sat, 29 April - Made a sluggish start and had some breakfast with Netia until noon, then I went to the library, saving more Orange emails for a couple of hours - why, for God's sake? Did trench digging - have run into some compacted hardcore, like concrete. Visited John, to Duke's Bar on the way back and the Central Fish Bar for sausage and chips. Drank home brew. The Beatles' *Sergeant Pepper* fifty years old. I loved it at fifteen or sixteen. I never thought I'd be a carer in fifty years time. I thought I'd have a wonderful life - something more in the line of being rich and famous myself.

Sun, 30 April - Wrote diary, had a library computer hour. Reheated some chips for lunch and a bit of chicken. Did a trench digging hour - very hard going. Visited John, finding him tearful, with trembly lips. He's been telling the staff he wants to die. The sooner he does die the better now, but we encourage him to keep going. He has become a quivering, frightened, skeletal thing in his bed - what a way to end. Heated tinned stewing steak with some cherry tomatoes, carrot, onion and mushy peas - not bad. Drank home brew lager.

Mon, 1 May - May Day holiday. I think, after sleeping off a hangover, that I stayed at the cottage doing some Registry filing, and also a script stint and work on the trench. I visited John, I'm sure. Have a slight sore throat - could be a cold coming.

Tues, 2 May - Did an early trench digging hour. Did film script and library computer hours, to Lidl supermarket and Sainsbury's for John. Phoned Sweet Tree, declining the prospective new client job, as it requires one permanent carer. Accepted a three night Live-in job starting tomorrow. Visited John, he seems marginally better, doesn't talk, just stares unblinkingly at me. Had a couple of brandies with orange juice before bed.

Holland Park, Fri, 5 May - After helping the client shower and put on clean clothes and have breakfast, I left at 10 am, after the arrival of Jenny.[15] Sunny morning, bus to Marble Arch, had Park Lane walk then bus to Victoria, fortuitously getting the 11.30 am Folkestone coach (£13). Cottage 3 pm, had a read and nap, then visited John, still going on, just about. Fed him some orange juice and milk. They have begun giving him a *complete diet* food drink. I had a tinned herring evening meal

Sat, 6 May - Followed my weekend getting up routine, breakfast comprising of porridge and custard cream biscuits. Pecked at the film script and did two trench digging stints during the day. Visited John. His eyes were closed all the time on this visit. Had drunk some home brew; had more back at the cottage with a Central Fish Bar sausage, fish cake and chips.

Mon, 8 May - I don't recall the day in detail (looking back from Sunday). Daily film script and library computer hours? I think I did some daily trench digging before 8 am and after 7 pm. Visited John, who has picked up somewhat, to the relief of the staff. Macron the new French President.

Tues, 9 May - I had declined a return to the last client on Saturday, due to Tuesday's Malaga flight, but today I relented and bought another flight for £52. Did daily trench digging. The film script is in abeyance again. John is not now looking deathly and is eating *Complan* liquid diet and taking his medication. Fed him some of his evening mealtime sweet.

Wed, 10 May - Netia phoned and I went for breakfast. She asked if I'd help strengthen Flo's garden fence against the wind. We went by bus to Dymchurch Road, Hythe. The fence is tall and difficult to stabilize with just posts, which is what Flo and Netia want, rather than further temporary props. Netia thought I could be expected to do it immediately - she thinks completely impractically. We looked at some posts at the

---

[15] Jenny, the client and client's wife's Personal Assistant.

nearby Jewson's, then I left. Visited John, drank beer, saw Netia again, she still miffed.

Thurs, 11 May - At 10 am I phoned Netia (out), then I got a bus to Jewson's, Hythe, and bought eight ten foot, four by four inch fence posts, £48 cut price cost, and carried them to Flo's house - a gift for Netia, not Flo. Cottage lunch, read, doze, visited John. Today I began positioning the pipe with earth backfill, twelve feet done. A solitary bee has been entering a crack in the gable end and nosing in the rafters the last week or two, and I did think I might be having a problem...

Fri, 12 May - ...I was woken in the night by a strange sound , like air escaping from a balloon, then that of a swarm, not large, but in the bedside cabinet, I thought. The sound stopped, but in the morning I found they'd started a nest, right by the bed on the floor, already around a six inch lump. Startled, I scraped it up and chucked it out of the window, bees and all. The cone tasted of honey - started by the rafters Queen Bee? I put the nest in a hastily made hive on the railway bank. Saw Netia at breakfast time, John at 5pm. Packed for London and Spain. Have had no more trouble with rats since doing the door repair and cutting that Ivy down.

La Herradura, Wed, 24 May - I felt in agony on waking, the pain now right up into my neck, preventing me turning my head and making it hard to get up.[16] I felt worried and pessimistic about being able to do any more cleaning work, even one or two jobs every couple of months. However during the day it began feeling better - quite recovered, in fact, as if I'd twigged something in the night to put it right. Bus, flight and trains from Herradura to Folkestone, arriving 5 pm to visit John, who has unexpectedly picked up and is talking audibly again. Drank home-brew.

Folkestone, Thurs, 25 May - Did my Folkestone getting up routine to 10 am. To NatWest bank and Lidl supermarket, went on a library computer, Chris was using one too. At 12.19 pm I

---

[16] Diarist's left arm had been feeling painful for two days.

met John's half sister, Thea, who lives in Kansas, at Folkestone West station and walked with her to Wells House. She and I had some lunch in Sandgate (on her), then we returned to John before walking back to the station. A spry seventy nine, Thea is a very agreeable lady. The UK is as warm and sunny as Spain. Returned to the cottage then saw John a third time, taking bottles of fruit juice and squash for him.

Fri, 26 May - Last night and early this morning I resumed work on the trench, hoping it won't be detrimental to my arm/shoulder, still faintly painful. Bought and began brewing a Wilco/Geordie beer kit. Went on a library computer and am now changing my lesser used *social* or personal Orange email address to Gmail. Did another trench digging stint in the evening after visiting John.

Sun, 28 May - Felt OK again.[17] The arm feels OK - what a let off from Wednesday morning and the past three or four months! Wrote diary, had library computer hour and cottage lunch, did a trench digging stint before going to see John from 5 pm to 6.50 pm. Fed him his supper plus chocolate and Refresher sweets and fruit juice. He has stabilized and is no longer at death's door. Lovely temperate walk there and back, a hazy, sunlit France visible off the Leas Cliff Hall.

Tues, 30 May - Have run into an extra hard bit, maybe where they were melting tarmac, which has slowed me right down to just inches a day. Did a library computer hour, saving Orange social/personal email account emails. Marvellous sunny weather, visited John at 5.30 pm with bottles of fruit squash for him. Walked there and back via the Leas grass, with its panoramic English Channel view.

Thurs, 1 June - After a trench digging stint I saw *A Hologram for the King* at the Classic Film Club, starring Tom Hanks and based on a David Eggers novel, a film in the Robert Mitchum/*Lost in Translation* culture shock vein. Emerged in 1 pm sunshine to go to the Poundland shop, have cottage lunch and

---

[17] Having had a headache the previous evening.

do more trench digging. Visited John, he's getting bed sores, a bad one on his elbow.

Sat, 3 June - Did some trench refilling, arm OK and in fact I'm fitter all round and can now use the pickaxe, making progress on the hard bit. Neighbour, Mick, asked if I had any five inch bolts he could have, which I did. Drank a pint then visited John and suggested he make a Will in favour of his sister and mother. Drank more home brew, had a drink at Duke's Bar and chat with hotelier, Mick, on politics. Labour is closing the gap on the conservatives - unbelievable, with Corbyn as leader. Had Central Fish Bar chicken and chips meal, went to bed pretty drunk.

Tues, 6 June - A routine day, as I struggle to recall. Did a trench stint before 8 am and another before dusk, after returning from seeing John. I think I did some financial admin in the morning. Phoned Affinity Water, requesting another site visit and quote. Oh, I helped John write his Will today, witnessed by staff member, Shirley.

Wed, 7 June - A day like yesterday. Bought some more Movelat cream from Lloyd's Pharmacy (£12.94). Did some financial admin. Visited John. Felt weary, arm painful again, though I did some more trench digging before dusk, while drinking home-brew. Vegetable *Cup-a-Soup* meal, the soup added to some torn up and steamed cabbage leaves and eaten with wholemeal bread.

Fri, 9 June - Arm feeling better, after a rest. The election has been disastrous for Theresa May, now left hanging onto power after riding high when she called the election. The Corbyn/Labour resurgence was due to EU *remainers* exercising a protest vote, I'd have thought, though it seems social welfare issues also had an effect. May was the right person to conduct the EU Brexit negotiations, but everything is in a mess now. To think I never thought Corbyn would win fifty seats! Saw John. Emailed R Pelling[18] the erotic content of VTITB.

---

[18] Rowan Palling, editor of the *Amorist* magazine. The diarist had been to its *Alternative Election Night* party in London the previous day.

Sat, 10 June - Worked mostly on the trench, pickaxe digging from 8 am to 10 am, then I had a sunny walk into the town. Bought a copy of *The History of Mr Polly* at Marrin's Bookshop, requested by John. Cup-a-Soup/cabbage lunch. At 4 pm I began drinking home brew and had a wheelbarrow walk to Wickes for sand. Did more trench infilling then had a dusk walk to Duke's Bar (closed), the new View Bar at the former Salisbury hotel (too busy), and the Norfolk hotel basement bar,[19] where I had a half. Had chip shop meal. The trench works now look neater, about half now done.

Sun, 11 June - At 10 am I rang Netia and she gave me breakfast, Chris visiting. Felt fit, dug and picaxed another five feet of trench, arm perfectly OK. Did another hour after a 3 pm break then visited John. Fed him his supper and did some correspondence. Did trench refilling to dusk then began heating some tinned stew in the dark, spilled a pint on the table, then I upset the camping gaz stove, then I found I'd made the stew with tinned chicken curry instead of stewing steak.

Holland Park, Mon, 10 July - The client's wife returned at 9 am, driven in her car from Heathrow by *Chicago Mike.*[20] I left and bussed to Edgware Road, going to the shop where I bought the Roberts portable radio to see if I could get the speaker repaired, but then I bought a better external plug-in speaker there instead, for £69. Folkestone 5 pm, bought and began brewing a beer kit. Visited John, says he's begun hearing voices again and wants his schizophrenia medicine changed. I doubt they can - the sooner his ordeal is over the better. Drank several pints of home-brew. I can't understand Corbyn's recent popularity, it's social media driven, I hear tell, whereas I still get my (opinion forming) news from the newspapers and radio. Would I have supported him when I was young? I was anti authoritarian, but I was always cynical about soviet communism and Stalin. We can't elect him Prime Minister.

---

[19] Harvy's Wine Bar.
[20] Chicago Mike, clients' occasional chauffeur, ex pop band roadie.

Gatwick Airport, Tues, 11 July - Slept off a headache. Wrote diary, bought a thousand euros at the Post Office, for rent and car insurance. I'll have to do this again - I haven't got the rent money sitting in La Caixa bank any more. Visited John at 5 pm, then returned to make departure preparations and have a pint and get the 8.09 pm Tonbridge train, thence to Redhill and Gatwick. Slept on North Terminal seating after finishing the journey's home brew there.

La Herradura, Wed, 19 July - Got the 7.10 am Malaga bus, 11.50 am Monarch flight to Gatwick, trains to Tonbridge - crowded with uniformed school kids - and to Folkestone, arriving cottage 5 pm. Visited John - he looked more at ease, is now having morphine, as I discovered. Called on Netia and had some of her elderflower wine, Chris visiting. Felt cheered; I was perfectly OK again.[21] Bottled some home brew after dark.[22]

Folkestone,Thurs, 20 July - Got up at 5 am to make ready for the 7.09 am St Pancras train, bussed to Semour Place, walked to Marble Arch, bussed to Holland Park, arriving at the client's home at 9 am. The client's wife, Anne, and PA, Kellie, were there too. At 1 pm I drove the client's wife in her Mercedes to Heathrow, Terminal 4, for her flight to China. She is addressing a convention on dance at the Normal University, Beijing. Called on Nick on the way back - not in. Cooked a frozen Thai stir-fry meal for the client, which I bought at Lidgates[23]last time I was here. This morning I bought John's wheelchair with me from Folkestone, which was used at Heathrow airport.

Holland Park, Wed, 26 July - Read the last chapter of *Madame Bovary* this morning. A quite affecting and controversial book, even today. Flaubert does have artistry and a big sensibility. I think VTITB compares quite well. To Kensington library on my 11.50 am break, walked past Lord Leighton's[24]house off the High Street. Bought a return flight to Malaga at the end of September, for £53. For lunch I bought some peanut butter eaten with my forefinger on the walk. Sent

[21] Diarist had been feeling out of sorts in Spain.
[22] Diarist had left it to ferment while he'd been in Spain.
[23] Holland Park butcher.
[24] Lord Leighton, Victorian painter.

a postcard to John. At 2 pm an American set designer friend of the clients, Jim Graham, visited for coffee and biscuits.

Mon, 31 July - 9 am I left the client's house after helping him shower. Got buses to Marble Arch and Hyde Park Corner then a Mall walk to Charing Cross for 10.40am train, cottage 12.40 pm. Bottled some home-brew then I walked to plumber D.E. Sutton's house at the top of Dover Road and talked to him about the water pipe. Called on Etelle on the way back and she gave me a sandwich and glass of wine.

Folkestone, Tues, 1 Aug - Am in email correspondence with Network Rail about getting permission to dig on their land. Now I've already started, I can't see any point in waiting before resuming the work - if they decline it, they decline it, although I don't expect them to. Resumed work on it today, aiming to get it done while the PRU school is on holiday. Visited John from 5 pm to 7 pm, with some mineral water he asked for. Had a pleasant summer evening walk back, had need of a shit Leas Cliff Hall toilets.

Fri, 4 Aug - After my getting up routine to 10 am, I went into town via Manor Road and the Leas, thence to the library, printing a government savings bond prospectus for John, which I have been thinking of investing in myself. Visited Netia on the way back, she awaiting the arrival of Tamsin for the weekend. Did trench digging, visited John, had tinned kipper evening meal. Weather cool and comfortable. Record *Lucifer* heatwave in southern Europe.

Sun 6 Aug - Felt a bit blank and made a sluggish start. Went to the library at 11 am, emailing a Land Registry map to Network Rail for the second time. Had to wait an hour to use the computer with the scanner. Fried an egg and reheated the remains of a chip shop meal for lunch. Did a trench hour then visited John. Met an odd character on the Leas on the way back, English, but with a Dutch registered car, back from living there with a long tale of woe - eviction, fights with neighbours, psychotic mental illness, a discontinued thousand euros a month pension. Called on Netia, Tamsin and Flo there. Drank home brew, heated tinned stewing steak and mushy peas.

Wed, 9 Aug - Had an eleven hour fitful sleep.[25] Had a fairly restful day, though I did an hour on the trench. To a library computer, bought the NS&I Guaranteed Growth Bond. Am still in correspondence with Network Rail, who want to know who is responsible for the pipe. Visited John, briefly, due to my cold. I met the senior nurse there on my arrival, who told me John's mother had died and together we went and told him the news. Drank six pints of home brew, which did their work.

Fri, 11, Aug - I take a sort of Zen attitude to the cottage renovation project as a whole. I'm prepared to do a certain amount of work every day, but whether I actually get there or not I'm not worried about. Had another fairly restful day, cold recovering. Did a little pipe extraction work.[26] To a library computer. Read a bit of the Tara Browne/Guinness family book.[27] Visited John at 5 pm. He asked to see any post cards and letters he had got from his mother, which I found and held up for him to read. He said he wished he'd been kinder to her.

Sun, 13 Aug - Had a crashing headache in the night when getting up for a pee. At 9.30 am I went to Morrisons for Netia, who gave me some Thai fish soup for breakfast. Did pipe work from 11.30 am to 2 pm, had fried egg and reheated chips for lunch, wrote diary then had a sunny Leas walk to Wells House. John was looking better and was in a confessional mood, talking about his daily boozing years and his dishonesty, stealing and giving the money to people to retain their friendship. Heated tinned stewed steak, drank beer, listened to a Radio 4 production of *Loot!*[28] United States and Korean presidents ranting at each other, war looking very likely.

---

[25] Diarist had a cold or the flu.
[26] Network Rail had declined to give permission and the diarist was removing the pipe from railway land.
[27] *I Read The News Today, Oh Boy*, by Paul Howard.
[28] By Joe Orton.

Tues, 15 Aug - Sent a cheque to Affinity Water head office. Did pipe extraction work - my current priority. Got a spare cottage key cut in town and went to Lidl supermarket and the library. Visited John at 5 pm, still confessing his sins; in fact he came back to life telling me about his money making scams (with chain letters mostly). He was actually smiling again! Drank some home brew.

Fri, 18 Aug - Went shopping for pumps and trousers this morning at Peacocks and Primark, also to Lidl supermarket. Am doing the last bit of trench refilling. Visited John at 5 pm. He seems fairly stable, although he said he had a bad trip last night on the morphine he'd been given, couldn't sleep; was having visions and hearing voices. Had a kipper meal at the cottage.

Sun, 20 Aug - Was a little wan, with a bout of diarrhoea. Netia gave me a fried duck egg breakfast. Did trench refilling. Wrote this diary, my recollection hazy. A 4 pm walk to see John. The odd character from Holland is still on the Leas with his car. Heated tinned stewed steak with cherry tomatoes, onion and mushy peas, drank home brew, felt OK   .

Sat, 26 Aug - Got another spare key cut. At 11.30 am I met Thea at Folkestone West station and we walked to Wells House. She told John about his mother's funeral in Salisbury, then she and I had lunch, at her invitation, at the Loaf café, Sandgate. Sunny weather. We returned to John and Thea looked at family photographs with him, then she and I returned to the railway station. Got some cupboard and door timber from a skip. Drank home-brew, to Duke's Bar and the Central Fish Bar for sausage and chips. Drank more beer at cottage.

Sun, 27 Aug - Slept off a nocturnal headache. Porridge and custard cream biscuit breakfast. Saw Chris and Netia in Netia's garden. Wrote diary, went to a library computer, putting photos on the old mobile (which Chris is buying) onto a flash drive and buying two flight tickets. Fried egg and reheated chips lunch. Used jigsaw[29] on skip wood. Visited John, not too good again - not eating and withdrawn. Drank home brew, ate tinned stewed steak, had a poor appetite myself.

Tues, 29 Aug - Began brewing some beer in the morning. Had an early lunch, sawed and placed some trench covering panels.[30] The tarmac along the side of the pathway is worn and easy to remove. Visited John, on the way buying some ginger beer and squash for him. Read a bit of *The History of My Polly* for him. Returned to the cottage with a chip board panel from a skip in Dixwell Road. Sweet Tree want me to start doing alternate weekends with a new client, which suits me fine for the rest of this year.

Wivenhoe, Fri, 1 Sept - We left the house at 10 am, Carol for a dental appointment, me for a sunny stroll to the quay, where I had a chat with Mark Paterson, he from up on his balcony after I'd rung his door bell. I then visited Hugh Brogan for coffee. He's inherited most of Little Hugh's estate, including ongoing pension entitlement, as they were in a civil partnership. Fixed his sticky front door with a handsaw. In London I walked in the Spitalfields market near Bishopsgate, now with ethnic street food stalls, and also over Millennium Bridge and along the South Bank to Waterloo East. Had to get a train from Victoria. Visited John at 6.30 pm.

Sat, 2 Sept - Had a custard cream biscuit breakfast, continued daily routine to 10 am, including public toilet slop-out. Did a film script stint, to the Smiths post office counter for John, returned with a skip plastic panel. Boiled egg lunch, read, dozed, worked on trench covering panels. Drank beer from 4 pm, had a beer at Duke's Bar, closed to other customers due to damage caused to the hotel by a freak rain storm on Thursday. Bought sausage and chips on the way back.

---

[29] A recent purchase.
[30] Diarist was now digging the water pipe trench along Ingles Lane pathway.

Sun, 3 Sept - A 7.30 am visit to Etelle, taking her *Sunday Times*. She gave me patatas bravas/chorizo breakfast and the use of her bath. Met Chris at Venetia's afterwards and sold him the mobile phone for £30. Wrote diary, had reheated chips and fried egg lunch. Dug and picaxed pathway tarmac. Visited John, so curled up it's hard to find his mouth to feed him. Drank home-brew, got more skip boards with the wheelbarrow. Had steam-heated Goblin steak and kidney pudding, with carrot and cherry tomatoes. North Korea has tested another atomic bomb.

Wed, 6 Sept - Felt wan, struggled to do anything useful. Phoned Halifax, cancelling my credit card, also Affinity Water. Printed the client Care Plan at the library. Bought Goblin steak and kidney puddings at Poundstretcher and powdered milk at Sainsbury's. Visited John. I wasn't going to tell him I'd been to Calais, but did.[31]

Thurs, 7 Sept - Felt recovered. At 6.15 am I jumped out of bed and did trench digging, working until 8 am before anyone was at the PRU school next door, term having this week started. Resumed wash/breakfast/toilet routine to 10.30 am. To a library computer. Positioned some trench boards, visited John. On the way back I dragged a large board from a skip in Jointon Road. Met Netia and she gave me some spinach tart. Hurricane *Irma* is devastating the Caribbean.

Tues, 12, Sept - Slept well, back feeling a little better.[32] The public toilet wasn't open, had a shit at Morrisons supermarket toilets. Did a film script hour - minimal progress. To a library computer, paying £50 to RBS credit card, my only credit card now, with a £850 debt. Had a 4.15 pm walk to Wells House Nursing Home and John; went via a skip in Shorncliffe Road and asked the builders there if I could have two doors in it, which I got later with the wheelbarrow. Drank some home brew.

---

[31] Diarist had been on a day trip to Calais the previous day.
[32] Diarist had been having some painful lower back spasms.

Thurs, 14 Sept - Am still using Morrisons toilets. Saw the 11 am Film Club screening of *The Promise*, about Turkish persecution of the Armenians during the First World War. Good production, simple plot and dialogue, ending a bit hammy, has some similarity to my own prospective film. Visited John from 5 pm to 6.30 pm, wrote one of his pen pal letters for him to a Palestinian. Swigged some home brew on the walk back, used the wheelbarrow to get some boards I'd seen earlier in a skip in Connaught Road.

Sun, 17 Sept - Toilets still not open until after 9 am. This morning I had some breakfast with Netia before a toilet slop-out. Wrote diary, did a film script hour. To Sainsbury's for John. Cottage lunch and read, did a trench digging hour then visited John. Had a pleasant evening promenade walk back to the harbour, where the Ska music festival was still going on. Saw Chris at Netia's, gave him a photocopied *Which* magazine booklet on smart phones. Drank brew, had a Goblin steak and kidney pudding meal.

Gatwick Airport, Mon, 18 Sept - Kim[33]and I came across a telephone line encased in a five inch ceramic pipe, and today I discovered that it does indeed seem to be on the exact line of my trench, dammit. Packed a bag for Spain and London, not heavy. Visited John. Resisted having a pint back at the cottage, ate a peanut butter sandwich and got 8.09 pm Tonbridge train, Gatwick 10 pm, slept North Terminal seating.

Gatwick Airport, Fri, 29 Sept - Security woke me at 7.30 am - they don't like sleepers. Had shave, got trains to Folkestone, arriving at noon - wet, autumnal weather. Unpacked. To a library computer, paying money to Capital One credit card, the outstanding balance not having been completely cleared, as I'd mistakenly thought. Hammered a hole in the concrete floor just inside the cottage door, to see how thick it was. Visited John, not looking very good - he's been refusing to let the staff

---

[33] Diarist's brother had come on Saturday to help with the water pipe trench.

wash him or change his position, says it hurts being touched. In La Herradura I had thoughts of being in Tangier rather than Spain. I could do with a change.

Sat, 30 Sept - Morning film script hour, to Sainsbury's for powdered milk and peanut butter. A fried egg and bacon and baked bean brunch. I began digging the trench going across the pathway and into the cottage, removing the tarmac to accommodate a thick door panel sawn to size previously. I'm aiming to get the cottage end of the pipe all done before the rest of the digging. Visited John, fed him some jelly and ice cream, got told off for eating his main course when he doesn't want it. To Duke's Bar on the way back, plus beer at cottage.

Mon, 2 Oct - Monarch Airways went bust this morning. I shall miss them, was lucky to have got the last flights in.[34] Feel OK physically - aches and pains have abated - but a bit doleful mentally. Here I am, back at the cottage, life going on and on with no point to it really. Tom Petty dead, my age.[35] To a library computer, did trench digging - I can see I'm going to have to get under the existing utility pipes and cables.[36] Visited John. Tinned chicken curry meal.

Wed, 4 Oct - Back to cottage reality.[37] To Boots at 9.30 am, to print one or two more Venice photos and to Sainsbury's. Saw Netia and Chris on return, Chris waterproofing Netia's porch roof. After lunch I dug and scraped some earth around the utility pipes in the trench for an hour, then visited John, looking dire again - apathetic and hardly eating. Swigged home brew on the way back, saw a big harvest full moon emerge from horizon clouds from the Leas Cliff Hall roof, my glare dimmed lights were on there. Started brewing some cider today.

---

[34] Diarist's last Monarch flight was on the 28th of September.
[35] Tom Petty, American singer, songwriter & guitarist, leader of Tom Petty and the Heartbreakers.
[36] Diarist had found that many pipes and cables ran under Ingles Lane pathway.
[37] Diarist had been to Calais the day before.

Thurs, 5 Oct - Today or yesterday I phoned the Team La Noria garage - the car passed its Spanish MOT test and Dave has parked it back at Herradura for me. Daily film script stint - miserable progress. To Asda supermarket, buying fruit juice for John. Visited him at 5 pm, he was looking a lot better. Yesterday I thought he was near the end and phoned Melissa to warn her. Today I phoned her again to reassure her. I had been going to return to Holland Park for a week today, but the client has gone into a nursing home. This week a sixty four year old white, disgruntled Las Vegas gambler shot dead fifty eight there and wounded several hundred with machine guns.

Mon, 9 Oct - The toilets are opening early again, which is good, as I was going at mid morning last week at the same time as some druggies injecting themselves there. I can see if the toilets are open from just outside Ingles Lane gate. Evone from Sweet Tree rang about a possible medication error with the Highgate client, which alarmed me, but on reflection I think I'm in the clear. To Asda supermarket. Visited John. Tinned Asda Chicken Vindaloo meal.

Tues, 10 Oct - The Ingles Lane pathway trench is hard to do, not *the least problematic option*.[38] Am trying to get under the utility/mains pipes running along the path and also under the concrete inside the cottage door, so my pipe can come up through a hole. Am not making much daily progress, God knows how long it will take. At least I know no one can stop me.[39] Visited John again from 5 pm to 6.15 pm.

Thurs, 12 Oct - Did a film script stint, then I went to the 11 am Film Club,[40] seeing *Rules Don't Apply*, written and directed by Warren Beatty, who played Howard Hughes. It was a reasonably good effort, all a bit fanciful, I thought. Felt a bit out of sorts walking out of the cinema into the sunshine. Cottage

---

[38] A previous opinion held by the diarist, or of someone advising him.
[39] Ingles Lane was classed as Unadopted Land by the Land Registry.
[40] Classic Film Club.

lunch, work on trench, visited John. He does eat a little and, dire as his condition is, seems to have stabilized again.

Sat, 14 Oct - Woke at 3 am and drank three or four pints of beer in bed, then slept again until 7 am. Worked on the concrete hole and excavations an hour, then I decided to view the 2017 Folkestone Triennial.[41] I followed the map around side streets (Amelia Pica shell souvenirs on residents' window sills), thence to the Baptist burial ground (Emily Peasgood sound installation), thence to Tontine Street and the town (Hoycheong Wong mosque minaret, Sintra Tantra painted Cube building), and to the harbour (Richard Woods, Anthony Gormley). Warm day, I enjoyed the tour but also felt uncharitable. Visited John, to Duke's Bar on the way back and the chip shop, drank home-brew.

Mon, 16 Oct - The PRU school kids are unruly. Today they were climbing on a car parked next to me to get on the wall and jump down into the path. They also open their Fire Door into Ingles Lane, which is supposed to be out of bounds to them. I put a note of complaint on the car, owned by head of school, Rachel. Worked on the trench and bought a November flight at the library. Visited John.

Wed, 18 Oct - Worked on Harry, succeeding in breaking through to Dick,[42] under existing pipes and cables. I am working at arms reach with the miscellaneous collection of tools I have. It was yesterday I left the note. Visited John, did an hour on the Tom hole through the concrete on return at dusk.

Thurs, 19 Oct - Before breakfast I worked on Tom, breaking through to Dick, then before lunch I got some water piping running through the tunnelling - my first bit of progress. Felt relieved. Visited John, buying some Asda *Summer Fruits* squash on the way with sugar in it - hard to find, as they are all now

---

[41] Urban open air art exhibition held every three years.
[42] Diarist was trying to join up three *Tom, Dick and Harry* holes.

labelled *with no added sugar*. Had a couple of pints on return to the cottage. Bottled some beer.

Temple Fortune, Thurs, 26 Oct - Permanent carer, Librado, returned at 10 am. Bus to Victoria, sitting on the top deck eating nuts and raisins. Noon Ashford train, cottage 2.30 pm. Repacked bag for tomorrow, 4 pm walk to Wells House Nursing Home. John is still stable, though he eats very little, drinks fruit squash and milk. Swigged home brew on the way back, calm autumn weather. Drank four more pints at the cottage, which went down well. Received a note of thanks from the Holland Park client's wife.

Folkestone, Wed, 1 Nov - Washed hair, as I do on Wednesday and Saturday, with tepid water from the public toilet hand basin. I went into the town and to the library, paying the credit card. I felt a bit fraught and on my 1 pm return drank a couple of pints of cider. I continued tippling during the walk & visit to John and back to the cottage. I was quite jovial with the care home staff, John remained uncheered. Today I also walked to a plumbers' merchant, trying to buy a stop cock for my 32mm. pipe - may not find one locally. Britain has lately adopted plastic bank notes. The new Jane Austin £10 plastic bank note is rather beautiful. It looks like all cash in notes and coins will be obsolete pretty soon, what with instant card payment. I'm hardly using much cash even now. Last week Catalonia declared independence, Madrid has imposed direct rule.

Thurs, 2 Nov - To the 11 am Film Club, seeing *The Hippopotamus*, based on Stephen Fry's novel. Not great - self indulgent, with the main character based on Fry himself, or how he is - or was - in private, I would guess. Netia gave me some lunch then I did some trench digging. Visited John. He ate his ice cream sweet and drank squash, but his weight still declines and he seemed apathetic and introverted again.

Mon, 6 Nov - I got up at 8.30 am and at 9 am went to Wells House - sunny blue-sky day walking on the Leas grass. John seemed brighter in the morning. I went because I was expecting to have to go on a five day Live-in care job later, but on the walk back I got a text cancelling it. Shopped at Asda for powdered milk and their tinned curry. Did a bit of trench work before 4 pm dusk. Heated the tinned curry, early to bed.

Wed, 8 Nov - I had agreed to do an 11 am to 7 pm day shift in London today, but that too was cancelled. I presently only have the Highgate job every other weekend, which does suit me, as I need to get on with the water pipe. There's also John, who surely must be getting near the end. On Monday I said I wouldn't be able to visit him again until Friday. Phoned Melissa this morning.

Fri, 10 Nov - I'm sleeping about ten hours a night. Weather chilly but I'm warm in bed. Did another 7 am trench digging hour. To the library, putting some more of the film script onto a memory stick/flash drive. Lay on my bed after lunch then had a 4 pm walk to Wells House. John is declining again. His fingers are all bent and twisted and today I saw his right thumb is bent the wrong way at the first joint and looks about to drop off. Ate tinned kippers back at the cottage, drank some of John's sugary squash.

Sun, 12 Nov - Did trench digging from 11 am to 1 pm and again from 2 pm to 4 pm. There's still no sign of the big pipe on the line of my trench as I dig the other side of the nearby British Telecom inspection cover. Phoned Kim. Had another lunch time fry-up with baked beans. Visited John from 5 pm to 7 pm. He said he felt in pain, like torture, from head to foot and wished he would die. They are giving him strong pain killers/morphine. Drank cider on the walk back, more at cottage, heated tinned stewing steak with cherry tomatoes and mushy peas.

Mon, 13 Nov - At 3.30 pm, on my way to visit John, I went to Jewson's near Folkestone West station, to see if I could buy a few feet of bendy pipe to protect some lagging as the water pipe goes into the cottage. I also tried hardware shops in Cheriton High Street. John ate some yogurt and a little milk, nothing else. Every night I dream vividly, usually featuring people known to me.

Wed, 15 Nov - I did a 7 am trench digging hour, resumed wash routine then at 10 am I phoned Netia, who gave me some fried breakfast, featuring Blewit fungi from West Hythe. To a library computer, emailing Jack. Visited John from 5 pm to 6.30 pm. He is now refusing to eat; says he can't swallow, but I think he's doing it deliberately. I said he must do what feels best for himself. Swigged beer on the way back, drank more at cottage.

Thurs, 16 Nov - Did a 7.15 am trench digging hour. Netia gave me some more breakfast at 10 am, then we went to the Film Club, seeing a documentary on French cinema presented by Bertrand Tavernier. It was long and with an intermission, during which we viewed some Fred Cuming[43] paintings next door, then Netia went shopping and I saw the second half which was not so interesting. Visited John, found a length of corrugated plastic bendy pipe beside a skip on the Lower Sandgate Road and took it on the way back. John is still refusing to eat or drink or take his medication.

Stansted Airport, Mon, 20 Nov - Bought six hundred euros at the post office (£566), printed Ryanair flight boarding card and bought a coach ticket at the library. After lunch I packed my bag and began bottling some beer, before a 4 pm dusk walk to Wells House. Blow me down! John has started eating again, fed him some gravy, his sweet and some milk and also orange squash. Finished bottling the beer in the dark. Got 9.09 pm Charing Cross train, 11 pm Mall walk to Victoria coach station, got 11.59 pm coach to Stansted.

---

[43] Fred Cuming RA, lived locally.

Gatwick Airport, Mon, 27 Nov - Got the 7.10 am Malaga bus for the 11.50 am Ryanair flight to Gatwick. Trains to Folkestone West station, had a rain-drizzly walk to Wells House. John is about the same, he asked for some fruit squash and drank three beakers then fell asleep. I ate some chocolate of his - I hadn't eaten all day. Back at the cottage I had some tinned curry then went to sleep too, pretty promptly.

Wed, 29 Nov - Did intermittent work getting the first few yards of the barrier pipe into position, from the stop cock to near where I've got to in the trench, where the remaining length of pipe is now rolled. Went to see John in the evening, swigging beer before, during and after. He ate a little yogurt and drank a little milk. He has the *Daily Mail* in his room, which I read, showing him anything about the Royal Family. Cold weather, am OK in bed. I have received the £200 cold weather heating allowance payment.

Thurs, 30 Nov - Did a 7.15 am to 8.30 am trench digging stint, before the PRU school opening. Noon walk to the library, but I met Netia outside and went for a coffee with her at the Asda supermarket café instead. After lunch I sawed the bendy pipe to the correct size then visited John. He ate a few tea spoons of gravy and some yogurt and a little milk.

Mon, 4 Dec - Had cold toes in bed. A receipt says I went to Asda supermarket. Film script stint? Did no early trench digging. Pulled the stop cock end of the pipe out a bit, to lag the bit between where it enters the cottage and comes out through the hole. Visited John, who was asleep, but when his meal arrived I woke him and fed him three tea spoons of the sweet and a little milk. I've strained my right side now, carrying my weighty flight bag, I think - it's painful under my right ribs somewhere. Christine Keeler[44] died. Also Johnny Hallyday[45] in France.

---

[44] Christine Keeler, nightclub hostess, featured prominently in 1961 Profumo Affair or scandal.
[45] Johnny Hallyday, French rock & roll singer.

Wed, 6 Dec - Made leisurely departure preparations. To the library, checking in for the Ryanair flight and buying a coach ticket. Cottage lunch, began putting foam lagging tubes on the the pipe, a tight fit and slow job. Visited John, he was rather better than on Monday. He is still eating and taking his medication. Got the 9.09 pm Charing Cross train, walked via Trafalgar Square, Haymarket and Piccadilly to Victoria coach station. I was booked on the 12.30 am coach to Stansted but I got on the 11.59p m coach.

La Herradura, Tues, 12 Dec - At 9.30 am I met Sunday's customer, Phil, at Burriana beach to see if I'd left the plastic bag inside his house, but I hadn't.[46] I just can't account for the loss, except for that bottle of brandy - or equivalent - I drank on Saturday night. I returned to Herradura, meeting Englishman, Dave, at the Best Alcazar hotel at 11 am and cleaning a sofa in a flat he manages near there. Finished curry and went to bed early. I was still reading when the phone rang and it was Melissa to say that John had died yesterday evening.

Wed, 13 Dec - I feel discomposed, annoyed about the wallet more than anything. It had belonged to John, as a matter of fact - perhaps he wanted it back! I don't feel sad for John - his ordeal is over, but I have been feeling apprehensive about the effect of his death will have on myself - no more pleasant strolls to Wells House for a warm up on a dark night, etc. Today I drove via Competa and Archez to Canillas de Albaida, to clean carpets at the hotel El Cerillo, for owners, Sue and her husband. It's very quaint - I would like to stay there myself. Had a walk in Canillas afterwards - very quiet. Had a coffee and brandy at the café in Archez.

Thurs, 14 Dec - Have been seeing perfect sea horizon sunsets in Herradura, and this morning I saw a perfect horizon sunrise through the palm trees on Malaga beach, as the 7.10 am bus arrived in Malaga. Got 11.50 am Ryanair flight to Stansted,

---

[46] Diarist had lost his wallet.

National Express coach to Victoria, trains to Faversham and Canterbury and bus to Folkestone. Met Henry (or Torrence) on the bus, an odd character I've known in Folkestone for years, lives in a dilapidated house in Christchurch Road and goes to Canterbury every day on the bus. Drank three pints at the cottage. I'm going to be lonelier without John - probably I needed him more than he needed me in the end.

Highgate, Fri, 15 Dec - At 10 am I arrived at Wells House to see the ward nurse and then have a chat, as arranged, with Tania in John's room. She was the nurse closest to John and she talked of his last days and weeks. She is very amusing, was once an actress who like Kim went to Mountview Theatre School. I got the 1.09 pm Charing Cross train then a 24 bus to Hampstead Heath, for a heath walk to Highgate. To Sainsbury's Local shop and the library there, then I arrived Wood Lane at 6 pm for a handover with Clarise.[47] Nice[48] and I gave the client his evening meal and helped him to bed at 9.30 pm, Nice left at 10. pm.

Folkestone, Mon, 18 Dec - At 11.15 am I met Melissa and her husband, Paul - me with John's birth certificate and Will - at the library and they registered his death there. We then drove to Wells House and walked down to Sandgate for some lunch at the Loaf café - sunny calm day. Back at Wells House I helped them clear John's room of his possessions. They gave me a few things, including his Roberts digital radio.

Wed, 20 Dec - Went by bus to Margate, walked from the beach to Colin and Harold's flat, arriving at 12.15 pm for a gin and tonic and good natter about John. They gave me a chicken curry lunch and wine, and another G&T and Christmas pud. Good to see them. To the Turner Gallery on the return walk, seeing an Arp exhibition plus Tracy Emin's unmade bed. A pint at the Mechanical Elephant.[49] Visited Netia again back in Folkestone,[50] still drinking some brandy and water I had on me.

---

[47] Clarise, client's permanent carer.
[48] Nice, carer.
[49] Weatherspoons pub on Margate sea front.
[50] Diarist had seen her the previous day.

Ate more of her sausage rolls, Chris there again, a most enjoyable day.

Thurs, 28 Dec - Did a film script stint, my first for some time. I then did some gentle trench digging - about eight bucketfuls - before it was dusk, with a muesli and egg sandwich lunch eaten on the job. Had a 4.15 pm walk, buying a beer kit at Wicos and a £12.99 wrist watch at Argos, the last one I bought there having broken. Cold evening, heated tinned Oxtail soup which came from John's flat. To bed wearing thick socks and a fur lined hat.

Highgate, Sun, 31 Dec - New Years Eve. Alex came 9 am to 2 pm, covering for Oliver.[51] We got the client up and gave him a body wash and breakfast. On my 11 am to 1 pm break I went to a charity shop nearby and bought a child's wooden jig saw puzzle, then walked to Archway and bought a *soft bunny* toy/ball in a charity shop there, both for the client's use. Found his electric shaver in a cupboard. Cooked a stew from a recipe book of his, Nice and I having some too. Am staying here until tomorrow morning, as requested by Clarissa.

It's been a year to forget, so we all say, but pretty good for me personally. I haven't achieved much though, apart from making a living. I haven't got the mains water supply yet, nor have I really got on with the film script. But I have enjoyed the year and have kept busy. I've kept busy the last five years and doing that has worked to get me by. In Spain I still like the sunshine and a coffee and tapas, though I do get lonely and am living in the past there. The cottage is my home now, though I'm glad I'm not there all the time. My big fear is to be stuck there one day. I'm OK there though. I don't really mind roughing it; I've got a dry, warm bed and my home-brew. I probably enjoy the thought of the cottage more when I'm away from it, though, than when I'm there. In London I've been feeling relaxed and happy and have loved getting to know it properly this last year or two. I also enjoy the care work I do.

[51] Alex & Oliver, carers.

John's dead. It's also been a bumper year for celebrity deaths. I can't help feeling 2017 will seem like a pivotal year - the start of my old age? What now for me? More of the same, I suppose. I can't see any big changes happening. I envisage going on as I am until I am 70, say, then spending a quiet retirement at the cottage. I feel mournful about my unfulfilled artistic potential; I always have done. I would like to have been successful artistically. I also wish I was with a woman, a woman I loved. I'm tired of always being on my own. I'm so lonely really. I'm too organised and self reliant. I don't love anyone and no one loves me. Now I'm losing my few friends and it feels like everyone has left and left me to carry on alone.

There may be some debt and poverty and homelessness at one end of the scale, and inequality at the other, but it seems to me that for the average person in the country life has never been so prosperous. People look well fed and clothed. On the face of it they seem contented and motivated and positive minded. You don't see many old cars on the road. It's a kinder, more egalitarian society now and life has never been so good - that's how it seems to me. As for myself, I can't say I'm unhappy - just sort of mildly perplexed. I wish I could end writing this diary. I wonder if I can? Probably not. I feel fit; I've nothing to complain about health wise. All my aches and pains have abated. I know I have been drinking too much lately, or binge drinking

POSTSCRIPT

Folkestone, Fri 5 Jan - Slept ten hours. So here I am at the cottage, another year ahead to be utilized somehow. This diary is my friend, I can't afford to lose you. Went 8 am to the Manor clinic, enquiring about a flu jab. Continued breakfast/wash routine and unpacked. To Wickes after lunch, returning with three metres of copper pipe and a tap. At dusk I went to the library with my early diaries, looking for the first mention of John.

Sat, 6 Jan - A 10 am walk to Wells House for a cup of tea with Tania, and to collect some post. On the way back I got a cupboard door from a skip outside the Burlington hotel, which after lunch I cut and laid as more trench covering. To the library at dusk with my old diaries - am thinking of publishing another selection, under the title *The John Diaries.* Instead of visiting John these dark evenings I can go to the library and work on this. Drank six pints.

Tues, 9 Jan - My priority, I suppose, is to get the mains water installation finished. I do something towards it each day. I'm working on the bit of plumbing between the cock stop and outside tap in the patio. I try and do some film script work and at dusk go to the library, to work on *The John Diaries* until it closes at 6 pm. Donald Trump isn't coming to open the new US London Embassy, or to the Royal Wedding,[50] or on any state visit. He feels unloved by Britain - bodes ill for post Brexit UK-US trade deal.

Tues, 16 Jan - Trains to Salisbury (£75) for John's 11.30 am funeral. Paul met me outside the Rose and Crown pub and we went to his and Melissa's home, then with Melissa and Thea to the London Road cemetery. Two other relatives were there and a former Scottish neighbour of John's parents. There was then a service back at All Saints' church. We all had tea and cakes at Melissa and Paul's house, then Paul took me to the bus station for coaches to Victoria and Stansted. Melissa gave me £100 for the journey cost - I didn't argue about it.

[50] Marriage of Prince Harry and Meghan Markle.